CAMBRIDGE STUDIES IN LAW AND SOCIETY

The broad area of law and society has become a remarkably rich and dynamic field of study. At the same time, the social sciences have increasingly engaged with questions of law. In this process, the borders between legal scholarship and the social, political and cultural sciences have been transcended, and the result is a time of fundamental re-thinking both within and about law. In this vital period, Cambridge Studies in Law and Society provides a significant new book series with an international focus and a concern with the global transformation of the legal arena. The series aims to publish the best scholarly work on legal discourse and practice in social context, combining theoretical insights and empirical research.

The vagabond is by definition a suspect.

Daniel Nordman

THE INVENTION OF
THE PASSPORT

Surveillance, Citizenship and the State

John Torpey
University of California, Irvine

CAMBRIDGE UNIVERSITY PRESS

PUBLISHED BY THE PRESS SYNDICATE OF THE UNIVERSITY OF CAMBRIDGE
The Pitt Building, Trumpington Street, Cambridge, United Kingdom

CAMBRIDGE UNIVERSITY PRESS
The Edinburgh Building, Cambridge CB2 2RU, UK   http://www.cup.cam.ac.uk
40 West 20th Street, New York, NY 10011–4211, USA   http://www.cup.org
10 Stamford Road, Oakleigh, Melbourne 3166, Australia
Ruiz de Alarcón 13, 28014, Madrid, Spain

First published 2000

Typeset in New Baskerville 10/12 pt

A catalogue record for this book is available from the British Library

National Library of Australia Cataloguing in Publication data
Torpey, John C.
The invention of the passport: surveillance, citizenship and the state.
Bibliography.
Includes index.
ISBN 0 521 63249 8 (hbk).
ISBN 0 521 63493 8 (pbk).
1. Passports – Europe – History – 19th century. 2. Passports – History.
3. Passports – France – History – 18th century. 4. Citizenship –
History. I. Title. (Series: Cambridge studies in law and society).
323.67

Library of Congress Cataloguing in Publication data
Torpey, John C.
The invention of the passport: surveillance, citizenship, and the state
John Torpey.
p.   cm.
Includes bibliographical references and index.
ISBN 0-521-63249-8 (hardback: alk. paper). — ISBN 0-521-63493-8 (pbk.: alk. paper)
1. Passports—United States. 2. Freedom of movement—
United States. 3. Passports—Europe, Western. 4. Freedom of
movement—Europe,Western. I. Title.
K3273.T67 1999   99-33083
342'.082—dc21

ISBN 0 521 63249 8 hardback
ISBN 0 521 63493 8 paperback
Transferred to digital printing 2002

CONTENTS

ACKNOWLEDGMENTS

While I was confident from the outset that a book about "the history of the passport" was a clever idea, I was less convinced at first that this was a subject of any real significance. I therefore owe a great debt to several historians who helped persuade me very early on that this would indeed prove a worthwhile undertaking: Paul Avrich, Eric Hobsbawm, Stephen Kern, Eugen Weber, and Robert Wohl. While I had the good fortune to enjoy an extended colloquy with Robert Wohl in the context of a National Endowment for the Humanities-sponsored seminar on intellectuals and politics during the summer of 1994 when the idea for this study was first formulated, the others simply responded to an unsolicited query from a young scholar unknown to them. This generosity only increased the admiration I had for them, which was of course what had led me to write to them in the first place. Todd Gitlin also reacted with enthusiasm to the idea of the book. Todd's endorsement of the project as well as his steadfast support for me and my work have been a source of great satisfaction over the last decade and more; I feel honored to have his friendship and encouragement. Without the generosity of these people, this project would never have become more than an idle curiosity.

Once I had seriously embarked on the project, two other people, Gérard Noiriel and Jane Caplan, lent their enthusiasm and provided shining examples of the kind of scholarship I wanted to produce. Noiriel's writings on the history of immigration, citizenship, and identification documents in France have been a major inspiration for me; the citations of his work in the text point only to the visible peak of an iceberg of scholarly debt. Jane Caplan's support for this project quickly led to a collaborative undertaking on related issues concerning the practices that states have developed to identify individuals in the modern period, to be published elsewhere. Working with her has been both a real pleasure and an extended private tutorial (entirely unrecompensed) in scholarly professionalism. I feel profoundly fortunate and grateful that David Abraham put us in touch, somehow intuiting – as a result of my work on passports and Jane's on tattooing – that "you're working on the same kind of stuff."

Next, I am particularly indebted to Aristide Zolberg, whose work on the dynamics of international migration in the modern world has deeply influenced my own thinking about these matters. Although we had met on a couple of occasions earlier and I was familiar with a number of his writings on this subject, it was as a result of my participation in the German American Academic Council–SSRC Summer Institute on Immigration, Integration, and Citizenship, organized by Ari and the impressive Austrian migration scholar Rainer Münz during the summers of 1996 and 1997, that I came to a fuller grasp of Ari's approach to understanding migration processes. His ideas pervade this book, which I can only hope will provide a useful complement to his work on the role of states in shaping migration processes.

Although the list of others I wish to thank is long, I hope this will not be regarded as merely a surreptitious effort at self-congratulation. The fact that these people and institutions are to be found in several countries on three continents is both a measure of the good fortune I have had in carrying out this project and testimony to the reality of an international community of scholars, of which I am thrilled to be a part.

Much of the research for this book was carried out while I held a Jean Monnet Fellowship at the European University Institute in Florence, Italy during 1995–96. Upon my arrival in the world's most beautiful city, a young legal historian, Stefano Mannoni, insisted that the place for me to conduct the research I wanted to do was the Library of the Chamber of Deputies, situated happily in the shadow of the Pantheon in Rome. Stefano called his friend, *bibliotecario straordinario* Mario di Napoli, on my behalf, and the rest was smooth sailing. I am greatly indebted to Mario's colleague Silvano Ferrari, who tracked down many an obscure source for me and, if he couldn't find it, invited me to join him in the otherwise closed stacks for the search. At the EUI, Raffaelle Romanelli's enthusiasm for the project helped sustain me through some uncertain times; my friend Christian Joppke pushed me forward, and provided plenty of good company.

For kindnesses, criticisms, assistance, suggestions, hospitality, citations, and occasionally quizzical looks, I wish to extend my sincere gratitude to Peter Benda, Didier Bigo, Scott Busby, Kitty Calavita, Craig Calhoun, Mathieu Deflem, Gary Freeman, Bernard Gainot, Janet Gilboy, Phil Gorski, Valentin Groebner, Virginie Guiraudon, David Jacobson, David Laitin, Leo Lucassen, Michael Mann, John McCormick, Bob Moeller, Daniel Nordman, Giovanna Procacci, Marian Smith, Peggy Somers, Yasemin Soysal, Anthony Richmond, Tim Tackett, Sara Warneke, the late Myron Weiner, and Bruce Western. I am especially grateful to Susan Silbey for inviting me to contribute this volume in the Cambridge series on Law and Society.

In the course of writing this book, I have benefited greatly from the largesse of several other institutions that have provided funding for research or time away from regular academic duties, as well as congenial surroundings in which to carry out the project. At a time in which public support for scholarship is under sharp attack in the United States, I wish to make special mention of a fellowship from the National Endowment for the Humanities, the award of which I regarded as a particular honor. I was also delighted that the German Marshall Fund found my work worthy of its support. In Paris, I enjoyed the assistance of Professor Catherine Duprat at the Institut de l'Histoire de la Révolution Française and the hospitality afforded by the Maison Suger/Maison des Sciences de l'Homme, whose director, Maurice Aymard, has been most helpful. The University of California at Irvine has been supportive of me and of this project, for which I am grateful.

I have talked about aspects of this project in venues too numerous to indicate here, but I would nonetheless like to take this opportunity to thank Charles Maier, Director of the Center for European Studies at Harvard, and Nancy Green, a distinguished historian of migration at the École des Hautes Études en Sciences Sociales, for invitations to speak about this project at their respective institutions and for the helpful comments I received on those occasions.

An earlier version of Chapter 1, together with the Conclusion, appeared previously as "Coming and Going: On the State Monopolization of the Legitimate 'Means of Movement'," *Sociological Theory* 16(3) (November 1998): 239–59. That article has also appeared in French as "Aller et venir: le monopole ètatique des 'moyens légitimes de circulation," *Cultures et Conflits* 31–2 (Automne–hiver 1998): 63–100. A French translation of parts of Chapter 3 was published as "Le contrôle des passeports et la liberté de circulation: Le cas de l'Allemagne au XIXe siècle," *Genèses: Sciences sociales et histoire* 30 (March 1998): 53–76.

I must also thank my research assistants, Derek Martin and Sharon McConnell, who helped me get under the trap door just before it came down. Alas, unlike when Harrison Ford is involved, the door did not remain open until there was time for one last act of heroism. I am grateful to Phillipa McGuinness and Sharon Mullins at Cambridge University Press for their enthusiasm about the project, and for holding the door open just a little longer than they might have liked. I hope the result justifies their patience.

Finally, my deepest thanks to Caroline, who made it all worthwhile.

INTRODUCTION

In an obscure paragraph of a package of immigration reforms adopted in 1996, the United States government committed itself to developing "an automated system to track the entry and exit of all non-citizens, thus providing a way of identifying immigrants who stay longer than their visas allow." At the time that the legislation was supposed to be put into effect, however, some in the government came to regard this measure as likely to cause undue complications for millions of border-crossers, and the implementation of the law was postponed for two and a half years. The postponement was also deemed advisable in part because the Immigration and Naturalization Service, the agency mandated to design the system, was far from having amassed the technology "to process information estimated to be so vast that in one year it would exceed all the data in the Library of Congress."[1] Clearly, this program would be an enormous and unprecedented undertaking.

This book examines some of the background to such efforts to identify and track the movements of foreigners. The study concentrates on the historical development of passport controls as a way of illuminating the institutionalization of the idea of the "nation-state" as a prospectively homogeneous ethnocultural unit, a project that necessarily entailed efforts to regulate people's movements. Yet because nation-states are both territorial and membership organizations, they must erect and sustain boundaries between nationals and non-nationals both at their physical borders and among people within those borders.[2] Boundaries between persons that are rooted in the legal category of nationality can only be maintained, it turns out, by documents indicating a person's nationality, for there simply is no other way to know this fact about someone. Accordingly, a study that began by asking how the contemporary passport regime had developed and how states used documents to control movement ineluctably widened to include other types of documents related to inclusion and exclusion in the citizen body, and to admission and refusal of entry into specific territories.

I argue that, in the course of the past few centuries, states have successfully usurped from rival claimants such as churches and private enterprises the "monopoly of the legitimate means of movement" – that

1

is, their development as states has depended on effectively distinguishing between citizens/subjects and possible interlopers, and regulating the movements of each. This process of "monopolization" is associated with the fact that states must develop the capacity to "embrace" their own citizens in order to extract from them the resources they need to reproduce themselves over time. States' ability to "embrace" their own subjects and to make distinctions between nationals and non-nationals, and to track the movements of persons in order to sustain the boundary between these two groups (whether at the border or not), has depended to a considerable extent on the creation of documents that make the relevant differences knowable and thus enforceable. Passports, as well as identification cards of various kinds, have been central to these processes, although documentary controls on movement and identification have been more or less stringently developed and enforced in different countries at various times.

This study focuses on the vicissitudes of documentary controls on movement in Western Europe and the United States from the time of the French Revolution until the relatively recent past. I begin with the French Revolution because of its canonical status as the "birth of the nation-state." Yet the transformation of states inaugurated by the French Revolution turns out to have had much more to do with the gradual process of inclusion of broad social strata in the political order than with the construction of an ethnically "pure" French population, although I examine efforts along these lines as well. The shift toward broader incorporation of the populace in political decision-making is reflected in the controversies chronicled in Chapter 2, where I recount how the French revolutionaries publicly debated the issue of passport controls on movement for the first time in European history. Because I was intrigued by the question of who supported and who opposed documentary controls on movement in various contexts and why they did so, I have discussed subsequent debates over these matters in other countries wherever I have been able to find source materials. The narrative addresses the legal history of passport controls in these countries until shortly after the Second World War. I have said relatively little about the postwar period, mainly because others have analyzed the process of European unification and its attendant relaxation of documentary restrictions on movement in greater detail than I could hope to do.[3] Instead, I have said only enough about the postwar era to indicate some doubts about whether we have entered into a period of "post-national membership," as some commentators have recently suggested.[4]

The geographical frame of the study derives from my belief that the dominance of Western states in the period examined has been relatively clear-cut, and that the imposition of Western ways on most of the rest of the world has been one of the most remarkable features of the era. Here I am only echoing what I take to be common wisdom about the rise and dominance of the West during the modern age. This should not be taken to imply any denigration of non-Western cultures, but only the recognition that those societies have not been sufficiently powerful to impose their ways upon the world. Indeed, I would be delighted if this study were to stimulate studies of systems of documentary controls on movement and identity in other parts of the world and in other periods.[5] For now, however, it seems worthwhile to begin to make sense of the processes that spawned the world-girdling system of passport controls on international movement that arose from the gradual strengthening of state apparatuses in Europe and the United States during the past two centuries or so.

Because the passport system arose out of the relatively inchoate international system that existed during the nineteenth century, I have not undertaken strong, systematic comparisons of one country versus another. I argue that the emergence of passport and related controls on movement is an essential aspect of the "state-ness" of states, and it therefore seemed to be putting the cart before the horse to presume to compare states as if they were "hard," "really-existing" entities of a type that were more nearly approximated after the First World War. Moreover, what is remarkable about the contemporary system of passport controls is that it bears witness to a cooperating "international society" as well as to an overarching set of norms and prescriptions to which individual states must respond.[6] This does not mean, as some seem to think, that there is no such thing as "sovereignty," but only that this is a *claim* states make in an environment not of their own making. To paraphrase Marx, states make their own policy, "but they do not make it just as they please; they do not make it under circumstances chosen by themselves, but under circumstances directly found, given, and transmitted" from the *outside*.

The following study seeks to demonstrate that passports and other documentary controls on movement and identification have been essential to states' monopolization of the legitimate means of movement since the French Revolution, and that this process of monopolization has been a central feature of their development *as* states during that period. The project has been motivated in considerable part by the uneasy feeling that much sociological writing about states is insupportably abstract, failing to tell us how states actually constitute and maintain themselves as ongoing concerns. By focusing not on the grand flourishes of state-building but on what Foucault somewhere described as the "humble modalities" of power, I hope to contribute to a more adequate understanding of the capacity that states have amassed to intrude into our lives over the last two centuries.

3

COMING AND GOING: ON THE STATE MONOPOLIZATION OF THE LEGITIMATE "MEANS OF MOVEMENT"

In his writings, Karl Marx sought to show that the process of capitalist development involved the expropriation of the "means of production" from workers by capitalists. The result of this process was that workers were deprived of the capacity to produce on their own and became dependent upon wages from the owners of the means of production for their survival. Borrowing this rhetoric, Marx's greatest heir and critic, Max Weber, argued that a central feature of the modern experience was the successful expropriation by the state of the "means of violence" from individuals. In the modern world, in contrast to the medieval period in Europe and much historical experience elsewhere, only states could "legitimately" use violence; all other would-be wielders of violence must be licensed by states to do so. Those not so licensed were thus deprived of the freedom to employ violence against others. Following the rhetoric used by Marx and Weber, this book seeks to demonstrate the proposition that modern states, and the international state system of which they are a part, have expropriated from individuals and private entities the legitimate "means of movement," particularly though by no means exclusively across international boundaries.

The result of this process has been to deprive people of the freedom to move across certain spaces and to render them dependent on states and the state system for the authorization to do so – an authority widely held in private hands theretofore. A critical aspect of this process has been that people have also become dependent on states for the possession of an "identity" from which they can escape only with difficulty and which may significantly shape their access to various spaces. There are, of course, virtues to this system – principally of a diplomatic nature – just as the expropriation of workers by capitalists allows propertyless workers to

4

survive as wage laborers and the expropriation of the means of violence by states tends to pacify everyday life. Yet in the course of each of these transformations, workers, aggressors, and travelers, respectively, have each been subjected to a form of dependency they had not previously known.

Let me emphasize that I am not claiming that states and the state system *effectively* control all movements of persons, but only that they have monopolized the *authority* to restrict movement vis-a-vis other potential claimants, such as private economic or religious entities. Such entities may play a role in the control of movement, but they do so today at the behest of states. Nor am I arguing that states' monopolization of the legitimate means of movement is a generalization valid for all times and places; the monopolization of this authority by states emerged only gradually after the medieval period and paralleled states' monopolization of the legitimate means of violence. My argument bears strong similarities to that of John Meyer when he addresses the delegitimation of organizational forms other than the nation-state in the emerging "world polity." Various non-state associations, Meyer writes

> are kept from maintaining private armies, their territory and property are subject to state expropriation, and their attempts to control their populations are stigmatized as slavery . . . although states routinely exercise such controls with little question. A worker may properly be kept from crossing state boundaries, and may even be kept from crossing firm boundaries by the state, but not by the firm.[1]

To be more precise, firms may keep a worker from crossing the boundaries of the firm, but they do so under authority granted them by the state.

An understanding of the processes whereby states monopolized the legitimate means of movement is crucial to an adequate comprehension of how modern states actually work. Most analyses of state formation heretofore have focused on the capacity of states to penetrate societies, without explicitly telling us *how* they effect this penetration. Such analyses have posited that successful states developed the ability to reach into societies to extract various kinds of resources, yet they typically fail to offer any specific discussion of the means they adopted to achieve these ends. Foucault's writings on "governmentality" and the techniques of modern governance represent an important corrective to this tradition. For all their preoccupation with policing, population, and "pastoral power," however, Foucault's considerations of these matters lack any precise discussion of the techniques of identification that have played a crucial role in the development of modern, territorial states resting on distinctions between citizens/nationals and aliens.[2]

Meanwhile, analyses of migration and migration policies have tended to take the existence of states largely for granted, typically attributing migration to a variety of socioeconomic processes ("push–pull" processes, "chain migration," "transnational communities," etc.) without paying adequate attention to territorial states' need to distinguish "on the ground" among different populations or to the ways in which the activities of states – especially war-making and state-building – result in population movements. The chief exception to this generalization has been to be found in the writings of Aristide Zolberg, who has been urging for two decades that the state-building (and state-destroying) activities of states should occupy a central role in studies of human movement or its absence, alongside the more routine examination of states' immigration policies.[3] Rather than ignoring the role of states, studies of immigration policies take them as given and thus fail to see the ways in which regulation of movement contributes to constituting the very "state-ness" of states.

These approaches are inadequate for understanding either the development of modern states or migration patterns. In what follows, I seek to supersede these partial perspectives and to show that states' monopolization of the right to authorize and regulate movement has been intrinsic to the very construction of states since the rise of absolutism in early modern Europe. I also attempt to demonstrate that procedures and mechanisms for identifying persons are essential to this process, and that, in order to be implemented in practice, the notion of national communities must be codified in documents rather than merely "imagined."[4]

In the remainder of this chapter, I undertake four tasks. First, I show how and why states have sought to monopolize the "legitimate means of movement" – that is, to gather into their own hands the exclusive right to authorize and regulate movement. Next, I argue that the processes involved in this monopolization force us to rethink the very nature of modern states as they have been portrayed by the dominant strands of sociological theories of the state. In particular, I seek to show that the notion that states "penetrate" societies over time fails adequately to characterize the nature of state development, and argue instead that we would do better to regard states as "embracing" their citizenries more successfully over time. Then, I analyze the need for states to identify unambiguously who belongs and who does not – in order to "embrace" their members more effectively and to exclude unwanted intruders. Finally, I examine some of the efforts of early modern states in Europe to implement documentary restrictions on movement, and thus to render populations accessible to their embrace.

MONOPOLIZING THE LEGITIMATE MEANS OF MOVEMENT

States have sought to monopolize the capacity to authorize the movements of persons – and unambiguously to establish their identities in order to enforce this authority – for a great variety of reasons which reflect the ambiguous nature of modern states, which are at once sheltering and dominating. These reasons include such objectives as the extraction of military service, taxes, and labor; the facilitation of law enforcement; the control of "brain drain" (i.e., limitation of departure in order to forestall the loss of workers with particularly valued skills); the restriction of access to areas deemed "off-limits" by the state, whether for "security" reasons or to protect people from unexpected or unacknowledged harms; the exclusion, surveillance, and containment of "undesirable elements," whether these are of an ethnic, national, racial, economic, religious, ideological, or medical character; and the supervision of the growth, spatial distribution, and social composition of populations within their territories.

States' efforts to monopolize the legitimate means of movement have involved a number of mutually reinforcing aspects: the (gradual) definition of states everywhere – at least from the point of view of the international system – as "national" (i.e., as "nation-states" comprising members understood as nationals); the codification of laws establishing which types of persons may move within or cross their borders, and determining how, when, and where they may do so; the stimulation of the worldwide development of techniques for uniquely and unambiguously identifying each and every person on the face of the globe, from birth to death; the construction of bureaucracies designed to implement this regime of identification and to scrutinize persons and documents in order to verify identities; and the creation of a body of legal norms designed to adjudicate claims by individuals to entry into particular spaces and territories. Only recently have states actually developed the capacities necessary to monopolize the authority to regulate movement.

To be sure, despotisms everywhere frequently asserted controls on movement before the modern period, but these states generally lacked the extensive administrative infrastructure necessary to carry out such regulation in a pervasive and systematic fashion. The *successful* monopolization of the legitimate means of movement by states and the state system required the creation of elaborate bureaucracies and technologies that only gradually came into existence, a trend that intensified dramatically toward the end of the nineteenth century. The process decisively depended on what Gérard Noiriel has called the "*révolution identificatoire*," the development of "cards" and "codes" that identified people (more or less) unambiguously and distinguished among them for administrative purposes.[5] Such documents had existed previously, of course, but their uniform dissemination throughout whole societies, not to mention their worldwide spread as the international passport with which we are familiar today, would be some time in coming. Once they became available to (almost) anyone, however, they also became a requirement for legitimate movement across territorial spaces.

Things have not always been this way. The great migrations that populated many of the world's inhabited regions would otherwise have been greatly hampered, if not rendered impossible. Where the right to authorize movement was controlled by particular social groups before the coalescence of the modern state system (and indeed until well after it had come into being), these groups were as often private entities as constituted political authorities. Indentured servants' right to move, for example, was under the control of their masters. Under serfdom, the serfs' legal capacity to move lay in the hands of their landlords, who had jurisdiction over them. Slavery, even when it did not involve actual shackles, entailed that slaveholders held the power to grant their slaves the right to move.[6]

As modern states advanced and systems of forced labor such as slavery and serfdom declined, however, states and the international state system stripped private entities of the power to authorize and forbid movement and gathered that power unto themselves. In doing so, they were responding to a considerable extent to the imperatives of territorial rule characteristic of modern states, as well as to the problem of "masterless men"[7] as personal freedom advanced. The phenomenon is captured nicely in Karl Polanyi's discussion of the emergence of "the poor" as a distinctive group in early modern England:

> [T]hey became conspicuous as *individuals unattached to the manor,* "or to any feudal superior[,]" and their gradual transformation into a class of free laborers was the combined result of the fierce persecution of vagrancy and the fostering of domestic industry . . .[8]

The transition from private to state control over movement was an essential aspect of the transition from feudalism to capitalism.

The process through which states monopolized the legitimate means of movement thus took hundreds of years to come to fruition. It followed the shift of orientations from the local to the "national" level that accompanied the development of "national" states out of the panoply of empires and smaller city-states and principalities that dotted the map of early modern Europe. The process also paralleled the rationalization and nationalization of poor relief, for communal obligations to provide such relief were an important source of the desire for controls on movement. Previously in the domain of private and religious organizations, the administration of poor relief gradually came to be removed from their purview and lodged in that of states. As European states declined in number, grew in size, and fostered large-scale markets for wage labor outside the reach of landowners and against the traditional constraints imposed by localities, the provision of poor relief also moved from the local to the national arena.[9] These processes, in turn, helped to expand "outward" to the "national" borders the areas in which persons could expect to move freely and without authorization. Eventually, the principal boundaries that counted were those not of municipalities, but of nation-states.

The process took place unevenly in different places, following the line where modern states replaced non-territorial forms of political organization[10] and "free" wage labor replaced various forms of servitude. Then, as people from all levels of society came to find themselves in a more nearly equal position relative to the state, state controls on movement among local spaces within their domains subsided and were replaced by restrictions that concerned the outer "national" boundaries of states. Ultimately, the authority to regulate movement came to be primarily a property of the international system as a whole – that is, of nation-states acting in concert to enforce their interests in controlling who comes and goes. Where pronounced state controls on movement operate *within* a state today, especially when these are to the detriment of particular "negatively privileged" status groups, we can reliably expect to find an authoritarian state (or worse). The cases of the Soviet Union, Nazi Germany, apartheid-era South Africa, and Communist China (at least before the 1980s) bear witness to this generalization.[11]

The creation of the modern passport system and the use of similar systems in the interior of a variety of countries – the product of centuries-long labors of slow, painstaking bureaucratic construction – thus signaled the dawn of a new era in human affairs, in which individual states and the international state system as a whole successfully monopolized the legitimate authority to permit movement within and across their jurisdictions. The point here is obviously not that there is no unauthorized (international) migration, but rather that such movement is specifically "illegal"; that is, we speak of "illegal" (often, indeed, of "undocumented") migration as a result of states' monopolization of the legitimate means of movement. What we now think of as "internal" movement – a meaningless and anachronistic notion before the development of modern states and the state system – has come to mean movement within national or "nation-states." Historical evidence indicates clearly that, well into the nineteenth century, people routinely regarded as "foreign" those from the next province every bit as much as those who came from other "countries."

None of this is to say that private actors now play no role in the regulation of movement – far from it. Yet private entities have been reduced to the capacity of "sheriff's deputies" who participate in the regulation of movement at the behest of states. During the nineteenth and into the twentieth century, for example, governments in Europe pressed steamship companies into overseeing for them whether particular people should be permitted to travel to the destinations they had chosen. Since the development of air travel, airline companies have been subjected to similar obligations. Both shipping enterprises and air carriers have frequently resisted carrying out the sheriff's deputy function, mainly because they fear that their participation in such quasi-governmental activities will hurt their profitability. Not wanting to appear guilty of mere cupidity, however, they are likely to say that they regard the regulation of movement as the proper province of the state – and so it is. [12]

If, along with their efforts to monopolize the legitimate use of violence, modern states also seek to monopolize the legitimate means of movement, they must have means to *implement* the constraints they enunciate in this domain. In order to do so, they must be able to construct an enduring relationship between the sundry agencies that constitute states and both the individuals they govern and possible interlopers. This fact compels us to reconsider the principal line of sociological argumentation concerning the way modern states have developed.

MODERN STATES: "PENETRATING" OR "EMBRACING"?

Previous sociological discussion of the development of modern states has focused attention primarily on their growing capacity to "penetrate" or "reach into" societies and extract from them what they need in order to survive. Discussions of states as "penetrating" societies more effectively during the modern period can be found in almost any major recent sociological discussion of the nature of modern states. [13] Going the state theorists one better, Jürgen Habermas expanded the metaphor of "penetration" to characterize the activity of both the modern bureaucratic state and the capitalist economy. Habermas thus speaks of the "colonization of the life-world" by the "steering media" of money and power. [14] Yet Habermas's analysis shares the weaknesses of the "penetrationist" paradigm of state theory, for "money" is rather more concrete than "power" as a mechanism for enabling and constraining social choices. But we may correct for the abstractness of "power" relative to that of money by seeing that identification papers of various kinds constitute the bureaucratic equivalent of money: they are the currency of modern state administration.

The traditional (and unmistakably sexual) imagery of societies being "penetrated" by the state, however, unnecessarily and misleadingly narrows our analytical vision about the nature of modern states. In particular, the "penetrationist" approach has had little to say about the mechanisms adopted and employed by states to construct and sustain enduring relationships between themselves and their subjects, the "social base" of their reproduction. The metaphor of the "penetration" of societies by states thus distorts the nature of the process whereby states have amassed the capacity to reconfigure social life by focusing our attention almost exclusively on the notion that states "rise up" above and surmount the isolated societies that seem, in this metaphor, to lie prostrate beneath them. Willingly or unwillingly, the now-standard imagery of penetration suggests, more or less weak societies simply receive the advances of more or less powerful states. Having been penetrated, societies give up – to a greater or lesser extent – what states demand of them. But how does this actually happen? How are the people who make up "societies" compelled to "render unto Caesar what is Caesar's"?

In order to extract resources and implement policies, states must be in a position to locate and lay claim to people and goods. This fact suggests an alternative imagery to that of "penetration" for understanding the accumulation of infrastructural capacity by modern states. Foucault has of course stressed the importance of "surveillance" in modern societies, but it often remains unclear in his writings to what particular purposes surveillance is being put. I believe we would do well to regard states as seeking not simply to penetrate but also to *embrace* societies, "surrounding" and "taking hold" of their members – individually and collectively – as those states grow larger and more administratively adept. More than this, states *must* embrace societies *in order to* penetrate them effectively. Individuals who remain beyond the embrace of the state necessarily represent a limit on its penetration. The *reach* of the state, in other words, cannot exceed its *grasp*. Michael Mann is correct that the "unusual strength of modern states is infrastructural,"[15] and their capacity to embrace their own subjects and to exclude unwanted others is the essence of that infrastructural power.

My use of the term "embrace" derives from the German word *erfassen*, which means to "grasp" or "lay hold of" in the sense of "register." Thus, for example, foreigners registered at the *Ausländerbehörde* (Agency for Foreigners) are said to be "*ausländerbehördlich erfasst*" – i.e., registered for purposes of surveillance, administration, and regulation by that agency. People are also "*erfassen*" by the census. It says something important about the divergent processes of state-building on the European continent and in the Anglo-American world that we lack ordinary English equivalents for the German "*erfassen*" (as well as for the French verb *surveiller*). Whether or not our language adequately reflects this reality, however, the activities by which states "embrace" populations have become essential to the production and reproduction of states in the modern period.

In contrast to the masculinized image of "penetrating" states surmounting societies, the metaphor of states' "embrace" of societies directs our awareness to the ways in which states bound – and in certain senses even "nurture" – the societies they hold in their clutches. In this regard, the imagery of "embracing" states shares similarities with Michael Mann's notion of the way states "cage" social activity within them, particularly the way in which the rise of national states tended to reorient political activity from the local or regional to the national level.[16] Yet Mann's "caging" metaphor fails to get at the way in which states metaphorically "grasp" both entire societies and individual people in order to carry out their aims. My metaphor of states "embracing" their populations is much more akin to James Scott's idea that states seek to render societies "legible" and thus more readily available for governance.[17]

The notion that states "embrace" individuals goes further, however, by calling to mind the fact that states hold *particular* persons within their grasp, while excluding others. This consideration is especially important in a world of states defined as nation-states – that is, as states comprising members conceived as nationals – and concerned successfully to monopolize the legitimate means of movement. In contrast, the imagery of "penetration" is blind to the peculiarities of the society that the state invades. Surely the metaphor of "embrace" helps make better sense of a world of states that are understood to consist of mutually exclusive bodies of citizens whose movements may be restricted as such.

Systems of registration, censuses, and the like – along with documents such as passports and identity cards that amount to mobile versions of the "files" states use to store knowledge about their subjects – have been crucial in states' efforts to achieve these aims. Though not without flaws and loopholes, of course, such registration systems have gone a long way toward allowing states successfully to "embrace" their populations and thus to acquire from them the resources they need to survive, as well as to exclude from among the beneficiaries of state largesse those groups deemed ineligible for benefits.

Modern "nation-states" and the international system in which they are embedded have grown increasingly committed to and reliant upon their ability to make strict demarcations between mutually distinct bodies of citizens, as well as among different groups of their own subjects, when one or more of these groups are singled out for "special treatment." The need to sort out "who is who" and, perhaps more significantly, "what is what" becomes especially acute when states wish to regulate movement across external borders. This is because, as Mary Douglas wrote some years ago, "all margins are dangerous . . . [A]ny structure of ideas is vulnerable at its margins."[18] The idea of belonging that is at the root of the concept of citizenship is threatened when people cross borders, leaving spaces where they "belong" and entering those where they do not.

Yet the nation-state is far more than a "structure of ideas." It is also – and more importantly for our purposes – a more or less coherent network of *institutions*. In this respect, recent developments in sociology turn our thinking in a fruitful direction when we try to make sense of how states actually embrace the societies they seek to rule, and to distinguish their members from non-members. Rather than merely suggesting the way institutions shape our everyday world, the "new institutionalism" directs our attention to the "institutional constitution of both interests and actors."[19]

This point has a special relevance with regard to identities. Too frequently in recent academic writing, identities have been discussed in purely subjective terms, without reference to the ways in which identities are anchored in law and policy. This subjectivistic approach, given powerful impetus by the wide and much-deserved attention given to Benedict Anderson's notion of "imagined communities," tends to ignore the extent to which identities must become codified and institutionalized in order to become socially significant. Noiriel has made this point in the strongest possible terms with respect to immigrants: "It is often overlooked that legal registration, identification documents, and laws are what, in the final analysis, determine the 'identity' of immigrants."[20]

But the point is more general. The cases of "Hispanics" (as opposed to Caribbeans or South or Central Americans, for example) or "Asian Americans" (as opposed to Japanese-Americans, Korean-Americans, etc.) in the United States, categories designed for the use of census-takers and policy-makers with little in the way of subjective correlates at the time of their creation, are here very much to the point. Whether substantial numbers of people think about themselves subjectively in these terms is an open, empirical question; that they would not be likely to do so without the institutional foundation provided by the prior legal codification of the terms seems beyond doubt.

As nation-states – states of and for particular "peoples" defined as mutually exclusive groups of citizens[21] – modern states have typically been eager to embrace their populations, and to regulate the movements of persons within and across their borders when they wish to do so. Their efforts to implement such regulation have driven them toward the creation of the means uniquely and unambiguously to identify individual persons, whether "their own" or others. In order to monopolize the legitimate means of movement, states and the state system have been compelled to define who belongs and who does not, who may come and go and who not, and to make these distinctions intelligible and enforceable. Documents such as passports and identity cards have been critical to achieving these objectives. Beyond simply enunciating definitions and categories concerning identity, states must *implement* these distinctions, and they require documents in order to do so in individual cases.

GETTING A GRIP: INSTITUTIONALIZING THE NATION-STATE

In order to make sense of the notion that states exist "of and for particular peoples" generally understood today as "nations," we must first consider what a "nation" is. The concept of the nation, according to Weber, entails that we may "expect from certain groups a specific sentiment of solidarity in the face of other groups," without there being any determinate "empirical qualities common to those who count as members of the nation."[22] Following in Weber's footsteps, Rogers Brubaker has stressed the "contingent, conjuncturally fluctuating, and precarious" quality of "nation-ness," pointing out that: "We should not ask 'what is a nation' but rather: how is nationhood as a political and cultural form institutionalized within and among states?"[23] Brubaker's institutionalist constructionism provides an important corrective to those views (typically held above all by nationalists themselves) that suggest that "the nation" is a real, enduring historical entity. Failing their institutionalization, "nations" must remain ephemeral and fuzzy.

How, indeed, is nationhood institutionalized? More specifically, precisely how is the nexus between states, subjects, and potential interlopers generated and sustained? In order to extract the resources they need to survive, and to compel participation in repressive forces where necessary, states must embrace – that is, identify and gain enduring access to – those from whom they hope to derive those resources. Alternatively, states must be in a position to establish whether or not a would-be entrant matches the criteria laid down for authorized entry into their domains. Charles Tilly has noted that the French Revolution's inauguration of what he aptly calls "direct rule" gave rulers "access to citizens and the resources they controlled through household taxation, mass conscription, censuses, police systems, and many other invasions of small-scale social life."[24] Yet this listing leaves the matter too vague for adequate comprehension of the way in which states have, in fact, "invaded" small-scale social life and sought to render populations available to their embrace.

In particular, Tilly's enumeration of invasions leaves unclear how taxation and conscription grew to depend decisively on mechanisms of surveillance such as censuses, household registration systems, passports (internal and external), and other identity documents. The activities classically associated with the rise of modern states only became possible on a systematic basis if states were in a position successfully to embrace their populations for purposes of carrying out those activities. Such devices as identity papers, censuses, and travel certificates thus were not merely on a par with conscription and taxation as elements of state-building, but were in fact essential to their successful realization and grew, over time, superordinate to them as tools of administration that made these other activities possible or at least enforceable.

Sociologists of the state have begun in recent years to address more adequately the problem of how states construct a durable relation between themselves and their subjects/citizens in furtherance of their own aims. This concern has been especially prominent in the work of Anthony Giddens. In his important study *The Nation-State and Violence*, Giddens pays considerable attention to the growing role of surveillance in the development of "direct rule." In contrast to "traditional states," Giddens noted that modern states presuppose a regularized administration and that much of the necessary administrative capacity of modern states is rooted in *writing*. It is through written documents – such as identification papers – that much of the surveillance entailed by modern state administration is carried out: "[A]dministrative power can only become established if the coding of information is actually applied in a direct way to the supervision of human activities . . ."[25] Max Weber had earlier noted the importance of "the files" as an important element of bureaucratization, of course, but he failed to indicate their enormous role in the construction of states' enduring embrace of their citizens. Yet despite the heightened attention to the relationship between states and their subjects/citizens in recent writing on the development of state capacities, we still have little idea of how this relationship is actually constructed and sustained.

The essence of the problem can be couched in terms of states' need to be able to embrace their populations and to distinguish them from others. From the point of view of states' interests in keeping track of populations and their movements, people are little but "stigmata," appropriately processed for administrative use. The classic analysis of the operation of and responses to stigmata in informal interaction is Erving Goffman's discussion of *Stigma*,[26] where the burden of the analysis is on the management of "spoiled identity." But the problem is more pervasive than Goffman indicated, a fact that surely would have been clear to him if he had devoted more attention to the operations of bureaucratic institutions.

In one of his few sustained treatments of formal institutional environments, the irreplaceable essay on "total institutions" in *Asylums*,[27] Goffman shows that the effort to impose control in such environments begins with systematic attempts to annihilate the "identities" – the selves – of their inmates. In total institutions, the point is to deprive individuals of the personality resources that they might use to mount a defense against their condition. "On the outside," however, obliteration of individual identity would be ruinous to the state, for it would short-circuit the essential process of identifying individuals for administrative purposes. This outcome

15

would frustrate the performance of those universal and indispensable state activities, the extraction of resources from subjects to nourish the administrative and coercive agencies that constitute and (assuming the state continues to function coherently) continuously replenish states.

Michel Foucault extrapolated these basic insights into a nightmarish, dystopic, even absurd vision of modern society as a "carceral" world pervaded by "gentle" means of discipline and control carried out under and through the watchful eye of the "individualizing gaze."[28] Foucault dramatized this intuition by suggesting that Bentham's (never-built) "Panopticon," in which individual prisoners could be seen by a centrally located guard who was himself invisible to them, had become the basic model of modern social organization. In a sense, Foucault only drew the logical consequences from Weber's persistent fears about the juggernaut of bureaucratic rationalization. Yet Foucault's emphasis on the intimate connections between power and knowledge, and on the crucial importance of individual surveillance in modern administrative systems, has proven enormously suggestive.

Indeed, the following passage from a manual for driver's license tests issued by the State of California offers remarkably clear evidence of the profound importance that identification practices have assumed in modern times:

> IDENTIFICATION: The issue of identification (ID) – its reliability, integrity, confidentiality, etc. – is of prime concern to all levels of government, and the private sector as well. The eligibility for government services, the issuance of various licenses, the assessment of taxes, the right to vote, etc., are all determined through evaluations based in part on the identification documents you present. *It becomes critical that ID documents and systems be completely authenticated and accurate in order to positively and uniquely identify each individual.*[29]

By their own lights, then, states have come decisively to depend on the unique and unambiguous identification of individuals in order to carry out their most fundamental tasks.[30] The examination of individual stigmata, the essential form of which lies at the heart of all modern systems of identification, "places individuals in a field of surveillance [and also] situates them in a network of writing; it engages them in a whole mass of documents that capture and fix them."[31] The document held by the individual as "ID" thus corresponds to an entire series of files chronicling movements, economic transactions, familial ties, illnesses, and much else besides – the power/knowledge grid in which individuals are processed and constituted as administrative subjects of states.

The achievement of this administrative knowledge was a long time in coming, however; state-sponsored identification practices with the aim of extending states' embrace of their populations have evolved significantly over time. Prior to the French Revolution, for example, descriptions of a person's social standing – residence, occupation, family status, etc. – were generally regarded as adequate indicators of a person's identity for purposes of internal passport controls in France.[32] Thereafter, the growing preoccupation with surveillance and the progress of modern science combined to render insufficient these earlier, more homespun practices. States wanted to embrace their inhabitants more firmly, and to be able to distinguish them from outsiders more clearly, than was possible with such methods. Achievement of this aim necessitated greater precision in identifying them. Yet at the same time, the rise of liberal and natural law ideas proclaiming individual freedom and the inviolability of the person cast into disfavor older habits of "writing on the body" such as branding, scarification, and tattooing, as well as dress codes as means for identifying persons (except when these methods of marking are voluntarily assumed, of course).

As a result, states with a rising interest in embracing their populations had to develop less invasive means to identify people. The approach they adopted employs roughly the same principle that underlies ju-jitsu: the person's body is used *against* him or her, in this case as evidence of identity. Techniques for "reading off the body" have become more and more sophisticated over time, shifting from unreliable subjective descriptions and anthropometric measurements to photographs (themselves at first often considered unreliable by police), fingerprinting, electronically scanned palm-prints, DNA fingerprinting, and the retina scans dramatized in the recent film version of *Mission: Impossible*. The persistent tinkering with these techniques indicates that states (and other entities, of course) have a powerful and enduring interest in identifying persons, both their own subjects and those of other countries. The ability of states uniquely and unambiguously to identify persons, whether "their own" or others, is at the heart of the process whereby states, and the international state system, have succeeded over time in monopolizing the legitimate means of movement in the modern world.

Against this background, let us briefly examine the imposition of passport controls in early modern European states, as rulers increasingly sought to establish untrammeled claims over territories and people. Such rulers began to move away, however unintentionally, from a "political map [that] was an inextricably superimposed and tangled one, in which different juridical instances were geographically interwoven and stratified, and plural allegiances, asymmetrical suzerainties and anomalous enclaves abounded."[33] In doing so, they cleared away some of the medieval underbrush that stood between them and the nation-state.

THE PREVALENCE OF PASSPORT CONTROLS IN ABSOLUTIST EUROPE

Passport controls in Europe are hardly a recent invention. The exigencies of rule in early modern Europe led states to take a considerable interest in strengthening their power to regulate the comings and goings of their subjects. The mercantilist policies pursued by these states entailed the general presupposition that population was tantamount to, or at least convertible into, wealth and military strength. Accordingly, these rulers had a powerful interest in identifying and controlling the movements of their subjects. This they sought to do with a variety of strictures on movement that frequently involved documents as the means for their enforcement.

For example, with Prussia's Imperial Police Ordinances of 1548, beggars and vagrants "were banned as a threat to domestic peace, law, and order." Shortly thereafter, an edict of the Imperial Diet prohibited the issuance of "passes" to "gypsies and vagabonds [*Landstreicher*]," suggesting both that these two groups were in bad odor and that passes were required as part of the normal procedure for removing from one place to another, at least for those of the lower orders.[34] By the seventeenth century, German rulers made laws intended to tie servants more firmly to their masters, and thus also to squelch those bogeys of the officialdom, vagrancy and itinerancy.[35]

Meanwhile, across the Channel, similar developments had been afoot for some time. Despite the guarantee of the English subject's freedom to depart in the Magna Carta, a statute of 1381 forbade all but peers, notable merchants, and soldiers to leave the kingdom without a license.[36] Early modern English rulers were especially concerned that uncontrolled departures would facilitate religious deviance.[37] Then, not long after the English Civil War, an alleged upsurge in itinerancy generated by the desire of the destitute to turn up more generous rates of poor relief than were available in their native villages led the English monarch Charles II to adopt a law severely restricting movement from one parish to another. The "Act for the better Reliefe of the Poore of this Kingdom" of 1662[38] empowered the local authorities to remove to their place of legal settlement anyone "likely to be chargeable to the parish" – or, to put it in terms that would later become familiar in American immigration legislation, anyone "likely to become a public charge." At the same time, the law allowed migration for purposes of performing seasonal or other temporary labor, provided that the person or persons involved "carry with him or them a certificate from the minister of the parish and one of the churchwardens and one of the overseers for the poore" attesting to their legal domicile, to which they were required to return upon completion of such work. These laws governing movement helped to codify in law – and to implement in practice – a distinction between "local" and "foreign" poor, and notably referred to the place to which illegal settlers should be removed as their "native" residence. The act of removing oneself from one's place of birth thus appears to have been regarded as an anomaly, and may indeed have constituted a violation of the law without proper papers.

To the east, trends toward enhanced documentary controls on movement received a powerful boost from Russian Czar, Peter the Great. Eager to advance Russia's standing among the Continental powers, Peter's modernizing reforms arose primarily from a desire to improve the country's military capabilities. In this enterprise Peter was smashingly successful, for by 1725 he had created the largest standing army in Europe.[39] Such armies required extensive recruitment and, consequently, systematic access to the young men of the country. One means for the state to gain such access was to restrict mobility by requiring documentation of movement and residence. Consistent with this aim, the Czar in the early eighteenth century promulgated a series of decrees regulating the domicile and travel of Russian subjects. An edict of 1719 required anyone moving from one town or village to another to have in his (or less likely her) possession a pass from his superiors.[40] This ukase only broadened the provisions of the legal code of 1649 that had originally consolidated the Russian pattern of serfdom, the very essence of which lay in its controls on peasant movements.[41] The use of documents as mechanisms of control made serfdom's legal restrictions on peasant movements easier to enforce.

These examples demonstrate clearly that restrictions on personal freedom of movement related directly to two central questions facing burgeoning modern states: (1) how the economic advantages available in a particular area were to be divided up, whether these involved access to work or to poor relief; and (2) who would be required to perform military service, and how they would be constrained to do so. In other words, documentary controls on movement were decisively bound up with the rights and duties that would eventually come to be associated with membership – citizenship – in the nation-state.

Until the ultimate triumph of capitalism and the nation-state in nineteenth-century Europe, however, controls on movement remained predominantly an "internal" matter. This fact reflected the powerfully local orientation of life and the law, as well as the persistence of mercantilist ideas about population-as-wealth and the relatively inchoate character of states and the international state system. Gradually, competition among states set in motion processes of centralization that resulted in a winnowing of the number of competitors, such that only those states capable of mobilizing sufficient military and economic resources survived.[42]

In the course of these developments, rulers seeking to expand their domains and their grip on populations increasingly asserted their authority to determine who could come and go in their territories. For example, during the late medieval period in France, the legal concept of the "foreigner" shifted from the local to the "national" level (at this point the term can still only be applied anachronistically), and from the private realm to that of the state, as a consequence of the royal usurpation from the *seigneurie* of the so-called *droit d'aubaine*, according to which foreigners had been defined as those born outside the *seigneurie*.

> This [shift] created for the first time a kingdomwide status of foreigner and, correlatively, an embryonic legal status of French citizen or national. The legal distinction between French citizen and foreigner thus originated in the late medieval consolidation of royal authority at the expense of seigneurial rights.[43]

The monopolization of the legitimate means of movement by states entailed their successful assertion of the authority to determine who "belonged" and who did not. The state's complete expropriation of the power to authorize movement would take some time to achieve, of course, but they were well on their way to making this monopoly a reality.

To these more strictly political considerations must be added Karl Polanyi's compelling portrayal of the decisive role of the early modern state in weaving together local into national markets, a process that frequently involved the triumph of the central state against fierce local resistance. This gradual transformation facilitated a sea-change in conceptions of "internal" and "external" territory and thus in the nature of the restrictions on who could come and go, and with whose authorization.[44] As markets for labor power, in particular, became "nationalized," states asserted dominion over the right to determine who could move about and under what conditions. The general result of the process was that local borders were replaced by national ones, and that the chief difficulty associated with human movement was entry into, not departure from, territorial spaces. The spread of identification documents such as passports was crucial to states' monopolization of the legitimate means of movement. But this would take some time to achieve in practice, and began by facing a sharp challenge from the libertarian elements in the French Revolution. It is to the events of that upheaval, typically thought of as the "birth of the nation-state," that we now turn.

CHAPTER 2

"ARGUS OF THE *PATRIE*": THE PASSPORT QUESTION IN THE FRENCH REVOLUTION

THE PASSPORT PROBLEM AT THE END OF THE OLD REGIME

In his recent history of the state built by the French revolutionaries, Isser Woloch has noted that "passports and certificates of residence [became] extremely important documents as conscription became a way of life," and that "birth registers [were] the key to the whole process" of conscription, a process Woloch rightly regards as the revolutionaries' most significant, enduring, yet improbable institutional achievement.[1] While Woloch is correct that the success of conscription depended on bureaucratic mechanisms designed to identify and regulate the movements of the citizenry, this approach to state administration would first have to overcome vigorous antipathy toward such means by many of the participants in the revolutionary project.

Passport controls, in particular, had been a vital mechanism of domination under the old regime in France, and were clearly regarded as such by those who made the revolution there in the late eighteenth century. Among the many restrictions to which the French revolutionaries objected was a 1669 edict of Louis XIV that had forbidden his subjects to leave the territory of France, as well as to related requirements that those quitting the Kingdom be in possession of a passport authorizing them to do so.[2] In addition, commoners on the move *within* eighteenth-century France were technically required to have one of two documents: a passport issued by the town hall in the traveler's native village or the so-called *aveu*, an attestation of upright character from local religious authorities.

The principal purpose of these documentary requirements was to forestall any undesired migration to the cities, especially Paris. They were at least occasionally effective in achieving their aims. Yet, as Richard Cobb has pointed out: "France had a population that, in its vast

21

majority, walked; and there is no one more difficult to control than the pedestrian."[3] Rather than issuing documents, under these circumstances simply closing the gates of the town was a highly successful means of controlling pedestrians, as viewers of the film version of Victor Hugo's *Les Misérables* may recall. People who do not move in a container of some sort are difficult to constrain, and the effort to restrict them may entail turning the area to be controlled itself into a container.

Notwithstanding the documentary requirements in force in old regime France, passports had a notorious propensity to go "lost," in which case replacements were to be secured in the area in which the traveler then found him- or herself (arrangements drastically at odds with the situation today, where those who attempt to cross an international border without satisfactory documentation are normally denied entry or returned immediately to their point of departure). Even the most unsavory figures apparently found it possible thus to get their hands on the papers they needed, even though they might have been denied them by the authorities in their place of origin. "Hence," as Olwen Hufton has put it, "possession of a passport was not conclusive evidence of innocence, and lack of one did not prove guilt."[4] Passport restrictions were a nuisance for many, to be sure, but administrative laxity and the well-meaning assistance of a variety of benefactors frequently made a mockery of the state's use of documentary controls as a means of regulating movement.

Despite the relative ease with which passport requirements could often be skirted, these controls on movement appeared among the many complaints regarding royal government and feudal organization that were presented in the *cahiers de doléances* during the meeting of the Estates General convened at Versailles in early 1789. Thus article 2 of the *cahiers* of the parish of Neuilly-sur-Marne pleaded:

> As every man is equal before God and every sojourner in this life must be left undisturbed in his legitimate possessions, especially in his natural and political life, it is the wish of this assembly that individual liberty be guaranteed to all the French, and therefore that each must be free to move about or to come, within and outside the Kingdom, without permissions, passports, or other formalities that tend to hamper the liberty of its citizens. . .[5]

On this view, passport controls and other "formalities" associated with physical mobility undermined the natural and civil rights of the French.

In a debate that would last throughout the revolutionary period and beyond, however, other petitioners to the Estates General demanded more vigorous enforcement of the existing passport controls in the interest of greater public security. For example, the order of the *noblesse du bailliage* of Montargis urged in its *cahiers* that those charged with the maintenance of public security be required to exercise "the most meticulous oversight over the certificates and passports of vagabonds and those without an *aveu*."[6] Yet one should bear in mind Georges Lefebvre's estimation that the *cahiers* of the bailiwicks (*bailliages*) are even less representative of the popular will than the grievances expressed by other jurisdictions – which already tended to mute the voices of the peasantry – because their betters often "simply eliminated from the original lists those demands which displeased them or did not interest them."[7] As the passport and the *aveu* were instruments of social control that plagued primarily the lower orders, the demand of the Montargis notables may well have reflected a bias in favor of the views of the privileged strata.

The representatives to the Estates General thus vied contentiously over the liberty of people to circulate in France without documentary attestation, and the issue carried over into the discussions of the Constituent Assembly after the fall of the Bastille. As a consequence of the Tennis Court Oath, according to which the revolutionaries had pledged in late June 1789 not to leave Paris without completing work on a new constitution,[8] the assembly ironically found itself on 9 October 1789 discussing the freedom of its own members to move about. The "October Days" had begun, and the Assembly was under intense pressure to resolve food shortages that had galvanized the common people into action.

The debate was joined after the president of the house sought the authority to issue or deny the passports that had been requested of him by various members of the Assembly. Dividing the two sides of the debate was the question whether one could limit the freedom of the deputies by denying them passports, on the one hand, and whether deputies should leave their posts in the country's hour of need, particularly given that the foot-soldiers of the nation would not be allowed to do so, on the other. In the end, the Assembly granted its president the authority to issue passports to its members, thus making the liberal choice that freedom of movement was to be preferred to constraint, even under conditions of substantial domestic political tension.[9] The forces supporting free movement seem to have gained the high ground more generally as well, for according to Donald Greer, a prominent historian of the revolutionary emigration: "During the greater part of the period . . . 1789–1792, Frenchmen were free to go and come as they pleased."[10]

Yet Greer's judgment here is misleading in at least two respects. First, contrary to what our contemporary sensibilities might lead us to expect, the freedom to come and go to which Greer refers was not restricted to the native population. With the outbreak of the revolution, France had welcomed into its bosom a considerable number of persons not of French origin, many of whom were political refugees from their noble-dominated countries and favorably predisposed toward revolutionary ideology. Such "friends of liberty" were widely indulged in the cosmopolitanism of the revolutionaries.[11] Second and more importantly, one must bear in mind that this was a period of grain riots, rural revolt, and ultimately the threat of foreign invasion and war. Many people long familiar with the restrictions on movement characteristic of the *ancien régime* remained anxious about the idea of free-floating marauders and the footloose poor coming and going as they pleased. Greer's estimate thus misleads because it focuses upon the freedom of the French to enter and leave their country rather than on the liberty to move *within* the Kingdom, which at this point remained very much a live issue – indeed, for most of the French, the primary one.

Greer's optimistic view of freedom of movement among the French during this period sits awkwardly, for example, with the evidence of a decree of the National Assembly dated 30 May – 13 June 1790. The measure was provoked when the Assembly learned that "a great number of foreign mendicants" were taking advantage of the poor relief in Paris to the detriment of the indigenous indigent. The term "foreigner" here applied principally to French citizens from outside the capital. In order to assert greater control over eligibility for poor relief in France's principal city, the decree required every non-French beggar or person without an *aveu* who had not been domiciled in Paris for at least one year, as well as mendicant French persons resident in Paris for less than six months, to leave Paris and to obtain a passport indicating the route they would follow in leaving the Kingdom or returning to their native place. Those who departed from the route indicated in their passports, or who stopped along the way for any length of time, were to be arrested by the national guards or departmental police and required to explain themselves.[12]

The persistence of these kinds of restrictions soon provoked the ire of a commentator named "Peuchet," who was given space in *Le Moniteur*, one of the principal outlets for revolutionary debate, to publish a scathing indictment of "the slavery of passports" in mid-1790. Insisting that the French state had delivered up the individual's "movements and his conduct to a surveillance as extensive as it is dangerous" and that every person should be free "to breathe the air he chooses without having to ask permission from a master that can refuse him that right," Peuchet declared passports "contrary to every principle of justice and reason" and demanded their abolition. He also noted that, as the provisions of the law discussed above suggest, the constraints on freedom represented by passport requirements fell especially hard on "the poor and obscure class of people."[13] In Peuchet's liberal view, passport controls were part and parcel of the tyrannical, freedom-choking strictures of the *ancien régime*. In response to criticism of his remarks, which were interpreted by his detractors as "favoring those guilty of crimes" because the abolition of passports would allegedly allow them to escape the grasp of the law, Peuchet retorted that this was far from his aim, which concerned the fundamental human right to come and go: "To allow a man to travel is to allow him to do something that one has no right to deny: it is a social injustice."[14].

THE FLIGHT OF THE KING AND THE REVOLUTIONARY RENEWAL OF PASSPORT CONTROLS

These criticisms of the restraints on freedom of movement notwithstanding, attitudes toward free circulation in France changed dramatically with the flight of the King on 21 June 1791. The stage had already been set for a backlash against free movement during the previous months. In February, the departure of the King's aunts had caused a furor in the radical press and given rise to stillborn efforts of the Constituent Assembly to stiffen emigration controls.[15] Then, in March and April, Pope Pius VI officially condemned both the principles of the revolution and the Civil Constitution of the Clergy, and "in an act of incalculable importance the Church of Rome opposed its doctrine to the Declaration of the Rights of Man and Citizen."[16] Those inclined toward counterrevolutionary activity were greatly heartened by the Church's stance. Against this background, Louis XVI absconded for Varennes disguised as a valet. In a state of shocked alarm at the King's attempted escape, the National Assembly mandated a complete halt to departures from the Kingdom and the arrest of anyone attempting to leave.[17]

The Assembly debate over responsibility for authorizing the passports under which the King's party had traveled revealed considerable administrative confusion in this area. In order to clarify the circumstances under which the royal retinue had sought to make off, the Assembly summoned Louis XVI's foreign minister, Montmorin, to its chambers to explain how they had come into possession of their passports. The foreign minister was accused of having furnished the passports under assumed names, and thus of collaborating in the King's escape attempt. In response to the Assembly's inquiry, Montmorin noted that "with the large number of passports [the foreign minister] signs, it is impossible for him to verify whether the name of the persons who request them is true or false." Clearly, a great deal of administrative rationalization would be required before we would reach our present state, in which the effort to acquire documents under an assumed name involves considerable difficulty and ingenuity.

Ultimately, Montmorin was absolved of having surreptitiously issued the passports under assumed names. The King had masqueraded as a valet during the escape attempt, but he was able to do this because passports for the nobility typically included a number of persons listed by their function but without further description ("a valet"), and not as a result of any connivance on the foreign minister's part. The judgment of his innocence came none too soon for Montmorin, whose house was being besieged by crowds who held him responsible for facilitating the King's getaway. The Assembly immediately sent four representatives to announce its findings and thus, it hoped, to forestall any harm to Montmorin's person or property at the hands of the angry mob.[18]

Tempers and apprehensions flared throughout France in the aftermath of the royal escape attempt. According to Georges Lefebvre, "no one doubted that the King's flight heralded invasion," and the National Assembly thus added to its prohibition on departures a call-up of 169 infantry battalions to be raised from among the National Guard. Frontier garrisons prepared for invasion. A "great fear" swept the country, provoking violent retribution against aristocrats and refractory priests as well as attacks on their property.[19]

With the spectre of aristocratic conspiracies stalking the land, the King's flight not only provoked the deputies of the Constituent Assembly to seal the borders; it also appears to have inflamed rogue popular forces to throttle departures from Paris of which they disapproved. On 22 June 1791, the city's mayor issued an order enjoining the Parisian citizenry to permit the exit from the city of those equipped with passports, which he promised would be issued with "discretion and prudence."[20] Under these conditions, possession of a passport bore witness to the revolutionary state's approval of movement by its bearer; it thus functioned as a "safe-conduct" of a kind that would later be associated only with movement into other sovereign jurisdictions, at least in times of peace. This would not be the last time that extralegal elements would contest the state's monopoly on the legitimate right to authorize movement. Indeed, this sort of popular usurpation of the "legitimate means of movement" is typical of situations in which states are being revolutionized or have disintegrated.

Despite the move to close the borders in response to the King's flight, the revolutionary Assembly was, like the Parisian authorities, beset by a concern to insure freedom of movement throughout the interior of the country. Accordingly, the Constituent Assembly only three days later decreed that it was necessary to uphold the right to "free circulation of persons and things," at least up to a distance of ten *lieues* from the border, and that all the administrative, municipal, and military authorities should cooperate to guarantee such freedom. The proponent of the decree defended it above all on administrative grounds, noting that the Assembly's various measures to defend the Kingdom would be futile "if the couriers carrying these orders are stopped in every municipality along the way in order to undergo verification of their passports."[21] At this point, at least, the leaders of the revolution wanted to open up the French territorial space to free movement on administrative, commercial, and liberty grounds. Frontier areas were regarded as "hot," however, for here the administrative and municipal organs were to "keep watch meticulously."[22]

Then, just a week after slamming shut the gates to departures of French citizens from France, the Assembly also decreed that foreigners and French merchants would be free to leave the Kingdom. Before doing so, however, foreigners were to be in possession of a passport supplied by the ambassador from their own country or by the French ministry of foreign affairs, whereas the French merchants were required to obtain a passport from their own or the nearest district capital. In order to avoid a repetition of the sort of disguised escape attempted by the King, article 7 of the decree mandated that "all passports are to contain the number of persons to whom they are given, their names, their age, their description, and the parish inhabited by those who have obtained them, who are obliged to sign both the register of passports and the passports themselves."[23] This provision had been included in the final decree after a member of the Assembly had found insufficient the passport requirements for departure from the realm. Without descriptions (*les signalements*), this critic admonished, those who wished to slip out of the country would have had little difficulty doing so.[24]

In early August 1791, the Constituent Assembly sought to enhance French strength by encouraging the many frightened and disillusioned emigres who had departed after the outbreak of the revolution to return home. As Greer has put it, this was "a prelude *dolce* to the later harsh legislation" on emigration and the emigres. The law upheld the ban on departures from the country and enjoined those who had left after 1 July 1789, to return within one month. "Those who complied were to suffer no penalties; those who disobeyed were to be fined by the triplication of their taxes concurrent with their absence." But the law was weak and remained in force only a little more than a month, when the National Assembly nullified it.[25] Despite the apparently conciliatory attitude toward the emigres expressed by the Assembly in this law, worse – much worse – awaited those who had left France after the onset of the revolution.

What is remarkable about all these regulations from our contemporary standpoint is that the group whose movements the defenders of the revolution were concerned to regulate consisted primarily of their fellow French citizens. Not without reason, the revolutionary leadership regarded the emigres – as potential enemies of the revolution in league with the King, reactionary priests and nobles, and foreign powers – as a profound threat to its survival.[26] And of course there were many others who were viewed with suspicion, and hence as deserving of surveillance and sharpened control. A notion of "foreignness" underlay this attitude, but it was not the same as that now-familiar version that reflects the rivalries of narcissistic nation-states. In his famous pamphlet "What is the Third Estate?" of January 1789, the Abbé Sieyès had written of the nobility: "This class is assuredly foreign to the nation because of its do-nothing idleness."[27] This "political" rather than national definition of the foreigner owed everything to the fact that the revolution had burst upon the stage of world history by defining "the nation" principally in terms that excluded a slothful, parasitic nobility, rather than people from other countries.

At this point, at least, the term "foreigners" therefore applied as much to those who opposed the revolution, regardless of their "national" origins, as it did to persons not of French birth. Reflecting this cosmopolitan view, one contemporary commentator tellingly remarked, "The only foreigners in France are bad citizens."[28] Foreignness in the legal sense remained a murky business. The clarification of the legal concept of the foreigner, whose movements were to be restricted as such, would first require much impassioned debate and bureaucratic development, and would ultimately be forged in the fires of military conflict.[29] Noiriel has written that the modern conception of the "foreigner" came into being with the French Revolution as a result of the elimination of feudal privileges on 4 August 1789, which formally created a national community of all French citizens.[30] This Act was, however, in inherent and insoluble tension with the Declaration of the Rights of Man and Citizen, which proclaimed the equality of all *individuals* and thus tended to promote the rights of foreigners as such. Ever since, politics have been driven by the dynamics deriving from that tension.

In an important contribution to the newly proclaimed equality of French citizens, the revolutionaries began to move during this time toward the codification of a uniform national space in which goods and persons would be permitted to circulate freely. One of the first steps taken by the leaders of the revolution to obliterate local particularism in favor of national integration had been the creation of *départements* to replace the old provinces into which France had traditionally been divided. In the process, it took the names of the eighty-three new departments from their geographical features and replaced the thirty-six royal intendancies with new departmental capitals in order to sweep away the spatial relics of the *ancien régime*. The departmentalization of France was designed to achieve the aim laid out by Sieyès in September 1789: "France is and ought to be a single whole, uniformly subordinated in all its parts to a single legislation and one common [system of] administration."[31] In furtherance of this objective, the National Assembly gradually pushed outward to the "national" borders the toll barriers for goods.[32] Georges Lefebvre counted the smiting down of internal frontiers among the chief results of the revolution; a uniform administration was created before which each and every French citizen stood equally, at least in theory, and "the national market was realized, insofar as means of communication permitted it."[33] Yet the right to untrammeled internal freedom of movement still remained to be achieved.

THE CONSTITUTION OF 1791 AND THE ELIMINATION OF PASSPORT CONTROLS

Not long after the uproar sparked by the King's flight and the attendant restrictions on the movements of the French, the National Assembly completed its new constitution for France after two and a half years' work. When it did so, the matter of controls on movement occupied a central place in its deliberations. The first three "natural and civil rights" promulgated by the Assembly were relatively general provisions dealing with equality before the law. Then, the very first concrete "natural and civil right" guaranteed by the Constitution of 3–14 September 1791, was that of the freedom "to move about, to remain, [and] to leave."[34] Although the ordering of the articles may have been somewhat arbitrary, this article preceded even the Constitution's enumeration of those rights that Americans, at least, normally think of as foundational – namely, freedom of speech and assembly.[35]

The Assembly became more specific about its defense of the freedom of movement on 13 September. During that day's deliberations, the Marquis de Lafayette proposed – and the Assembly greeted with sustained applause – the abolition of all controls, especially including passports, on the movements of the French citizenry, as well as an end to the order mandating the pursuit and arrest of emigres that had been imposed in the 21 June decree barring departures.[36] The decree as adopted stated that "there will no longer be any obstacles impeding the right of every French citizen to travel freely within the realm, and to leave it at will," and specifically eliminated passports. Flush with the glow of having set out a document recognizing the equality of all French citizens before the law, the revolutionaries were in an expansive mood that extended even to forgiveness for the emigres. The records of the proceedings indicate that the members of the Assembly believed they were making a major contribution to the cause of human freedom when they abolished passport controls on the French people, which they viewed as part and parcel of the arbitrary power of the *ancien régime*.[37]

Soon, however, the practical implications of this much-ballyhooed liberalization began to make themselves clear. Greer has described the results as follows:

> The consequences were ominous. The emigres of yesterday met the emigres of tomorrow on the roads to the frontiers, and the latter outnumbered the former. Those who had hoped that the amnesty would inaugurate a phase of reconciliation were disillusioned and alarmed.[38]

There was reason enough for alarm; hostile armies, of emigres and their allies, were massing beyond the Rhine.

In response, the Legislative Assembly – a newly constituted body with entirely different membership and perspectives than its predecessor – passed a decree on 9 November 1791, declaring all French persons gathered outside the borders of the Kingdom to be under suspicion of conspiracy against the *patrie*. Anyone still so assembled after 1 January was to be considered guilty of such conspiracy and subject to the death penalty.[39] The decree was rendered ineffectual, however, when the King, whose approval was required for the enactment of the Assembly's laws, vetoed it. The Bill nonetheless reflected a dramatic shift in mood from the ebullient September days. It was during this period that the Gironde rose to prominence under the leadership of Brissot, Vergniaud, and others, and "leftist" measures found increasing resonance in the Legislative Assembly.[40]

At the same time, the change of mood within and the growing fears of invasion from without led some *départements*, especially on the frontiers, to intensify passport and other controls on foreigners. For example, the *département du Nord* issued regulations in mid-December 1791 requiring foreigners (*étrangers*) entering its villages and towns to present themselves to the authorities to have their passports checked and to receive (or be denied) permission to remain. A census was also to be kept so that the authorities would be in a position to inform the departmental directory about "the measures taken by the municipalities to prevent gatherings of foreigners" and "to insure the most exact policing with respect to foreigners."[41] It was not only frontier departments that went ahead and abrogated the National Assembly's pronouncements when they felt the need; in the debate over the reintroduction of passport controls in the Assembly in early 1792, one member noted that the *département* of Maine-et-Loire, north-east of the Vendée, had also decided to reinstitute passport controls during the preceding months.[42]

It was with little steps such as this that the definition of the "foreigner" during the revolution slowly drifted toward the notion which nowadays has come to be taken for granted: that is, a foreigner is someone from another country whose trustworthiness is questionable. Indeed, according to Sophie Wahnich, with this ordinance the surveillance of foreigners becomes institutionalized "not simply in the order of normalized police practices, but in the order of writing . . . [T]he process of identification comes into conflict with the free circulation of persons . . ."[43] State officials were beginning to recognize that surveillance of untrustworthy elements defined in *a priori* terms – separate and apart from any actions they might have committed – had to be codified in writing, for there is no other way to identify "the foreigner."

The matter of revolutionary hospitality toward foreigners had hardly yet been definitively decided, however. Only two weeks after the promulgation of the *département du Nord* decree, the philosopher Condorcet delivered himself of an eloquent speech insisting that France would never give itself over to a narrow-minded nationalism, even in time of war:

> The asylum that [France] opens to foreigners will never be closed to the inhabitants of countries whose princes have forced us to attack them, and they will find in its womb a secure refuge. Faithful to the commitments made in its name, [France] hastens to fulfill them with a generous exactitude. The dangers it faces may not permit it to forget that French soil belongs entirely to freedom, and that the law of equality must be universal. It presents to the world the novel spectacle of a nation truly free, subject to the rules of justice despite being caught up in the storms of war, and respecting everywhere and at all times with regard to all people the rights that are the same for all.[44]

Yet Condorcet's revolutionary cosmopolitanism would be put to the test soon enough. Brissot declared on 31 December that "the time has come for a new crusade, a crusade for universal freedom."[45] Whether this beautiful crusade was intended to install human freedom or French domination in the territories to which it advanced depended, however, on the eye of the beholder. In any case, many in France itself did not share Condorcet's openness to outsiders – whether legal foreigners or mere "strangers" – as war loomed on the horizon.

Around this time, for example, the municipal government of Paris found it necessary to rein in the confusion surrounding another type of document used by the state to "embrace" individuals, the "certificates of residence." The commissioners responsible for their issuance had informed the city's leaders that these important papers were "multiplying toward infinity." Thenceforward, instead of being issued by the authorities immediately upon demand, the certificates were to be requested, signed, and registered by two different agencies, and were only to be delivered after a hiatus of two days from the initial request.[46] By slowing the process down and making it more complicated, the municipal government decided, the administration would be less likely to give out these valuable documents to undeserving persons – a matter of some concern to a city plagued by the intensifying demands of revolutionary upheaval.

Aside from merely authorizing domicile in particular places, certificates of residence were closely tied in to the provision of public welfare, particularly pensions. A decree handed down by the Legislative Assembly in December 1791 required that anyone – with the exception of merchants appropriately vouched for by municipal authorities – receiving a variety of payments from the public purse had to produce a certificate attesting that he or she currently resided in the French Empire, and had done so without interruption for the previous six months. The certificate of residence was to be issued by the municipality where the person was actually domiciled, and visaed within eight days by the district directory.[47] In a move that presaged practices that would grow commonplace as welfare states began to take hold on a national scale, the Legislative Assembly sought to ease the strain on French coffers by tightening eligibility for state transfer payments – as well as its documentary attestation. Although they go unmentioned in the text of the decree, this measure was obviously directed at the emigres, who were thought to have rendered themselves unworthy of public largesse during the previous six months by fleeing the *patrie* in its hour of need.

THE DEBATE OVER PASSPORT CONTROLS OF EARLY 1792

The ranks of those in the Assembly inclined to reverse course regarding the freedom of movement in general, and passport controls in particular, swelled in proportion to the darkening of the clouds of war. Controversy in the Legislative Assembly over the reintroduction of passport restrictions thus grew boisterous early in 1792, as war came to seem increasingly imminent. On 7 January Assembly Member Le Coz, Bishop of the Breton *département* of Ille-et-Vilaine, rose to demand that the Assembly take action on a steady stream of petitions from the *départements* throughout France which, at least so he claimed, complained of the upsurge in brigandage that had followed the suppression of passport controls, and pleaded with his colleagues for their reestablishment.[48]

Le Coz was very much on the side of those who wished to restore passport restrictions. During the course of the parliamentary debate that his pleas initiated – a debate that extended over several days and generated considerable passion and eloquence – Le Coz would dub passports the "Argus of the *patrie*."[49] (In classical mythology, Argus was a monster with many eyes who was therefore regarded as a good watchman.) It is perhaps noteworthy that Le Coz coined this phrase almost simultaneously with Jeremy Bentham's proposal in the early 1790s of what Karl Polanyi called Bentham's "most personal utopia," the Panopticon.[50]

The participants in the controversy over the reintroduction of passport controls during the French Revolution gave expression to a number of motifs that would reappear later as prominent features in other legislative debates about passport restrictions. It is thus useful to examine the debate in some detail. To begin with, however, both sides in the debate recognized that the requirement that travelers be in possession of a passport entailed a certain presumption of guilt – a presupposition that travelers were up to no good and might be moving about under pretenses contrary to those deemed acceptable by the revolutionary regime.

For the advocates of the reinstitution of passport controls on the French citizenry, however, such requirements comprised a tolerable infringement on freedom in defense of the revolution's broader achievements. Joseph François Lemalliaud, an Assembly representative from the Breton *département* of Morbihan and a staunch supporter of the revolution,[51] articulated this view in his comments on an agitated letter from the Morbihan procurer-general demanding the reintroduction of passports in order to get the upper hand over the "brigands" who "infested the roads" of that region. Passport requirements, according to Lemalliaud, "may perhaps afflict the bad citizens, but the true friends of liberty would gladly support this minor inconvenience." In other words, genuine patriots would accept that their freedom might be modestly curtailed in order to defend the larger freedoms won by the revolution – freedoms that were being threatened by homegrown counterrevolutionaries, emigres, and autocratic foreign powers. These petty restrictions were not too much to ask of true defenders of the greater liberties won by the revolution.

Lemalliaud's proposal was seconded by another Assembly representative who noted that the nearby *département* of Maine-et-Loire (Anjou) had already felt compelled to reestablish passport controls and that "substantial contingents of troops composed of brigands and those without an *aveu* are forming at the borders" of Brittany and Anjou. In this view, the lack of an *aveu* was itself evidence of counterrevolutionary intent; the obvious remedy was to reassert and strengthen the authority of the state to authorize and regulate movement. The widespread enthusiasm for the reintroduction of passport controls among revolutionaries from these areas arose from the fact that they were plagued by popular disturbances during this period. In August, aristocrats and refractory priests had provoked disturbances in the Vendée, immediately south-west of the Maine-et-Loire, and rightists fomented trouble throughout the region during subsequent months.[52] One of the deputies objected that the passport could not simply be reintroduced without the matter being discussed by the Assembly's Committee on Legislation, but the Assembly declared passport requirements restored and directed that committee to report the following day on "how to make this measure effective."[53]

The *rapporteur* of the committee on legislation, an ally of Lemalliaud from Ille-et-Vilaine named Codet, responded to the Assembly's request with a proposed law to reestablish passport controls "temporarily."[54] The committee argued that, "in this moment of crisis," foreigners required "the particular attention of the administrative bodies." The hearts of .some foreigners were "entirely French," to be sure, but others were suspects, traitors prepared "to betray the sacred rights of hospitality." Therefore, "without molesting foreigners too much," the committee urged the Assembly to "watch them with the most scrupulous attention . . . to follow their paths and foil their plots." In order to facilitate the achievement of these ends, all travelers within France were to have their passports visaed in every district, while those leaving the Kingdom were to submit to this formality at the directory of the frontier *département* where they would be crossing the border. To carry out these bureaucratic tasks, the committee's proposal authorized all gendarmes and active National Guardsmen to examine passports, and empowered all officers of the *gendarmerie* to issue warrants for the arrest of those without a valid passport. The bill proposed penalties for those who refused properly to identify themselves to the state, for failure to do so "renders one culpable, manifests perverse intentions, contravenes the law . . ."

As he introduced the bill into the Assembly, Codet noted that the committee found important sources for its proposal in earlier decrees of the Constituent Assembly, particularly its "Law on the Municipal Police" of 19 July 1791.[55] That law included a requirement that municipal authorities conduct a census of all inhabitants, as well as a register of the declarations of those canvassed that was to include a variety of personal information such as name, age, place of birth, previous domicile, occupation, and means of subsistence. Those lacking the last mentioned were to indicate the name of a local resident who was prepared to vouch for them. Workers without either means of subsistence or a sponsor were to be registered as *gens sans aveu;* those who failed to indicate a previous domicile as "suspicious persons" (*gens suspects*); and, finally, those shown to have made false declarations were to be identified as "ill-intentioned persons" (*gens malintentionnés*).

The committee then recommended as an "indispensable condition" that every passport include an extract of the person's municipal declaration.

> If the traveler is honest, his passport will be an advantageous document for him, and it will flatter him; if he is not honest, it is necessary that his passport will put him under surveillance throughout the Kingdom . . . With this correspondence [of passport and municipal register], the law on passports will complement all the other measures already taken for the security of the realm.[56]

Despite the general perception that passport requirements constituted an illiberal restriction on the freedom of movement, Codet was arguing, in effect, that these documents would protect the "honest" man while helping to flush out the politically or morally dubious.

In the course of the debate, the Jacobin firebrand Jean-François Delacroix expanded upon this notion, suggesting that the passport, far from entailing a presumption of guilt, was in fact a "certificate of probity" insuring the security of those traveling in France.[57] There was something in Delacroix's view: if state authorities had the right to demand some independent verification of a person's identity and some justification of his or her whereabouts, as Codet had insisted they did, possession of a document attesting to these matters would provide a certain security to the would-be traveler. Only under conditions of pure freedom to come and go, irrespective of who or what a person is, would a passport constitute nothing but a restriction. Once the genie of the state's authority to identify persons and authorize their movements is out of the bottle, it is hard to get him back in. And, from long years of experience under the *ancien régime*, most of the French took for granted that that genie was loose on the world; perhaps, many of them must have thought, it had always been so. Gradually, however, a distinction would emerge between identification documents as such and passports authorizing travel, opening up the possibility for states to eliminate the latter without giving up their essential capacity to "embrace" individuals by means of documentary identification practices.

Those opposed to the resurrection of passport controls took a sharply different view of the probable consequences of their restoration. Far from regarding the reintroduction of passport controls as a small price to pay for defending the revolution's larger gains, these critics saw the resurrection of social control techniques characteristic of the *ancien régime* as a reversal of the newfound freedom that the revolution had inaugurated, and therefore as likely to undermine popular support for the revolutionary project. This view was expressed by Stanislas Girardin of the *département* of the Oise (north of Paris), a one-time pupil of Rousseau who moved from left to right in the course of the revolution. One of the most stirring and impassioned critics of the new passport law, Girardin besought his fellow deputies not to adopt such an "inquisitorial" law:

> A nation that claims to have a constitution cannot enchain the liberty of its citizens to the extent that you propose. A revolution that commenced with the destruction of passports must insure a sufficient measure of freedom to travel, even in times of crisis.

Certainly not all would agree with Girardin's characterization of the revolution's origins, but his statement suggests the significance that many of the deputies attributed to the passport question and its implications for the fate of the revolution. The royalist Viénot-Vaublanc of the neighboring *département* of Seine-et-Marne supported Girardin's motion to delay consideration of the "inquisitorial" law's individual articles until after the impending weekend, provoking cries from the gallery when he suggested that overhasty decisions might make of France "a convent in which liberty is recognized in name only."[58] Viénot-Vaublanc may have been extraordinarily prescient in his opposition to the renewal of passport controls; after the revolution of 10 August 1792, he was forced to go underground and to traverse France on foot.[59]

A DETAILED EXAMINATION OF THE NEW PASSPORT LAW

When the Assembly reconvened on Monday, 27 January, the matter of the passport law was their central preoccupation;[60] a vigorous debate then unfolded that lasted for the next three days. The Breton Codet began the discussion by defending the restrictions anew as a small sacrifice of liberty in favor of the defense of the larger liberty that, in his view, the revolution had wrought. He went on to remind the Assembly that the laws would, in any case, only affect the minority of the population that actually moved about. Codet asserted that the vast majority of those who traveled were honest people who, without passports, had no way of demonstrating that they were such, nor of being certain that the people they met on the roads would be well-disposed toward them. In short, according to Codet, only the tiny minority of *gens suspects* and *gens malintentionnés* could possibly be opposed to passport requirements for travel.

To this defense of the passport requirements, a deputy named Lémontey retorted that giving in to the demands of those *départements* that were demanding the reinstitution of the passport would result in disaster. It was true, he conceded, that there were foreigners with strong antipathies toward the revolution, and he had no objection in principle to keeping them under surveillance. Lémontey insisted that he was not far from supporting the passport restrictions, but only if the controls "leave nothing to arbitrariness" and would not "defame us in the eyes of Europe": "[T]he law that has been proposed is a symptom of weakness, of distrust, of internal sickness . . . What foreign power would desire the friendship of a government wracked with civil division and sacrificing its principles to its needs and its passions?" Lémontey objected to what he felt was the limitless, arbitrary power – "a permanent tyranny," he called it – that was being handed over to the municipal authorities. Like Girardin before him, Lémontey feared that a move such as this on the part of the revolutionary leadership would only "augment the number of malcontents. The welfare of the state is in this word: Make them love the Constitution; it is imperishable." Lémontey concluded by arguing that the law would stimulate massive emigration from France on the part of those "weak and fearful" persons who remain only because they assume they can leave if the situation becomes unbearable for them. There was an element of sophistry in this argument, of course, but the opponents of the passport law sensed that they were on the defensive.

Another deputy advanced a rather more creative response to the proposed law by turning its attack on vagabondage and brigandage into a justification for land redistribution: would it not be possible, he wondered, to give the itinerant indigent some of the lands lying fallow that were now in the possession of the nation as a result of the extensive confiscations of estates and Church lands? The landless poor would then have work and sustenance, and hence no reason for taking to the roads as they normally did in times of need. This member was not opposed in principle to restricting the movements of foreigners and enemies of the revolution, however; far from it. Indeed, he proposed that foreigners traveling in France be required to make a declaration to the municipal authorities wherever they found themselves, and urged that the machinery be set in motion to deport recidivists who were *gens sans aveu, gens suspects*, or *gens malintentionnés*: "This is the only means to purge our political body of that scum that causes fevered and convulsive movements throughout the country."

In response, Le Coz, the bishop from Ille-et-Vilaine, returned to the podium to mount a spirited defense of the need for the passport restrictions. Le Coz's remarks betrayed the classic illiberal assumption, embodied for example in many of today's drug-testing proposals, that anyone who refused to cooperate with the authorities in these procedures was guilty – of something. Bishop Le Coz went on to advance the ingenious argument that the law "would establish among our *départements* a chain of relationships and of surveillance that would be as favorable to the well-meaning man as it would be terrible to the scoundrel." In other words, such requirements would facilitate the administrative unification and domination of the country. Passport controls, moreover, would allow the national gendarmerie to ask "the unknown traveler, in the name of the law, 'Who are you?'" The fundamental point here, as Gérard Noiriel has pointed out, is that "written documents [are] the quintessential instrument of communication at a distance,"[61] and such means were necessary aspects of the development of a unified state before which all individuals stood equal, irrespective of where they came from.

In concluding his enthusiastic endorsement of the proposed passport law, Le Coz wondered aloud: "Had passports been required all along, how much less would we now have to bemoan the maneuvers of the aristocracy, the poisons of fanaticism, the crimes of the counter-revolutionaries?"

Even allowing for the much-inflated rhetoric routinely adopted by the revolutionaries in the parliamentary discussions, the adversaries in the debate over passport controls spoke as if the very fate of the revolution hung on the outcome of the passport question.

Once Le Coz had finished his remarks, the Assembly moved to an article-by-article consideration of the Bill submitted by the Committee on Legislation. Girardin, the implacable critic of passport restrictions, immediately went on the attack. He recognized that the horse was already out of the barn, and that the best he could do at this point was to seek to control the damage he believed the law would cause. In particular, Girardin worried that "inquisitorial laws are always advantageous to the executive power." He therefore proposed an amendment to the first article, which enunciated the basic requirement that travelers be in possession of a passport, that would limit the validity of the law to one year. If the law were not explicitly limited in time, he feared, "you run the risk of not being able to revoke it." His pleas fell on deaf ears, however; Girardin's amendment was rejected, and the Assembly moved on to deliberate on article 2.

The proposed article 2 would have required all passports to include the name, age, profession, description, domicile, and nationality of the bearer. The issue of the bearer's description provoked opposition to this part of the law. We have seen that the passport restrictions adopted in mid-1791 in response to Louis XVI's flight to Varennes had included a description of those traveling on the document's authority in order to forestall any disguised departures such as that of the King. Until that time, it had been thought adequate to identify people mainly in terms of their social station, geographic origins, and the like. Yet now the objection was raised that requiring descriptions in a passport would result in the arbitrary infringement of travelers' freedom because the various agents of the state involved in enforcing these controls were "inadequately informed" and might "not be able to distinguish exactly among descriptions." Half a century later, photographs would come into use in passport documents precisely in order to overcome this sort of objection – although photographs themselves would at first encounter the same objection from police officials who doubted their reliability.[62]

The doctor, naturalist, and Girondin sympathizer Broussonet countered with the proposal that the standard passport format be attached to the law as adopted, thereby leaving no ambiguity about the information each passport was to contain. "There isn't a municipal administration in the Kingdom," he insisted, "that is not in a position to distinguish between color of hair, of eyes . . ." Broussonet went on to make a crucial addition to the criteria for granting passports: henceforth, they should all be issued to *individuals*. Part of the reason the King had been able to get as far as Varennes, of course, was that he was traveling – undescribed – as a servant in a passport issued to someone else (the Baroness de Korff). The practice of issuing passports for groups of persons had, according to Broussonet, "given complete liberty to bad subjects." The Legislative Assembly found his arguments persuasive and adopted the version of the amendment that he had proposed, with the sole revision that passports were to be handed out exclusively by the municipal authorities. This change had been urged by Delacroix, who insisted that this power be removed from the hands of the ministers who, in his view, were issuing the passports with which the emigres were slipping off to Coblenz to join the enemies of the revolution.

The law's article 3 proposed that, in addition to the information required by article 2, each passport was to include a copy (*extrait*) of the declaration made before the municipal authorities in accordance with the aforementioned law on municipal police of 19 July 1791.[63] To this clause the objection was raised that the whole business would be superfluous and circular; "if a citizen is the bearer of a certificate that contains his age, his position (*qualité*), etc., it is perfectly useless for him to present a copy of the municipal declaration, for it is only on the basis of a copy of that declaration that the municipal authorities would give him a passport in the first place. This would unnecessarily burden the municipal officials." The Jacobin Jacques Alexis Thuriot, a member of the party that had stormed the Bastille in 1789 who became distinguished for his efforts to stymie the counterrevolution,[64] grasped the essential point – which was precisely the circular integration of these documents, their correspondence as state-sponsored verifications of identity – and demanded that the requirement be included in the final version of the law. Yet objections concerning the feasibility of implementing this provision led the Assembly to drop it.

Article 4 would have forbidden the municipal authorities to issue passports to those registered by their respective municipalities as *gens sans aveu*, *gens suspects*, or *gens malintentionées* without express mention of these designations in the passport. This proviso was clearly outrageous, and inevitably calls to mind Peuchet's insistence that the burden of the passport requirements fell most heavily on the "poor and obscure" elements of the population. The proposed amendment provoked immediate and indignant objections from several members including Vergniaud, the Girondins' "best orator",[65] who regarded it as "infinitely immoral and unworthy of the Assembly to allow the municipal authorities to inscribe defamatory remarks in the passports." Vergniaud went on to observe that this sort of defamation, often rooted in a malevolence and a desire to slander rather than in any legitimate motive, would have "a legal character, because it is certified by the municipal authorities."

Whereas the requirement that persons state their profession in passports was, as Paul Fussell has written in another context, an "open invitation to self-casting and social promotion, not to mention outright fraud,"[66] the bureaucratic codification of social marginality held grave dangers for those subjected to it. The Legislative Assembly recognized this proposal as the arbitrary constraint on the liberty of the poor that it was, and eliminated it from the law.

The proposed Article 6 would have allowed all French passport bearers to move about unhindered only within the *district* in which they resided. Yet upon departure from the district they would have been required to have their passports visaed by the directory of the district or *département* in which their municipality was situated. To this measure Delacroix replied simply that "it would dishonor the Assembly to propose such an article for its deliberation," and the matter was disposed of. The version of the law that was actually adopted required that those departing from the *Kingdom* – French or foreign – indicate this intention to the municipal authorities in their place of residence, and that this act be mentioned in their passports.[67] The law thus harmonized with the overall trend toward the replacement of local by national boundaries and the "nationalization" of French political space.

Next, the Committee on Legislation proposed to require that all foreigners who wished to depart the Kingdom be in possession of a passport and, in addition, that it be visaed by the directory of the district or frontier *département* from which the traveler in question intended to leave. Girardin and others objected that such a clause would frequently force people already at the border to return to the interior to get the necessary visa and would generally cause considerable inconvenience, and proposed instead that the visa authority be given to municipal authorities. The moderate Louis Becquey suggested that this article (and the next) should be rejected because "our intention is to prevent internal troubles and to guarantee individual security and general liberty," not to constrain emigration. Another member observed that French travelers in Spain were experiencing difficulties because the authorities there were refusing to recognize passports issued by the municipalities, and hence insisted that all passports be visaed by higher authorities (*les gouverneurs*).

Thuriot, an outspoken enthusiast of passport controls, argued that the Assembly needed to be in a position to know when people had left France in order to be able to determine which of them wanted to join up with the emigres. In effect, he said, the legislators wanted to have distinct passports for the interior and for exit, and thus proposed to require those wishing to depart to take a passport in which that aim was to be duly indicated. This proposal met with the objection that people might decide that it was necessary to leave the country while already away from their domicile in France, forcing them to return home before departing simply to get proper authorization. Backing Thuriot's proposal, Vergniaud noted that the essential point was to be able to distinguish between those who wanted "to leave the realm" and those who wanted "to abandon the *patrie*" – that is, the purpose of these measures was not to restrict emigration, but to be able to make ideological distinctions among those leaving.

One member, raising the "who will guard the guards" question, said he would support Thuriot's proposal only if it also regulated the behavior of the frontier municipalities charged with checking whether those leaving the country were going where they had said they would. Otherwise, he insisted, these departees might be on their way to join the enemy forces at Coblenz after dissembling about their motives when they originally received their passports. A number of legislators shouted that such a provision was unacceptable, for, as Becquey put it, "you have no right" to determine where people shall go. While it may be difficult for states to control movement outside their own borders, this has scarcely kept them from trying to implement such controls, and they may be able to do so effectively mainly because of their capacity to distribute rewards and punishments at home when the traveler returns.

By now the Assembly was churning with controversy, and a proposal to adopt Thuriot's amendment by acclamation drove the house wild. Pandemonium had erupted in the chamber in response to his proposal to require those wishing to leave the Kingdom to carry a passport in which that intention was inscribed. One legislator insisted on a roll-call vote, calling the provision "bloodthirsty"; another denounced it as "destructive of commerce and industry, and contrary to the interests of the people." That steadfast opponent of passport controls, Girardin, returned to the attack, demanding that the Assembly "not be permitted to destroy commerce and freedom without discussion . . ."[68]

Thuriot declared himself astonished that those who had defended the revolution from its very outset could regard as "bloodthirsty" a measure intended "to save the public good," but he revised his proposal to the effect that passports would be issued by the municipal authorities in the recipients' place of residence, and that mention would be made therein of their intention to depart. It was this version that was ultimately adopted as article 5 of the passport law of 1 February – 28 March 1792. After some further minor sparring about the inconveniences associated with the passport regulations, the Assembly adjourned. A tumultuous day's debate over the particulars of the new passport controls thus came to an end. Two more similarly rancorous days of discussion would follow before the final result was obtained.

In the end, under the influence of the siege mentality invoked by numerous speakers during the debate, the Assembly reversed a decision it had excitedly and unhesitatingly taken only a few months before. The atmosphere in which the Assembly adopted this course could hardly be better indicated than by Thuriot's remarks on 30 January 1792, which were met with exuberant applause: "At this moment, we cannot deceive ourselves: there are conspiracies of every kind against us, and we cannot be too vigilant." The forces favoring the restoration of controls – mostly from the revolutionary left – won out, and passport restrictions were reintroduced. Declaring that "the health of the Empire requires the most active surveillance," the National Assembly mandated that everyone – whether French or foreign – traveling within the Kingdom be in possession of a passport. Those wishing to leave French territory had to have a notation to this effect inserted into their passports by the authorities in their place of residence; those entering the Kingdom, if they did not already have one, were to take a passport from the authorities in the municipality where they crossed the border.[69] Surveillance had, indeed, become the order of the day.

By the summer, with war against Prussia and Austria heating up and the problem of emigration persisting, the Assembly on 28–9 July adopted a further "Decree on Passports" entirely suspending the issuance of such documents for departure from France, except to certain selected groups distinguished mainly by their need to travel abroad for commercial purposes.[70] Movement within France was once again heavily restricted and departure from the country made illegal for almost everyone.

In adopting these measures, the Assembly had taken a new departure as well. By subjecting foreigners as well as French citizens to these passport requirements, the new restrictions on movement were part of an important shift in the legal status of foreigners in European states. Under mercantilism, the foreigner, although otherwise treated like the subject in legal terms, typically enjoyed greater freedom to emigrate than native-born subjects.[71] Now, foreigners were increasingly being exposed to the same disabilities as Frenchmen with respect to departure from France. Moreover, they tended to be seen as a threat to the *patrie*, as would gradually come to be expected in any international conflict. Several protagonists in the early 1792 Assembly debate over passport controls had insisted that, notwithstanding their birth elsewhere, many foreigners were "true friends of liberty" and should therefore not be encumbered with extraordinary legal burdens. Their views failed to carry the day. The foreigner, increasingly defined exclusively in national rather than local terms, was perceived more and more *ipso facto* as a suspect.

The passport restrictions on movement voted by the Assembly in early 1792 held sway for a number of months as France faced intensified hostility from within and without. Toward the end of the year, however, the deputies came around to the view that the restrictions on movement within France, at least, were proving counterproductive. In response to claims that the provisioning of Paris was suffering greatly under the restraints on "the circulation of goods and people," the Assembly in early September adopted a decree reestablishing "free circulation" and abolishing the clauses of the law of 1 February – 28 March 1792 requiring a passport, except within ten *lieues* from the borders or from enemy-occupied territory.[72] This was a remarkable turnabout, coming as it did only a few days after the fall of Verdun and the declaration draped across the facade of the Hôtel de Ville in Paris that "the *patrie* is in danger." Yet less than two weeks later, the Assembly bolstered these provisions by decreeing that those found guilty of hindering the movements of persons or goods would themselves be subject to detention for a period equivalent to the duration of such hindrance.[73]

The tendency to equate "goods and people" when discussing the question of free movement was a striking aspect of the parliament's deliberations at this point. The proclivity appears to have been of older provenance,[74] deriving perhaps from a time when many of those traveling the roads of the country were subject to one form or another of unfree labor, and thus seen as little more than property capable of moving itself. Whatever its origins, the habit of viewing freedom of movement as contributing to both liberty and prosperity is a recurrent motif in subsequent discussions of passport restrictions, and a figure of thought that gathered strength with the rising prospects of economic liberalism in nineteenth-century Europe.

Despite the Assembly's decisive steps to guarantee free circulation when it adopted the new constitution in September 1791, those involved in constructing the new regime in France recognized that they had to be in a position to "embrace" the subjects of the state when the need to do so arose. Accordingly, it was necessary for the state to be in control of birth registries that until then had been in the hands of the parish priest. Because the Catholic Church was principally concerned to tend to its own flock, however, the church registers frequently ignored the births of Jews, Protestants, and others. This simply would not do for modern states, which – unlike the Church – are territorial *and* membership organizations that must thus be able to distinguish between members and non-members, those with rights of access to the territory and those lacking them.

On 20 September 1792, the government therefore decreed the establishment of civil status (*l'état civil*), a title denoting "standing" within a constituted political order. "From that moment on," Gérard Noiriel has written, "an individual could only exist as a citizen once his or her identity had been registered by the municipal authorities, according to regulations that were the same throughout the national territory."[75] In doing so, the French state enhanced its capacity to "embrace" its citizens and to keep track of them in order to achieve its aims. On the same day, ironically, Goethe famously declared that "this date and place mark a new epoch in world history"[76] after the bedraggled French "nation in arms" defeated vastly better-trained Prussian troops in the battle at Valmy. Enthusiasm for the nation and its definition by the state would mutually characterize that new epoch of which Goethe spoke.

PASSPORTS AND FREEDOM OF MOVEMENT UNDER THE CONVENTION

The legal fortunes of the freedom of movement and the extent to which travelers were encumbered by passport requirements rose and fell in response to the decrees of the revolutionary Convention, which looked for, and found, enemies everywhere. In late October 1792, the Convention banished the emigres from French territory "in perpetuity" and declared the death penalty for those who contravened the law.[77] Shortly thereafter, the emigres then on French territory were directed to leave the country.[78] The lot of the emigres, irrespective of why they had left France, had taken a decided turn for the worse.

Yet the picture was far from monochromatic. In late November, the Convention had suspended the delivery of certificates of residence, only to adopt a few days later a decree rescinding this suspension for merchants and their agents who found it necessary to travel "for their commercial affairs," and authorizing the issuance of certificates and passports to them.[79] Then, on 7 December 1792, the Conventionnels adopted a measure that softened the restrictions of the passport law of the previous July by allowing the distribution of passports to those wishing to leave the Kingdom for "their interests or their affairs." The legislation was cautious, however, in requiring would-be travelers to obtain a passport from the directory of the *département* in which they lived; the directory, in turn, was to rely on the judgment of the district and municipal authorities in deciding whether the request for a passport was "legitimate and sufficiently verified," and to issue the passports only under these conditions.[80]

The purpose of these restrictions on access to passports for departure, according to the law's proponent, was "to stymie the culpable maneuvers of the ill-intentioned, and to keep at their posts those citizens who want to permit themselves too easily to leave French territory at a time when the *patrie* may have need of their presence."[81] In short, the French state needed to be able to lay hold of miscreants, and to keep hold of its potential allies who might be overcome with *Wanderlust* at a time that the state regards as inconvenient. Later emendations of passport requirements would frequently recur to this law as the touch-stone from which they took their cue.

Soon, however, this relative laxity would become unacceptable to those at the helm of the Convention, who sought to gain firmer control of affairs. Their utter seriousness became unmistakably apparent when they voted to have the King beheaded in the Place de la Révolution on 21 January 1793. Shortly thereafter, in its justification of a new, standard passport form for seamen, the Convention voiced its distress about the administrative chaos it confronted: "It is a matter of the dignity of the French Republic to establish a uniform procedure in its government, and to abrogate this monstrous mélange of disparate forms." Henceforth, valid seamen's documents were to be made recognizable by bearing the superscription "Liberté, Egalité."[82]

In February, moreover, the pages of *Le Moniteur* indicate that a specifically revolutionary form of documentation, the so-called *certificats de civisme*, had begun to proliferate uncontrollably, and efforts were made to stem their availability. First introduced on 1 November 1792, the *certificats de civisme* had been made a requirement for all government functionaries with a law of 5 February 1793, and by June they were obligatory for all *pensionnaires de la République*. Such certificates could be denied to persons revealing a liking for foreigners or foreign customs. As attestations of revolutionary sentiment with significant advantages to those holding them, the distribution of *certificates de civisme* could be used as a way to terrorize those who did not have them. They were thus very valuable documents that people were prepared to lie about in order to get.[83]

Against this background, calls for the reinvigoration of passport controls were once again heard in the Convention. A member from the brigand-infested Breton *département* of Morbihan complained that the *patrie* was beset by enemies because of the lack of enforcement of the passport laws and demanded that they be "severely executed." That reliable supporter of passport restrictions, Thuriot, reminded the assembly that the passport law was on the books, but had been neglected during the preceding months. "But the only measure," he insisted, "that can force the volunteers to remain under the colors, and to prevent the actions of the malevolents, trouble-makers, and thieves is to put the law back in effect." Thuriot pressed for the renewed implementation of the laws of 28 March and 28 July 1792, to which it was replied that this would be acceptable only if the law of 7 December was not "derogated."[84]

Claiming that it was of "the greatest importance" that the "constituted authorities" be in a position "to know, to arrest, and to punish the malcontents that circulate in different parts of the Republic inciting the violation of the laws, and to prevent as much as possible all criminal intelligence with the external enemy," the Convention declared on

26 February 1793 that this trio of laws was to be implemented until otherwise ordered.[85] Two days later, the Convention seems to have felt that it had not written a sufficiently stringent regulation. As a result, it decreed that all French citizens away from their domiciles and not in possession of a passport issued more recently than August 1792 were to appear before the municipality where they currently resided within twenty-four hours after the promulgation of the decree to report "their description, and to give their name, age, occupation, and domicile."[86] This measure was designed to contend with the problem of issuing documents to those away from their municipality of domicile, the authority empowered by the law of 28 March 1792 to issue passports.

Six weeks later, in a decree primarily devoted to assuring the representatives of accredited foreign powers that they would be able to gain access to passports, the Convention "suppressed the usage of the *laissez passer* established by the city of Paris for exit from the barricades."[87] Clearly, in this chaotic period, the central government had no effective monopoly on the legitimate authority to control movement. Moreover, although the Convention demonstrated a charming faith in the efficacy of its pronouncements, it seems improbable that its regulations were implemented with any strict uniformity.

In fact, the Convention was losing its grip on the country, which in any case was not especially powerful in the first place. In early March, the counterrevolutionaries of the Vendée rose again, this time *en masse*, and lit a torch that ignited other parts of the region. During the ensuing weeks, General Dumouriez concluded an armistice with the Austrians with the intention of marching on Paris to restore the monarchy and the Constitution of 1791; the death penalty was invoked against armed rebels, refractory priests, and emigres; and, by the end of the month, the latter had died "civil death" and were subject to the physical variety if they returned to the country.[88]

During this period, control over administration of the repression increasingly slipped from the Convention's grasp. In particular, with the creation of the watch committees (*comités de surveillance*) on 21 March regulation of movement and enforcement of passport regulations fell more and more into the hands of rogue, *sans-culotte* elements.[89] Worse still, the rebels of the Vendée were issuing their own passports; in June, the Convention adopted a decree punishing with ten years' deprivation of the rights of citizenship those soldiers who, having been captured by the Vendéans, accepted a passport from them in order to return to the Republican ranks.[90] On 28 Frimaire Year II (18 December 1793), the Convention would nullify all passports issued by the municipalities situated in the areas where the "fugitive brigands of the Vendée" circulated – presumably because the Vendéans were getting access to legitimate passports as a result of the connivance of local officials sympathetic to them.[91] The paranoia of the Convention was growing, and would continue to do so until it issued in the draconian "Law on Suspects" of September 1793, which made the watch committees "all-powerful" and defined as suspects – among many other groups – those who had ever been denied a *certificat de civisme*.[92] In an effort to impose greater order on the administration of passport controls, at least, the *Conseil général* endorsed a Parisian measure to bureaucratize the distribution of documents, providing that the commissions on passports, certificates of residence, and *certificats de civisme* should consist of four members each who should receive an indemnity of 2000 *livres* for their efforts.[93]

Those from other countries suffered special antipathy during this period. On 18 March 1793 Barère, soon to be a member of the Committee of Public Safety, instigated a law that "chased" foreigners from the territory of the Republic. Exceptions were to be made only if the individual in question had made a declaration to the newly installed twelve-member committees instituted in each municipality to hear them. If they passed this examination, they were issued residence certificates; otherwise, they were to leave the country within twenty-four hours or eight days, depending on circumstances. With this law, "all foreigners are henceforth accused of being political enemies of the revolution."[94] Because it is impossible to identify a foreigner merely by sight, some means must be created to do so; it seems that at least some of those who passed the "examen de civisme" were required to wear armbands inscribed with the word "hospitality" and the name of their country of origin.[95] The watch committees assumed a special role in safeguarding France against "strangers," whether internal or "foreign" in our contemporary sense.[96]

Yet it should not necessarily be supposed that the regulation of "strangers" was the sole or even primary activity of the watch committees. Their mandate encompassed a wide array of suspects and their authority expanded with the drift toward unconstrained terror. On 24 February 1793 the Convention had embarked upon a levy of 300 000 men to be drawn from among bachelors and widowers between the ages of twenty and forty.[97] Enthusiasm for military service remained a spotty affair, however, and considerable energy had to be spent in tracking down the unwilling. As a result, "much of the time and effort of *comités de surveillance* was taken up in 1793–94 with tracking down deserters to their village, forest, or mountain hide-outs . . ."[98]

Recruitment problems multiplied with the Convention's declaration of the *levée en masse* in August 1793; Lefebvre concludes that, of those newly liable for service who absconded, "most of them certainly escaped."[99] Some of them may have been using public and postal vehicles to do so, for the *Conseil général* issued an order in early 1794 prohibiting such conveyances from taking on anyone not in possession of a passport visaed by the municipality and the revolutionary committees.[100] By early June 1794, the Great Terror of the Year II was in full swing, and with it the grim work of the guillotines.

With the fall of Robespierre and the Committee of Public Safety after the Thermidorian reaction (28 July 1794), a sense of relief was palpable in France. This mood extended to passport matters as well. At the same time that the watch committees were eviscerated, the Convention moved to liberalize documentary restrictions on travel. On 6 Fructidor Year II (23 August 1794), the Convention decreed that passports in the department of Paris would be issued by the *comité civil* without any longer having to be referred to the general assembly of the section, and would be visaed by the revolutionary committee of the *arrondissement*. The requirement that passports be visaed by the *département* was abolished as well. In addition, the passports of French travelers arriving in Paris were to be visaed exclusively by the *comité civil*.[101] By failing to specify whether this decree concerned both *internal* passports and passports for *exit* from the country, however, the measure aroused considerable confusion in the ranks of those responsible for administering these laws. This ambiguity was exacerbated by the fact that the Thermidorians held the municipality of Paris to have been engaged in a conspiratorial undertaking during the Terror, and would soon move to suppress that body.[102]

In late September 1794, the Convention's Committee on Legislation proposed a clarification of the terms of the 23 August decree. The committee's spokesman began by noting that the law of 7 December 1792 had not yet been abrogated; that law, it will be recalled, required that the *départements* were to issue passports for departure, after hearing the advice of the district and municipal directories concerning the legitimacy of the request. While this procedure had (supposedly) been followed in every other *département* in the Republic, "it is clear that the law cannot have applied in Paris, where a conspiratorial municipality has been justly struck down by the national sovereignty that it sought to usurp."[103] Once again, the central state found it necessary to assert its supremacy in the matter of authorizing legitimate movement against elements seeking to claim this authority for themselves.

The spokesman then announced that the legislative committee's reading of the law of 6 Fructidor Year II led it to conclude that the Convention had not, in fact, wished to change the requirements for external passports that had been dictated by the law of 7 December 1792. Thereupon the Convention adopted a decree affirming this interpretation, and reiterated the responsibility of the *département* of Paris for issuing passports – with the emendation that they should rely on the advice of the civil and revolutionary committees rather than on that of the municipality in determining the acceptability of a passport request.[104] In the process, and quite coincidentally, the revolutionary Convention took an important step toward distinguishing bureaucratically between internal and external passports: the one to be issued by local authorities, the other by higher-level – though not yet "national" – authorities.

The niceties of bureaucratic rationalization aside, however, much of this preoccupation with the details of passport procedure was, as a practical matter, little more than eyewash. For the central government in Paris was a paper tiger with scarcely any effective control in the country-side, over which were scattered all manner of brigands, dismissed officials,[105] deserting soldiers, and returning emigres, significant segments of whom were in rebellion. The steady stream of decrees and the frequency with which passport matters appear on the agenda of the Convention themselves point to this conclusion.

In fact, the passport laws were openly flouted and indeed mocked, as can be seen in the case of the emigres, who began a major reflux after Thermidor despite the persistence of penal legislation against them. Some had availed themselves of forged papers to facilitate their return, and saw easily enough the usefulness of such documents for their confrères (and perhaps a much-needed source of income for themselves). As the numbers of former emigres in France swelled, they established agencies in various cities dedicated to producing evidence of non-emigration, which was essential for their ability to evade hostile authorities. These counterfeits included hospital receipts, certificates of residence, and passports; quantity production of the latter "soon brought the price down to ten francs each and made them available to almost anyone."[106] It is axiomatic that fraud and forgery are more or less automatic responses to the imposition by states of documentary requirements of this kind.

Against this backdrop, it could hardly be surprising that one of the deputies harangued the Convention on 1 May 1795, with the charge that "the law on passports has not been implemented," as a result of which "the scum of the Republic seeks refuge here [in Paris], and we are surrounded by assassins."[107] By the end of the same month, and for the first time since 1789, troops would enter Paris to fight the rebellious citizenry of the city. When the Faubourg-St. Antoine surrendered without a struggle, the revolution – at least by Georges Lefebvre's reckoning – was over.[108]

A brief relaxation of documentary controls followed. First, the Committee of General Security endorsed the Parisian authorities' issuance of passports to disarmed citizens (citoyens desarmés) in order to facilitate "commerce" and "communication."[109] A month later, the government abolished the certificats de civisme, a measure heartily applauded as a contribution to the restoration of freedom.[110] The French would no longer require this documentary attestation of their adherence to the revolutionary cause, and even those who had taken up arms against the revolution would once again be free to move about to tend to their affairs.

The foreign-born did not get off so easily, however. In between these two measures, the Convention – at the advice of the Committees of Public Safety and General Security – banished from France all foreigners who had entered the country after 1 January 1792. The route which they intended to take on their departure from the country was to be recorded in the passports they would require to leave France. Conversely, upon arrival at the French border, foreigners were to deposit their passports with the municipal authorities, who were to send them on to the Committee of General Security to be visaed. In place of their passports, the municipal authorities were to give these individuals a provisional *carte de sûreté* indicating that they were to remain under surveillance while the passport was being checked out. Meanwhile, those foreigners who were permitted to remain – chiefly those from friendly or allied countries, those who had entered France prior to 1792, and those recognized for "their patriotism and their probity" – were to receive an identity card bearing their description. At the top of the cards were to appear the words *hospitalité et sûreté* and, if the person were from a country with which France was at peace, the word "*fraternité . . .*"[111]

While clearly analogous to the previously discussed practice of requiring foreigners to wear armbands, this may have been the first time that foreigners in France were to be compelled to carry a *document* attesting their foreignness but unrelated to movement control (i.e., an "identity card" rather than a passport). Only those from countries with which France was not at war received the inscription "*fraternité*" on their cards, suggesting the authorities' merely provisional attitude toward the "*sûreté*" of those originally from other countries. The regulation in any case bore witness to the undeniable fact that there is no way to identify a foreigner without some form of marking such as these cards. France had begun to take the necessary steps to distinguish clearly and effectively between natives and foreigners within its borders.

Shortly after the adoption of the Constitution of the Year III on 1 Vendemiaire Year IV (23 September 1795), the Convention once again tightened the screws on the movements of the French citizenry. In its "Decree on the Internal Communal Police," the government ordered that henceforth persons would be not permitted to leave the area of their canton without a passport signed by the administration of the municipality or of the canton itself. In the interest of bureaucratic consistency, each *département* was to supply the lower authorities with a model of the passport to be used. Those found outside their cantons without the required document and unable to establish satisfactorily the location of their domicile were to be treated as vagabonds, who might receive fairly harsh punishments including up to a year of detention – followed, in extreme cases, by "transportation," presumably to a French penal colony.[112]

If the government had had the teeth to make this measure bite, it would have turned France into a gigantic prison in which the cantons constituted the individual cells. As we have seen, however, the likelihood is that it would have been relatively easy to circumvent these requirements. Still, the decree bespoke a vindictive mood, especially against the poor. Indeed, these regulations reinvigorated a law from two years earlier that had been specifically directed toward the control of mendicity.[113] Having moved decisively to sharpen documentary restrictions on potential enemy foreigners, the Thermidorian Convention rejuvenated strictures against the lower orders that strongly resembled those of the *ancien régime,* and that the Constituent Assembly had proudly eliminated less than four years earlier. The revolution thus withdrew firmly from the prospect of untrammeled freedom of movement that had been heralded in the work of the Constituent Assembly.

PASSPORT CONCERNS OF THE DIRECTORY

Just as the Convention was adopting this most recent restrictive legislation, Napoleon was crushing the Parisian revolt of Vendemiaire Year IV. The Directory followed immediately on his heels. Despite the fact that it took a harder line against footloose elements, it, too, was unable to gain mastery over the country. The fact that the Directory felt it necessary to reiterate in late March 1796 the prohibition on passport-less departures from a canton enunciated the previous October suggests that the actual implementation of those restrictions left much to be desired.[114]

During this period, desertion from the army remained a major problem, and one that the government seems to have been largely helpless to curtail. Richard Cobb has offered a pungent description of the situation facing the government:

> [In the Year IV] we hear of a whole company of soldiers, in uniform, with their regimental numbers on their collars, walking from Sarrelouis [in Alsace], the length of a half-dozen Departments . . . without at any stage being challenged . . . The enormous extension of desertion in the year IV and the year V – probably the peak – is the most striking testimony to the powerlessness of the Directory almost anywhere outside Paris . . . There is something splendid about defiance of government on such an impudent scale . . .[115]

This impudence may have seemed splendid to one of its most brilliant historians, but it most assuredly did not warm the hearts of those running the Directory.

Perhaps as a result of its ineffectuality in governing movement within France, the drift of legislation under the First Directory was toward a more exclusive preoccupation with passport controls on those leaving and entering France. At least at first, the Directory held to the 7 December 1792 law concerning passports for departure from the country. In March 1796, however, the Directory took up a proposal to change that law to make it conform to the fact that the district directories – formerly responsible, along with the municipalities, for giving their recommendation to the *départements* with respect to the legitimacy of requests for passports for departure from France – had since been suppressed. According to the bill's preamble, it was also designed to "extend and activate the surveillance of the government over the acquisition of passports" for departure. It was to achieve the latter objective by requiring that the departmental administrations submit every ten days (the *décade* of the new revolutionary calendar) a list of the passports they had issued during the interim.[116]

Rising to defend the bill against critics who found it too lax, a speaker known as a vigorous devotee of the Constitution of 1791[117] waxed eloquent about the rights of a people that had lived "for fourteen centuries under the arbitrary power of kings and their ministers and that is surrounded by nations subject to a power of the same type," about absolute and relative freedom, and about natural rights and the rights of man and citizen – especially the right to move about and to leave that was guaranteed in the constitution. The speaker agreed that the times demanded sharper surveillance by the government and thus that it was admissible to require that those wishing to leave first obtain the state's permission to do so. Yet just as one inculcates timidity in a child too long kept in the crib, he insisted, "one robs the French people of a part of its energy" if one weighs it down too long with unnecessary restrictions. Ultimately, these views prevailed, and the Council of Ancients – the body now ruling France – adopted the bill. In view of the fact that both supporters and opponents agreed that this measure would lighten the burden of documentary requirements on those wishing to leave France, we may conclude that this outcome was not unwelcome to the leaders of the Directory.[118]

Whereas the government relaxed passport strictures with respect to French citizens, this period saw a harsh turn against foreigners, who were increasingly seen by the top officialdom as criminals. The pages of *Le Moniteur* from this period record an extraordinary diatribe by the Montagnard Julien Souhait regarding the need to impose a more severe passport regime on foreigners. Souhait began his remarks by noting that the government had required passports for all those leaving their domicile, "as proof of their good conduct and their respect for liberty and public tranquility." But if this were reasonable enough for French persons, he continued, there was all the more reason to require passports of foreigners, "men who cannot offer, like the French, the natural guarantee of their attachment to the *patrie*, nor the same means to repair the damage they might do through corruption or immorality." Souhait went on to decry the favoritism toward potentially dangerous co-nationals displayed by foreign ambassadors in the issuance of passports, and insisted that these foreign emissaries could not be trusted to take French security concerns into account in their passport practices.

Souhait then delivered himself of a statement that articulated directly the notion of the state's monopolization of the legitimate means of movement, as well as the shift toward making French political space a place "of and for the French":

> Passports are a police measure of the government on whose territory travelers circulate. None other than that government, or its agents, has the right to bestow them, for none other has the interest and none other has the right and obligation to watch over good order, liberty, and the public security. The agent of a foreign power cannot be your agent, even in his own interest; you cannot give him any authority, even less one that the constitution expressly delegates exclusively to the French and to the magistrates of the people. The foreigner, like every resident, is subject to the laws of the country in which he travels. This subjection is the price of the protection that he receives; it is the prerogative and the right of the public authority. A natural-born Frenchman (*un naturel*) may not travel in France without the permission of the government or the magistrates of the people; the foreigner must therefore [also] obtain permission.

One way to get around the problem of foreign undesirables entering the country with documents issued by foreign rather than French authorities, he suggested, would be to establish a system whereby French authorities *in the traveler's country of origin* would issue passports to those wishing to come to France. Unlike foreigners, French officials could be relied upon not to distribute passports to those who might be expected to undermine public order in France. Souhait envisioned, in effect, the international visa system that would gradually develop over the next century and a quarter. His main legislative point was to complain of the inadequacies of the law of 23 Messidor Year III (11 July 1795) that had banished from France all but the "patriotic" foreign-born, and to insist that foreigners circulating in France – whom he accused of instigating "tumultuous assemblies" and "provoking anarchy and demagogic furor" in the foregoing weeks – have their passports visaed by French authorities.[119] In all events, one senses in Souhait's remarks a decisive *adieu* to the revolutionary cosmopolitanism expressed by Condorcet and others in the early days of the revolution.

The xenophobic mood articulated by Souhait was not without issue. First, just before Christmas 1796, the Directory stiffened the provisions of the hostile law of 23 Messidor Year III (11 July 1795), requiring that the passports of foreigners arriving in France be deposited with frontier officials and sent on to the Ministry of General Police to be visaed. Now, in addition, duly certified copies of such passports were to be forwarded to both the public prosecutor and the Directory's commissioner at the departmental criminal tribunal.[120] Then, in April, the Directory declared null and void all passports issued or visaed by diplomatic emissaries of the United States.[121] This measure was taken in the atmosphere that produced the Alien and Sedition Acts, the first law empowering the American government to deport undesirable foreigners, and suggested the extraordinary discomfiture with which developments in France were being regarded abroad, even outside the Continent.[122] The earlier aim of exporting the revolution to other countries suffering under arbitrary rule had been transmuted into wars of conquest, and France had learned enmity of foreigners as it earned enmity from their respective fatherlands.

But the culmination of these trends was yet to come. With the coup d'etat of 18 Fructidor Year V (4 September 1797), anti-foreign and revolutionary sentiments welled up afresh as the dictatorship attempted to clean house of its opponents and enemies. For the French, this meant a wave of terror – "a reversion to the spirit of '93," Greer called it – against refractory clergy, emigres, and many who were confused with them in the ensuing fracas. The "Fructidorian Terror" thus spurred a new stream of emigration, not least of those members of the Council of 500 purged and condemned to deportation by the law of 19 Fructidor with which those who carried out the coup asserted their predominance.[123] By the end of September, the Directory moved to consideration of a new passport law intended to give them the upper hand in the midst of all the confusion. It soon adopted a statute that has been described as "the starting-point for modern aliens legislation."[124]

In fact, the law tightened passport requirements for both French citizens and foreigners. For the former, passports henceforth were to include mention of the bearer's destination. Within ten days after the promulgation of the statute, all passports issued prior to the date of promulgation were declared null and void. Those away from their place of domicile during that time were to obtain new papers from the administration in the canton in which they found themselves; the passports were to be issued, however, only on the basis of a declaration by two residents of the relevant canton who were familiar with the applicant. A copy of such passports was to be sent to the cantonal administration where the person had his or her domicile. In addition, article 6 pronounced penalties of one to two years in prison against those officials complicit in issuing passports for travel within France to those who had been ordered expelled from France pursuant to the law of 19 Fructidor.

Yet the regulations were even more stringent for those from other countries. Nonresident foreigners then in France were obliged to present their passports to the administration of the *département* – a higher-level authority – in which they happened to be, and the destination of their travels and their current residence was to be inscribed as for French citizens. Copies of these passports, however, were to be sent to the Ministry of Foreign Relations as well as that of the General Police. In a move presumably directed especially at the English, the surveillance measures already enjoined in law against those arriving in French ports were reaffirmed. Finally, article 7 brought the *coup de grâce*: all foreigners traveling within France, or resident there in any capacity other than that of an accredited official mission on behalf of a neutral or friendly power, and who had not acquired French citizenship, were "placed under the special surveillance of the executive Directory, which may withdraw their passports and compel their departure from French territory if it judges their presence susceptible to disturb the public order and peace."[125] The words of Julien Souhait had become deeds; the optimistic cosmopolitanism of the early days of the revolution had been obliterated; and the high-flown ambiguities of the Declaration of the Rights of *Man* and *Citizen* had been resolved in favor of the nation-state. Foreigners – made known by the papers they carried – were declared suspects as a matter of routine.

The reinstitution and strengthening of passport controls in revolutionary France – a process more or less unbroken after early 1792, punctuated by occasional attempts at liberalization – confirms Tocqueville's conclusion that the French Revolution went through "two distinct phases: one in which the sole aim of the French nation seemed to be to make a clean sweep of the past; and a second, in which attempts were made to salvage fragments from the wreckage of the old order."[126] Although much work remained to be done before the state could effectively assert its monopoly on the legitimate means of movement within France and across its boundaries, the "new regime" had made clear that it had no intention of adopting the attitude of the Constituent Assembly that passports should be abolished and freedom of movement should carry the day.

As we have seen, the revolutionary governments, beset by enemies domestic and foreign, real and imagined, sought to use passport controls and other documentary means – "fragments from the wreckage of the old order" – to regulate the movements of emigres, counterrevolutionary brigands, refractory priests, itinerant mendicants, conscripted soldiers, and the foreign-born, among others. While these devices may have been effective in many instances, the chaos and disorder ravaging the country, the efforts of dissident groups, and the lack of a well-articulated bureaucratic apparatus simply overwhelmed the government's capacity to assert a successful monopoly on the legitimate means of movement at this time.

Yet steps had been taken in this direction, as well as toward the implementation of effective distinctions between native and foreigner founded on documents. In part, of course, such efforts foundered on the incoherence of the international state system, especially during the various wars that plagued Europe until the end of the Napoleonic era. In the absence of an organized passport system, countries such as France that required passports to legitimate movement were forced simply to issue these to foreigners themselves, rather than being able to expect them to arrive with the required document, as we now take for granted must be the case. Still, by instituting civil status (*l'état civil*), the secular registration of each new addition to the French populace, the new regime in France had made a major advance toward enabling it to embrace its citizens and make them available for its own purposes.

Let us now turn to a consideration of the situation in nineteenth-century Europe, as the burgeoning fortunes of economic liberalism made free circulation appear an unavoidable necessity for industrial development, and the falling away of older documentary controls culminated in a period of extraordinary freedom of movement.

CHAPTER 3

SWEEPING OUT AUGEAS'S STABLE: THE NINETEENTH-CENTURY TREND TOWARD FREEDOM OF MOVEMENT

The defeat of Napoleonic adventurism and the stabilization of European interstate relations following the Congress of Vienna (1815) soon led to a relaxation of the controls on movement that had gone into effect during the revolutionary conflagrations, or that had existed since long before they began. The century-long period of relative peace that followed constituted the framework for the dissolution of feudal ties where they still held sway, a process that in Prussia began during the Napoleonic wars and was in part a form of compensation to those elements of the male population drafted into military service during those conflicts. Clausewitz and other reformers realized that German society would have to be transformed in a more liberal and egalitarian direction if it were to be in a position to match the fighting ability that had been newly demonstrated by the French "nation in arms."[1] Liberation from traditional dues and obligations also gained impetus, of course, from the example set by the abolition of feudalism in France in August 1789. In short, keeping the peasants bound to the land as they had been since the so-called "manorial reaction" of the sixteenth century grew increasingly untenable in western Europe, though the East remained as yet little affected by this trend.

This newly won freedom was deeply troubling to the guardians of social order. In the early nineteenth century (at least in Germany, but surely not only there), the nervous view was widespread among them that "nothing has appeared . . . to replace the previous patronage [of the lord] over the peasant."[2] Those responsible for superintending the "dangerous classes" were frequently rendered apoplectic at the heightened possibility that large numbers of "masterless men" might be found traveling the country's roads unhindered. The labor needs of an industrial capitalist economy *in statu nascendi* combined with the decline of serfdom, however, to promote a dramatic slackening of restrictions on movement in the course of the nineteenth century. Despite much hand-wringing on the part of the "better element," this trend culminated in 1867 with the Prussian-led North German Confederation's explicit abolition of all documentary requirements authorizing travel, whether these concerned citizens of the Confederation's member states or foreigners. At the same time that movement was liberalized, however, the Confederation reasserted its right to demand that persons "legitimate" themselves; the loosening of restrictions on travel could not be allowed, the state's guardians insisted, to diminish its capacity to "embrace" the population for policing and other purposes.

In this chapter, I concentrate primarily on the vicissitudes of documentary controls on movement in the German lands. The focus is on reconstructing the processes whereby this period gave rise to considerably greater legal freedom of movement, often irrespective of a person's nationality, than had been known in Europe since before the rise of modern states aiming to monopolize the legitimate means of movement.

FROM THE EMANCIPATION OF THE PEASANTRY TO THE END OF THE NAPOLEONIC ERA

From at least 1548, the German lands had known documentary restrictions on the movements of the lower orders. At Augsburg in that year, the Imperial Diet had mandated that the "masterless rabble" (*herrenloses Gesinde*) – those with "no master or spokesperson (*Vorsprecher*)" – be in possession of imperial travel documents in order to pass through those lands without hindrance, or otherwise risk expulsion. The language suggests the extent to which the state was acting in place of the feudal lord who would normally be expected to regulate the movements of the person(s) in question. Shortly thereafter, at least according to one mid-nineteenth-century observer, "passports" make their first entry into the language of the law.[3]

Early in the reign of Frederick William I of Prussia (1713–40), the so-called "Soldier King," a law intended to sharpen controls on beggars, vagabonds, and "other evil rabble" for the first time required foreigners (*Ausländische*) to have in their possession a passport, which was to be visaed nightly at the waystations along their route. Natives were to equip themselves with the "usual" passes.[4] During the course of his reign, the Soldier King would eventually prohibit all emigration by peasants, an order for the infraction of which the punishment was death.[5] Then, in 1753, a police measure mandated that "all traveling pedestrians and persons riding [horses] individually, insofar as they are not [army] officers or other distinguished persons, must be in possession of passports."

Innkeepers were to assist the authorities in enforcing these laws by report-ing each night on the presence of strangers in their accommodations.[6]

We should be careful not to take these draconian pronouncements too seriously, however. "The prohibitions on emigration," an Italian analyst of migration has noted, "could not stop a movement that had struck such deep roots in the country, and which political oppression, often accompanied by economic distress, rendered necessary as a release (*liberazione*)."[7] This was, after all, a period of substantial German emigration to North America, a flow engendered in part by the authori-ties' relaxation of emigration restrictions with the aim of ridding the country of religious squabbles.[8] But the major influx of Germans was still to come, and would have to await the emancipation of the peasantry and the decline of mercantilist attitudes toward population-as-wealth.

The liberation of the peasants in early nineteenth-century Germany would bring decisive steps to loosen restrictions on movement for the lower strata. With Napoleon's defeat of Prussia at Jena in 1806, the Holy Roman Empire of the German Nation had met its final demise. Given that a re-match with France was sooner or later inevitable, the Prussian King, Frederick William III, responded with measures designed to bring into existence a coherent body of subjects "with a sufficient stake in their nation so that they would be willing to fight and die for it." The so-called October Edict of 1807 freed the Prussian peasantry from hereditary servitude, traditional labor obligations and dues, and seigneurial restraints on their ownership of land. Many occupations were opened to all comers, stripping the guilds of their power to regulate access to employment. These measures were nothing less than the first strides down the road to a free market in labor. At the urging of the reformers arrayed around Karl Freiherr vom Stein, halting steps were also taken in the direction of popular participation in government.[9]

Despite some significant successes in a difficult period, however, the Prussian reforms could go only so far in a situation of (partial) military occupation and the imminent resumption of war. Following Napoleon's disastrous winter campaign in Russia, Czar Alexander undertook in late February 1813 an alliance with Prussia to save European Christianity from the godless French despot.[10] As the confrontation with France loomed, controls on movement were tightened anew. On 20 March 1813, a week before the official declaration of war against France, Frederick William III announced that it was necessary, "for the survival of the inde-pendence of our crown and our people," to promulgate a new passport law.[11] The punctiliousness of the regulations – their specificity regarding those affected, the precision concerning how border-crossings were to take place, the firmness with which the statute defined the relevant offi-cialdom – makes the measures we have examined in revolutionary

France seem haphazard and ramshackle by comparison. Unlike the French revolutionaries, of course, the Prussian King had no interest in debating fine philosophical points about the freedom of movement, at least not for publication. He had a realm to save.

As one observer has noted, the 1813 law was mainly designed to keep out the spies that "inundated" the country during wartime.[12] This interpretation is indeed suggested by the new documentary requirements. Upon entering Prussian territory, travelers from abroad were constrained to take possession of a Prussian passport issued not by local authorities (apparently the usual or at least an accepted practice), but by higher-level officials ranging from the Royal Chancellor down to the central government's police representative at the provincial level. The persistence of the practice whereby incoming travelers were furnished with a passport by the *receiving* state, rather than by the state of the traveler's origin, is notable here. Those who failed to have their passports visaed nightly in the town where they stayed, or who left the route inscribed in their passports, were subject to arrest and expulsion. Particular mention was made of the law's application to artisans and craftsmen, "irrespective of whether they have a journeyman's book [*Wanderbuch* – a document attesting to the craftsman's passage through the elaborate German apprenticeship system] or only a foreign passport." Russian and other allied troops and commanders were exempted from these requirements, as were certain groups of people traveling for business purposes, and diplomats.

At the same time, those subject to the restrictions on entry were forbidden to *leave* Prussia without a passport issued by authorities above the local level and duly visaed at the border. The foreigners and unknown persons circulating in the country were to be subjected to heightened scrutiny by the Prussian security forces, though not only by them: the law requested the assistance of landowners, innkeepers, cart-drivers, and others in its implementation. In addition, the statute forbade artisans to employ foreign or returning native apprentices, or to release them for work abroad. The serious penalties invoked for violation of this provision suggest that one may regard this aspect of the law as a forerunner of the "employer sanctions" associated with the immigration policies of our own time.

Despite the intensified surveillance to be exercised over those groups deemed to be potential spies, however, the law adopted an indulgent attitude toward Prussian subjects. The new passport formalities were not incumbent upon Prussian subjects returning from abroad, as long as they satisfactorily identified themselves (*sich legitimiren*) in some other way. Nor was there, in Frederick William's benign view, any need to restrict the movements of Prussian subjects in the country's interior. This lax posture was due, he said, to "our subjects' laudable devotion (*rühmliche Anhänglichkeit*) to the state." This may well have been a self-serving claim, but Frederick William's judgment of the popular mood reflected both rising anti-French sentiment among the Prussian populace and the King's conversion to the notion that a war for national liberation should be combined with a war for domestic freedoms.[13]

The new passport regulations were thus principally preoccupied with the movements of potential foreign enemies and spies, but they were remarkably lenient toward Prussian subjects themselves.[14] This relaxed attitude toward freedom of movement was sensible for a ruler eager to sustain the enthusiasm of those soon to be recruited into the army in order to restore Prussian sovereignty and regain Prussian lands lost to Napoleon. The spring offensive began in April, and a new conscription law followed within a few months. By August of 1813, "the decisive struggle for Europe's future" was underway.[15]

It was a battle that Napoleon would ultimately lose. In September, the rulers of Austria, Prussia, and Russia signed a series of treaties at Teplitz that committed them to fight together until Napoleon's ultimate defeat and to restore Austria and Prussia to their shape in 1805. The "battle of nations" (*Völkerschlacht*) that ensued at Leipzig in October 1813 signaled the end of the French Emperor's hegemony in Europe. Even if Waterloo (June 1815) was still nearly two years away, Prussia and its allies had crippled the power of the French war machine, and Napoleon would soon be packed off to exile on the island of Elba.

Against this background – "because the political conditions that required considerations of public circulation to be firmly subordinated to those of general security" in the previous year's passport law had changed so much for the better – Frederick William III in late February 1814 issued an edict to liberalize the regulations concerning the movements of lorry drivers, livestock dealers, and artisans, though the greatest attention was paid to the latter group. With the state of military emergency past, artisans entering from "friendly" states could now gain access to Prussian territory on the authority of a passport issued by municipal authorities in their country of origin, and no longer had to submit to annoying delays while awaiting a Prussian passport at the border, as had been the case since the promulgation of the March 1813 law. Upon due inspection by border guards of the passports they carried, however, they were to receive an unstamped "interim passport" that would authorize travel to the provincial or other appropriate office empowered by the 1813 law to issue the entry passport. The new regulation thus allowed the affected persons into Prussia without a time-consuming application for documents for which they had to wait at the border, instead allowing them to acquire the documents in their own time in a direct encounter with the relevant authorities. Yet mercantilist and feudal ideas about the retention of skilled workers maintained their grip largely unaltered; the restrictions enunciated in the 1813 law remained in effect for artisans wishing to depart.[16] Needless to say, these kinds of restrictions on departure, characteristic of most *ancien régime* states, anticipate later attempts to forestall "brain drain" out of the "Third World."

With Wellington's final defeat of Napoleon at Waterloo, the Great Powers of Europe proceeded to redraw the map of the continent. In this process, Prussia regained considerable portions of its old lands, as well as new territorial concessions that included two fifths of Saxony and extensive areas in the Rhineland and Westphalia. By absorbing parts of the more progressive and wealthy areas of the south and west, these acquisitions shifted Prussian geography sharply from its traditional eastern agricultural bastions. In addition, the treaties emerging from the Congress of Vienna erected a sort of halfway house on the road to German national unification. The German Confederation (*Bund*) created in 1815 included some thirty-nine members, among whom the leaders were Prussia and Austria (or more precisely those Habsburg and Hohenzollern lands that had previously been part of the Holy Roman Empire). The loose linking of the states of the German Confederation served the purposes of statesmen seeking to weigh down Prussian power on the one hand, and of small states worried about losing their sovereignty on the other. Yet it failed to satisfy enthusiasts of the German national project and thus imparted considerable impetus to their burgeoning cause.[17]

In this context, the Prussian King, Frederick William III, abolished the wartime statute of 1813 in order to reverse the earlier balance and now "pay as much regard to the freedom of travel and commerce as to security in the interior of our monarchy." The new passport law of 22 June 1817[18] liberalized the restrictive provisions of the earlier law mainly (paragraph 4) by restoring to local, border, and port officials the authority to issue valid documents for entry into Prussia. Also added to the list of those authorized to give out passports for entry were Prussian diplomats accredited at foreign courts, official trade emissaries and consuls, and – most notably – the "national" and provincial officials of *other* states (even, in the case of those coming to Prussia simply to "take the waters," local officials of other states as well). This was an innovation, at least since the Napoleonic era; heretofore, the Prussian government had jealously insisted that its indigenous organs alone should issue such documents. Those exempted from the requirements concerning an entry passport included ruling princes and the members of their households, returning Prussian subjects in possession of a valid *exit* passport, craftsmen with a valid *Wanderbuch*, women with their husbands, and children with their parents.

Exit from Prussia was, in the terms of 1817 passport law, another matter altogether. Technically, no one – whether native-born or foreign – was permitted to leave the country without a passport authorizing their departure. Exemption from these restrictions was provided for those not requiring a passport for entry and those who arrived from abroad with acceptable foreign passports, though these had to be visaed by the police in the Prussian town from which they were returning to their country of origin. In contrast to the situation with regard to entry passports, however, those for exit were not to be issued by local police officials, but only by authorities at the provincial level or higher. (Actually, officials of provincial governments were only permitted to issue passports if a passport from this relatively low level would satisfy the entry requirements in the country to which the person was traveling, "about which the [provincial] governments are to receive more detailed instructions from the Ministry of Police.") Foreign diplomats accredited to the Prussian court had the right to issue passports to other diplomatic personnel, but these still had to be visaed by the Ministry of Foreign Affairs or the Ministry of Police, depending on the rank of the personnel involved.

In the third section, the law said simply that native Prussians (*Inländer*) moving about within the country required no passport from the police, "but may travel freely and unhindered without one." Such persons were nonetheless required to identify themselves to the police officers who might demand that they do so, on pain of various penalties. The next paragraph of the statute offered the possibility of acquiring an "identity card" (*Legitimationskarte*) to facilitate such identification, obtainable from either the Ministry of Police, the provincial government, or the police in the place of domicile. The card was to include the person's description (*Signalement*), to be valid for one year, and to cost the relatively meager sum of four *Groschen* (including the two *Groschen* official stamp). Yet not all "*Inländer*" escaped the requirement of carrying a passport for internal movement; these non-exempt groups included certain types of journeymen, those traveling in postal conveyances, and non-citizen Jews.

All passports, whether for entry or departure, were to be visaed by the border police closest to the point of entry or exit, as well as by the police in those places where the bearer remained for a period exceeding twenty-four hours. The latter requirement was imposed upon internal passports as well.

The slackening of documentary restrictions on movement mandated by the law was not to result in a diminution of public order, however. The law directed the various security organs to exercise a "greater attention to and surveillance over travelers and strangers . . . so that, despite the facilitation of movement accorded to the innocent traveler, public and private security should not be endangered, and so that the work of vagabonds and criminals is not made easier." In order to avoid a situation in which the loosening of official documentary controls on movement would yield these results, the laws directed at these "dangerous classes and individuals" were to be sharpened. The point of all these regulations was to insure that the "innocent" travelers be in a position to identify themselves, and to see to it that the suspicious and the dangerous "come into contact as often as possible with the police."[19] In short, public security was not to fall by the wayside, however appropriate it might be to relax controls on movement during peacetime. The official response to the enhanced mobility of the lower classes, according to Alf Lüdtke, "was to create a seamless web of registration (permits, residence permits, etc.) combined with the vigorous, but futile injunction to the police authorities 'not to let travelers out of their sight'."[20]

The new passport law of 1817 was of a piece with a broader loosening of controls on movement in post-Napoleonic Germany and in keeping with the proto-national character of the German Confederation. As Brubaker has noted, the Act of Confederation (*Bundesakt*) extended to all its member states a number of earlier bilateral agreements permitting greater freedom of movement and settlement among German states.[21] Yet the evidence we have seen from the Prussian passport law of 1817 indicates clearly that Brubaker is premature in claiming that these treaties "abolished controls on exit but not on entry" and that "a person could leave any state [in the Confederation] without obtaining special permission . . ."[22] Even at mid-century, prospective emigrants from Germany typically "had to obtain certificates from the tax collector, the pastor, and from school district officials that he owed them no taxes or tithes; he had to be free or forgiven of private debt; he had to fill out elaborate forms, and relinquish his citizenship; by law he had to be officially informed that he was being foolish."[23] Although the actual enforcement of these strictures varied by time and place, and they were more or less ineffectual and easily skirted in any case, it is clear that the German states had not yet adopted a liberal stance with respect to departure of their subjects.

Nor was it only Prussia that sought to stem emigration. For example, Württemberg, a Confederation member, still had a prohibition against emigration on its books, though the provision was enforced only selectively and in fact most emigration from the German lands during this period came from the southwest. Thus several thousand Swabians left for Russia before that country's enthusiasm about their coming waned in the face of declining supplies of free land in the Transcaucasus. In May 1817, the Württemberg government therefore announced that it would no longer issue exit permits for Russia unless would-be emigrants had received certification to immigrate from the Russian authorities, who had no interest in absorbing destitute foreigners who would be unable to feed themselves without a plot of their own. The swarms of relatively impoverished prospective emigrants met similar responses from officials in western Prussia, the Duchy of Nassau, the Netherlands (at that time a province of the German Confederation), and Bavaria. As a result, by June of 1817, the government of Württemberg had broadened its requirements that emigrants meet the restrictions imposed by foreign governments; "this meant in effect that no passes would be issued to the sort of people who had been requesting them."[24] Even if people could get out of southwestern Germany, however, by 1819 the Russian government instructed its representative in Württemberg to visa no more passports for the Transcaucusus, which further complicated access to that region.[25]

Despite insistent pleas from local government officials who viewed emigration as a safety valve for their communities' straitened poor relief budgets and a last, desperate hope for the emigrants themselves, higher-level authorities equivocated. Grand Duke Karl of Baden said only that emigration "ought neither to be encouraged nor prohibited." In short, perhaps the best one can say is that policies regarding emigration from the German states were in some disarray, poised between older mercantilist attitudes chary of emigration and more liberal ones that viewed it as healthy for both the state and the emigrants themselves. Indeed, despite the official ban on emigration, the Württemberg government saw fit to establish a section for emigration affairs in the Interior Ministry in 1817. The barriers to departure posed by passport and other controls on movement were in all events hardly insurmountable; many – especially the indebted or those fleeing other obligations – simply left without them.[26]

I suspect that the confusion concerning Brubaker's claims about the freedom to exit lies in the translation of the term *Freizügigkeit*. The term may be rendered as "freedom of *movement*," but its more technical meaning in German treaties and laws of the nineteenth century concerned freedom of *settlement*. I am principally preoccupied here with the problem of *Bewegungsfreiheit* – literally (and exclusively), freedom of movement. While the scope of each had expanded during the period in question, freedom of exit – irrespective of the question of where one intended to live – had not progressed as rapidly as the legal freedom to *settle* elsewhere than in one's original domicile, though freedom of settlement was hardly unencumbered as yet either.[27]

Prussia, certainly, had not yet abandoned the mercantilist attitude toward population that led it to oppose (though it did not technically prohibit) emigration as a matter of course. In 1820, beleaguered by an exodus of its subjects that it blamed on commercial emigration agents (forerunners of today's "coyotes" in Mexico, and of migration smugglers more generally), the Prussian government imposed jail terms on anyone found guilty of inducing its citizens to leave the country, and such curbs would remain a staple of Prussian policy at least until mid-century.[28] Moreover, into the 1830s most of the German states denied passports to their departing subjects unless they could demonstrate that the destination country would admit them. The result was that an early version of the visa system as we know it today began to operate, as prospective emigrants went to the relevant foreign consulate to obtain the documents they needed in order to receive dispensation to leave their country.[29] While such measures obviously reflect the persistence of mercantilist attitudes, it may also have been designed to protect potential migrants from giving up their livelihoods in Germany without being certain of landing on hospitable soil. As we shall see, it is precisely this rationale that was later offered for the creation of the American visa system in the 1920s. Emigration restriction and paternalistic impulses commingled inextricably in laws such as these.

In all events, although controls on movement within Prussia were lightened considerably during this period, the sort of untrammeled freedom of exit which Brubaker identified as having taken place in the second decade of the nineteenth century would in fact still be some time in coming.

PRUSSIAN BACKWARDNESS? A COMPARATIVE LOOK AT THE SITUATION IN THE UNITED KINGDOM

In view of the apparent stringency at this time of Prussian restrictions on movement and especially on exit, it may be salutary to cast a sideward glance at the question of movement controls in the British Isles during this period. As the leading edge in the development of industrial capitalism, Great Britain should presumably have led the way in the creation of free markets in labor, of which an essential component was the dismantling of "feudal" restraints and the consequent mobility of labor. Manufacturing industry could hardly advance without being able to draw in the hands it needed from wherever they might wish to come.

As we have previously noted, the Elizabethan Poor Laws and the Act of Settlement and Removal of 1662 had created the legal foundations of "parish serfdom," which sharply restricted the movements of English subjects within the country. Given the social consequences of the enclosure of common lands, as a result of which "sheep ate men" and large numbers of peasants were forced off the land and into the arms of a still embryonic industry, it seems doubtful that the statute could have been very vigorously enforced. Still, in 1795 the British partially repealed the Act of Settlement in the interest of freeing hands to go where burgeoning capitalist enterprise needed them most. Parish serfdom was thus abolished and the physical mobility of English workers restored. Karl Polanyi has suggested that the simultaneous institution of the Speenhamland system, which provided poor relief in a number of English and Welsh counties regardless of earned income, discouraged workers from striking out in search of employment and thus stood in the way of a competitive national labor market.[30] Yet more recent research has indicated that the evidence is thin for "the notion of a rural population tied to its parishes by poor relief."[31]

To the enlarged freedom of internal movement enjoyed by English workers around this time was added a massive influx into England of Irish migrants, a flow considerably facilitated by the Act of Union in 1800. The Act gave the Irish masses common citizenship in the United Kingdom, and thus greater access to English soil. For extraordinary numbers of Irishmen, to be sure, the trip across the Irish Sea was only the prelude to emigration to America; cheaper and more accessible passage was to be had from Liverpool than from Irish ports as a result of the more regular triangular trade between England and the United States. The upshot of this Irish migration was that "in place of one, there . . . emerged two closely interacting Irish societies poised on the opposite seaboards of the Atlantic . . ."[32]

This pattern substantially lessened the impact of Irish immigration on the English population. In part for this reason, as one observer has put it, "throughout the bulk of the period of mass Irish immigration, the British state adopted a more or less *laissez faire* open-door policy to the regulation of the new arrivals."[33] This relaxed stance toward Irish immigration to England would wane along with the decline among the British governing elite of mercantilist attitudes that favored population growth and retention, but it would be some time yet before decisive segments of the ruling classes abandoned those views.

As in Prussia after the October Edict of 1807 emancipating the peasants, the enhanced freedom of internal movement within the United Kingdom after 1795 did not necessarily entail greater freedom to depart the realm. The specter of "depopulation," that bogey of the mercantilist mind, still haunted the sleep of the British notables. Accordingly, Parliament adopted in 1803 the first of the so-called "Passenger Acts." Despite avowedly humanitarian intentions, which were embodied in the law's regulations concerning accommodations for transoceanic passengers who were then typically regarded by ship captains as little more than a substitute for ballast, the Act was "cradled in mercantilism," and strict penalties were laid down for infractions of its provisions. While vigorous implementation of the 1803 Act would have improved the conditions of passage, it would also have cut down significantly on the number of those departing from England for American shores. Yet the first of the British Passenger Acts was never seriously enforced, according to their historian, Oliver MacDonagh. If it had been, in MacDonagh's view, the emergence of the "Great Atlantic Migration" would likely have been severely inhibited.[34]

Only after Waterloo did the mercantilist impulse in migration policy begin to give way definitively to free trade – or at least to those who draped their "emigrationist" sentiments in its spreading robes. The cessation of hostilities brought a surge of unemployment, depression, and "Malthusian forebodings." The riots at Peterloo (Manchester) in 1819, during which ten demonstrators were killed and hundreds injured while protesting for working-class demands, helped to shock the ruling elite into awareness that the "social question" was gaining in political significance. Thus "by 1819 we find a select committee on the poor laws virtually recommending emigration to the workless," and Parliament in the same year made its first grant for state-supported colonization.[35] The British sought to export their joblessness by loosening restraints on – or, indeed, positively encouraging – departures. A desire to regulate a labor market conceived in national terms thus increasingly determined British policies concerning departure from the realm.

As always, however, there were two sides to the migration coin. Just as the British were seeking to export their idle hands, economic distress led the United States – the chief destination of British emigrants despite government attempts to steer them towards Canada – officially to discourage, if not to restrict immigration. As the publicist Hezekiah Niles put it in his *Weekly Register*: "The time has been when we were pleased to see the progress of emigration [from Europe]. It is now painful to observe it because of the want of employment for our own people."[36] The city of New York responded to the emergency by taking steps to limit the landing of aliens likely to become public charges. In the event, the measures were circumvented with relative ease and rendered largely ineffectual.

The lean years faced by English laborers in the late 1810s and the social misery they engendered helped to concentrate the mind of the British elite in this respect. By the mid-1820s, free trade motives had come to dominate parliamentary debates over emigration policy. Long-standing bans on the departure of seamen and artisans – including a provision that every prospective emigrant present a certificate signed by the authorities in his native parish attesting that he was not a "manufacturer" or "artificer" – and various regulations concerning emigrants and their possessions fell by the wayside in 1824–25. "The last survivals of the ancien regime" in emigration policy had finally given way before the liberal onslaught.[37]

Yet if departures were made easier in order to take the burden off the domestic labor market and poor rolls, it only made sense that access to the territory should be restricted to avoid the incursion of excess hands. The Poor Law Amendment Act of 1834 abolished the Speenhamland system and took poor relief out of the hands of individual parishes. "The population of rural England," Marcus Lee Hansen has written, "after more than two centuries of stagnation, found itself in motion." This pruning back of disincentives to internal mobility further encouraged the national government to reduce the numbers of the indigent in England, for it now assumed greater responsibility for the country's poor. Not coincidentally, the Act authorized the use of local funds to assist in emigration schemes. As free trade replaced mercantilism, the labor market and poor relief were increasingly "nationalized"; poor relief legislation was extended to Ireland in 1837.[38] "Free trade" implied not open borders, but protection of the labor and welfare "markets" at the national rather than the local level.

This interpretation seems the only sensible way to understand why Great Britain in 1836 moved sharply toward the regulation of foreigners, for the English had long been remarkably open to outsiders. The Magna Carta of 1215 had guaranteed to merchants from other lands the right to come into and leave England at will "except in time of war and if they are of the land that is at war with us." Even then, such persons would remain unmolested if the King determined that his subjects were well-treated in the countries with which he was at war.[39] Yet war played no role in the 1836 legislation. Instead, bad harvests in Scotland and the breakup of traditional agriculture in Ireland made for hard times.[40]

The Aliens Restriction Act of 1836, coming at a time when the great powers in Europe were at peace with one another, heralded a new departure.[41] Henceforth ship captains arriving "from foreign parts" were to declare to the chief customs officer in the port of arrival the name, rank, occupation, and description of any aliens on board. Furthermore, any non-English person was required, upon disembarkation at any port of the Kingdom, to present to the customs officer "any passport which may be in his or her possession," or to make a declaration to him stating "to what country he or she belongs and is subject, and the country and place from whence he or she shall then have come." The language of the ordinance suggests that the British government was not expecting that every foreigner arriving on its shores would, in fact, be in possession of a passport and did not appear to make admission contingent on presentation of such a document. The British were nonetheless noticeably ahead of the Germans, at least in the letter of the law, when it came to recognition of the fact that travelers might be male or female.

Exempted from these requirements were authorized representatives of foreign governments and their domestic servants, as well as any alien who had lived continuously within the realm for three years, provided that this was certified by the appropriate officials. Yet exemptions from documentary evidence of nationality create their own problems; nationality cannot be read off a person's forehead, and thus it requires some sort of persuasive demonstration, usually involving *other* documents than those normally required. The Aliens Restriction Act thus noted that "if any question shall arise whether any person alleged to be an alien . . . is an alien or not . . . the proof that such person is . . . a natural-born subject of his Majesty, or a denizen of this Kingdom, or a naturalized subject, or that such person, if an alien, is not subject to the provisions of this Act or any of them . . . shall lie on the person so alleged to be an alien . . ."

Such provisos presumably stimulated the development of documentary attestations of a person's right to claim access to British soil, a function eventually assumed by the passport though at this point the requirement concerned precisely those who asserted claims to entry *without* need of a passport (i.e., British subjects). One imagines that, under these circumstances, well-dressed travelers speaking the King's English probably had no difficulty passing as Englishmen and -women, whereas "passing" in this manner was probably more difficult for a notional Italian shoemaker who, despite having plied his trade in London for two decades at his Majesty's pleasure, wished to return to his workshop after a visit to *la famiglia* in Turin. Our shoemaker would have needed some sort of papers demonstrating his claim to entry.

Foreshadowing later developments, the Act also required that customs officials keep an "aliens list," although at least one commentator has suggested that this was a "rather haphazard practice."[42] Rounding out the regulations was a requirement that aliens make known to those officials their intention to depart the realm before doing so. In addition to subjecting incoming aliens to heightened scrutiny that could provide the classificatory foundation for their exclusion by establishing their alienage, the Act thus promoted the creation of the administrative machinery necessary for the state to keep track of all aliens leaving and sojourning in the country at any given time.

Such legislation was hardly in keeping with any principled notion of free trade, which now carried the day in other respects, culminating in the repeal of the Corn Laws in 1846. The enhanced energy devoted to keeping track of aliens was consistent, however, with the policy of the so-called "emigrationists" to encourage and facilitate departures from "overpopulated" areas of the realm, especially Ireland, and with a broader British effort to reduce the size of the resident population and thus to ameliorate problems of unemployment. Even if it was no paragon of economic liberalism, the 1836 Act marked a departure from the "population is good" mentality characteristic of mercantilism. The

Aliens Restriction Act pointed to the rising inclination of European governments to create bureaucratic mechanisms that would allow them to keep track of entering persons' nationality – a capacity which, in turn, would permit them more successfully to limit unwanted foreign immigration when they wished to do so. The Act was also a salutary reminder that the expansion of the freedom of movement in Europe was by no means absolute. The British blazed the trail that led to the elimination of controls on "internal" movements and the displacement of those controls to the "national" borders. The "foreigner," once perhaps only from the next parish, was increasingly the alien, the non-national.

The United Kingdom moved to strengthen its capacity to identify and regulate the movements of foreigners at the same time that it inaugurated a domestic free market in labor. Great Britain thus preceded Prussia in achieving this essential precondition of industrial capitalism. Yet in the second half of the nineteenth century, when Germany finally pruned away the dense feudal underbrush still blocking the path toward a free labor market, the manpower needs of German industry would lead Prussia and its confederal partners to pursue a quite different course than that taken by the British. When the North German Confederation set about abolishing the last vestiges of the *ancien régime* in its lands, it would open its "domestic" labor market to all comers, whether "German" or foreign. The difference in approach can be attributed to timing: when the British brought their free national labor market into being, they felt they had too much labor power on hand; when the Prussians did so, they feared they had too little.

FREEDOM OF MOVEMENT AND CITIZENSHIP IN EARLY NINETEENTH-CENTURY GERMANY

The expanded freedom of mobility attendant upon the emancipation of the serfs in early nineteenth-century Prussia cast into bold relief the tension between presence in a particular place and the right to membership therein. In particular, the unwonted circulation of "masterless men" threw out of joint systems of social provision in which membership rights had been predicated on residence. The growing freedom to move around within the territory of the German states increasingly drove the individual states to determine who had access to their territories and to the benefits of membership in them.

Accordingly, the nineteenth century was a golden age of the codification of citizenship laws, a process directly motivated by the need to establish who did and who did not have a right to the benefits of membership in these states. In the German lands, the revision of membership statutes in response to the decline of serfdom and the attendant rise in mobility among the popular classes began shortly after the Congress of Vienna. First, in Bavaria, the new Constitution of 1818 stipulated that only those in possession of the so-called *Indigenat* (i.e., Bavarian "nationals") were to be permitted full enjoyment of citizenship (*bürgerliche*), public, and private rights. At the same time, acquisition of the *Indigenat* was made a matter of descent, replacing the principle of residence (*Wohnsitzprinzip*) that had previously held sway. Most of the other states of the German Confederation followed suit soon thereafter.[43]

Membership based on residence in a particular place may have been well suited to a context in which few people moved around. In contrast, membership rooted in descent was a means of coping with the fact that enhanced mobility made it more and more difficult to determine who belonged and who did not, and helped states "hold onto" population temporarily – or even permanently – living elsewhere than within the state's territorial boundaries. *Jus sanguinis* (the "law of the blood") might thus be thought of as a sort of migratory mercantilism, which "held onto" people wherever they might choose to go. In contrast to the migratory mercantilism of *jus sanguinis*, the *jus soli* (the "law of the soil") principle might be regarded as a sedentary mercantilism: hence its application in openly mercantilist (and physiocratic) *ancien régime* France, in late nineteenth-century France when population deficits were a matter of considerable concern in the face of growing German military power, and in the United States when it sought to encourage immigrants to spawn future citizens to populate its vast territories.[44]

Brubaker has argued that this process of defining who belonged to different states – who was or was not a citizen – "was not the product of the internal development of the modern state. Rather, it emerged from the dynamics of interstate relations within a geographically compact, culturally consolidated, economically unified, and politically (loosely) integrated state system."[45] While useful for suggesting the "international" components that help determine "domestic" citizenship laws, this point requires some modification. First, the state system – and hence the distinction between "internal" and "external" – remained in many respects inchoate at this time. Yet "internal" concerns surely played their part along with "interstate" considerations; Brubaker presumably means that citizenship laws were not *only* the product of internal developments. More importantly, perhaps, and unlike the situation in post-revolutionary France, many German towns during the first half of the nineteenth century retained rights to define membership and exclude non-members that were incompatible with citizenship systems conceived on the model of the internally unified nation-state, in which all were putatively equal before the central government.

The problem of municipal autonomy was less severe in Prussia than in the states and principalities of South Germany, where the towns had long enjoyed privileges that set them off from the larger cities and the countryside and which the towns defended jealously and zealously. This tradition would prove a major stumbling block to the first German unification that was ultimately consummated in 1871.[46] In Prussia, however, the situation was different "because local self-government there was a bureaucratic gift to apathetic townsmen."[47] Yet even in Prussia, the authority of towns to define who belonged and who did not, and to exclude those it did not wish to admit to its ranks, stood in the way of the legal and administrative unification of the territory.

In 1842–43, Prussia moved to overcome this barrier to its superordinate control over who came and went within its dominions. First, the "Law on the Acquisition and Loss of the Quality of Prussian Subject" systematically defined who was to be regarded as a Prussian subject. This pathbreaking statute subsequently served as a model for citizenship laws in a number of other north and central German states.[48] Brubaker has neatly described the underlying motivation for this redefinition of membership:

> Effective closure against the migrant poor required a sharper separation of membership and residence, and a reversal in their causal relationship. Domicile should be contingent on membership, not membership on domicile. Membership, defined independently of residence, should be the fundamental category.[49]

The membership law was enacted together with two others, which respectively regulated freedom of settlement within Prussia and the terms under which its municipalities were required to admit migrants from other parts of the Kingdom. The laws on internal migration guaranteed freedom of settlement to all but the currently indigent and limited the right of communal bodies to deny entry to such persons, which until then had been an important feature of their control over poor relief. These statutes thus deprived Prussian municipalities of their earlier authority to close their doors to those they merely *feared* might become public charges.[50] At the same time, Prussia affirmed the right of its subjects to emigrate, except those who owed military service obligations.[51]

Taken together, these laws constituted a major contribution to the construction of a labor market that was truly "national" in scope. By codifying the criteria associated with Prussian state membership (*Staatsangehörigkeit*), the government clarified the distinction between Prussian and non-Prussian. At the same time, by compelling local officials to accept as residents anyone at least initially able to provide for themselves, and to afford them poor relief if it subsequently became necessary, the Prussian government facilitated the internal migration of labor that was essential to the country's industrial development. The effect of these measures was to expand the horizons of mobility of Prussian subjects and to subject the communes increasingly to unified poor relief legislation of "national" scope. This transformation made of Prussia a larger, more coherent space from the point of view of free settlement and pushed outward the legal boundaries of alienage. In legal terms, the stranger (*der Fremde*) was increasingly transformed into the foreigner (*der Ausländer*), the person from another place into the person from another country, the local resident into the national.

Because the migration thus engendered was predominantly from east to west and from countryside to city, however, business elites in the more industrialized western portions of Prussia actually opposed these measures. They foresaw the potential for large numbers of needy migrants "falling on the rates" in periods of economic downturn, a fiscal responsibility that their municipalities would be forced to assume under the new arrangements. George Steinmetz has demonstrated that the Prussian bureaucracy regarded it as necessary under these circumstances to play the role of an "enlightened capitalist," overriding the narrow egoism of the commercial bourgeoisie that controlled the western German industrial cities in favor of a broader vision of Prussia's capitalist future.[52]

From the point of view of the sending regions, the system encouraged able-bodied villagers to make their way to the industrial districts of the west without fear that they would find themselves bereft of support in time of need. At the same time, the sending villages were absolved of the need to provide for their own non-resident poor, a fact that naturally helped secure their endorsement of the redistribution of responsibility for poor relief. It was not until the Poor Law was revised again in 1855 that the distribution of the burdens was reversed, as the principle of residency (*Wohnsitz*) was entirely eclipsed in favor of that of the "residence for purposes of poor relief" (*Unterstützungswohnsitz*). By mandating that municipalities' responsibility for poor relief accrued only after one year of residency, the 1855 law effectively reversed the earlier flow of liability for poor support and made sending areas once again responsible for their non-resident poor, at least for the first – and riskiest – year. Now it was the agrarians' turn to cry foul, for the new system would force those unable to support themselves to return to their home villages to seek poor relief.[53] In all events, these steps well served the functional requirements of capitalist industrialization in Prussia.

Although Prussia had gone a considerable distance in the direction of creating subjects with equal rights to establish themselves across the territory of the country, it still had some distance to go before it could claim to have created a free labor market of truly national scope in which Prussians were at liberty to move around as they wished. Documentary controls on their movements remained an annoying hindrance that would be removed only as Germany took the last, decisive steps on the road to "national" unification. In the event, the "national" labor market that was then called into being was, from our contemporary perspective, remarkably open to non-Germans.

TOWARD THE RELAXATION OF PASSPORT CONTROLS IN THE GERMAN LANDS

Until mid-century, the German states continued to throw obstacles in the way of would-be emigrants. Often the authorities pursued this aim by imposing taxes and fees (such as the so-called *Nachsteuer*) designed to discourage exit or to make it impossible for those with insufficient means. Shaken by the revolutionary upheavals that rocked virtually all of Europe in 1848, however, numerous German states relaxed such restrictions. In part, this shift was intended to provide a safety valve for social unrest, giving unhindered passage to those who were most troublesome to the authorities. Yet it also reflected the liberalism of the forces that spearheaded the Frankfurt Parliament, which included among its draft catalog of fundamental rights a provision that the state was no longer to be permitted to restrict the right of emigration except with respect to the fulfillment of military service obligations. This notion found its way into the majority of the new constitutions of the German states. Various proposals for the creation of an official *Reich* agency to regulate migrants – emigrants, not immigrants – failed to achieve consensus before the Frankfurt parliament was reduced to a cadaver; according to critics of these schemes, administrative resources for such offices were simply unavailable.[54]

Despite this insurgent liberalism in emigration policy, the ascent to the French throne of Louis Napoleon after his "Eighteenth Brumaire" alerted German rulers to the fact that they might soon need to muster the troops again. They therefore sought to keep young men from leaving indiscriminately, efforts that were stepped up as the Crimean War of 1854–56 approached. The actual difficulties of departure depended to a considerable extent upon where and how one sought to leave. "Passport formalities were more or less perfunctory" in France, making it relatively easy for those wishing to slip across the Rhine to escape their military obligations. In contrast, embarkation in Hamburg or Bremen was complicated by strict official supervision of steamship passengers, owing to these cities' concern to remain on good terms with interior states anxious to retain potential soldiers.[55]

As these developments suggest, the 1850s generally presented the picture of a continuing struggle between a liberal attitude toward freedom of departure and the persistence of mercantilist habits of mind concerning the value of population to state power. On the liberal side, a "Pass-Card Treaty" (*Passkartenvertrag*) of 18 October 1850 among "all the German states" except the Netherlands, Denmark, Hessen-Homburg, and Liechtenstein loosened passport requirements for travelers among them.[56] The treaty simplified and standardized the information that was to be included in pass-cards: the coat-of-arms of the issuing state; signature and seal or stamp of the issuing authority; name, status [*Stand*], and residence of the bearer; pass register number, and the bearer's description – age, "characteristics" (*Natur*), hair color, and distinguishing marks. The practice of taking away a traveler's pass-card for the duration of his or her stay was not expressly abolished, but in practice merely showing it to the authorities was generally regarded as adequate. (Those who have traveled from the territory of the former German Democratic Republic into West Berlin – where one's passport was placed on a conveyor belt and disappeared into a makeshift border control booth while it was being checked – will appreciate that this apparently minor change of practice would have contributed markedly to lessening the anxiety of those presenting their pass-cards for inspection.) Above all, however, visas were no longer required. Soon thereafter, an agreement between Austria, Bavaria, Württemberg, and other states mutually abolished visa requirements; Bavaria soon eliminated the practice altogether as "useless."

Yet the Pass-Card Treaty of 1850 bore signs of the persistence of the old regime as well. First, no subject of any of the participating states[57] had an absolute right to a pass-card. The document was to be issued only to those known to the authorities and considered to be "reliable" (*zuverlässig*), able to support themselves, and with their principal residence in the district where the pass-card was to be issued. Those found guilty of any crime, as well as tramping journeymen (*wandernde Gesellen*), servants, jobseekers of all kinds, and those practicing itinerant occupations, were not to receive pass-cards. "These limitations," according to a contemporary analyst of passport affairs, "have the advantage for the bearer of a pass-card that, simply by virtue of having this certificate (*Legitimation*), he is recommended to the police authorities as a reliable person." Under the circumstances, this was of course true; if pass-cards are required, then those lacking them are *ipso facto* lawbreakers. Clearly, however, these restrictions on access to a pass-card reflected a continued desire to regulate above all the "lower orders" of society, those always potentially "dangerous classes" whose desire or need to move about unsettled the authorities in a putatively sedentary society.

The German states were thus still divided over the matter of granting an unrestricted right of emigration to their members, as the Frankfurt Parliament had proposed. Indeed, when the Frankfurt Assembly of August 1856 created a commission to consider a federal law on emigration, the results of its investigation revealed a wide diversity of attitudes among the various German states concerning this issue. Twenty of the thirty-odd states of the German Confederation favored a requirement that would-be emigrants obtain an "authorization to emigrate," and that this authorization be shown before any transportation agreement could be entered into. Only twelve states opposed the first requirement and eleven the second.[58]

Despite lingering mercantilist attitudes, however, rulers in the German lands increasingly found themselves drawn ineluctably toward a more liberal stance in migration matters. Over the next several years, passport and visa requirements were relaxed or abolished between "German" states (including the Netherlands) and a series of other countries, such as England, France, Belgium, and the Scandinavian countries (although often such relaxation acquired force only where it was reciprocal). Saxony eliminated visa requirements entirely in 1862. The Prussian House of Representatives (*Landtag*) took up a bill to liberalize passport controls in the same year. Yet disagreements over the matter of the government's right temporarily to reintroduce passport requirements in times of emergency dragged out the discussion, and the Polish insurrection of 1863 intervened to kill the bill's chances of adoption.[59]

Also in 1862, Switzerland eliminated visa requirements and abolished the requirement of a passport for entry into or travel within its territory. A report from the Canton of Basel suggests the extent to which the abandonment of certain types of documentary controls was perceived in some quarters, at least, as simply an unavoidable capitulation to technological changes introduced by the arrival of the railroad:

> Insofar as travelers tend to stop only after great distances that they have traversed at great speed, and one simply cannot visa their papers after every little stretch, passports have lost their original value and have become simply an identification document, similar to local identity papers (*Heimathscheine*), pass-cards, etc. Moreover, the personnel responsible for passport control have made but few discoveries. The regular arrival of the trains and the telegraph are more important for the police. With the changed means of travel, the police have been forced to give up the more trivial things and have, so to speak, acquired an international type of activity with which previously they had nothing to do.[60]

From this perspective, the narrow, "internal" borders of old were crumbling before the onrush of the trains, simultaneously transforming "domestic" policing into an international undertaking. The massive improvement in transportation opportunities for the ordinary person would soon help persuade German political elites that passport controls had been rendered largely ineffective, contributing to their willingness to let them sink into obsolescence.

Yet despite the general trend toward relaxation of regulations that had required documentation authorizing a specific journey or travel in general, states were not prepared to give up entirely their ability to "embrace" mobile people in some fashion. Accordingly, in all of the cases in which passport requirements were abolished, the states in question simultaneously demanded that persons be in a position to identify themselves in some reliable and acceptable way. The loosening of states' control over *movement* did not – and indeed, without a slide toward a more anarchical state system, could not – mean the abandonment of its right and capacity to identify persons for purposes of administration and policing.

Within the various German states themselves, the 1860s were a period of intense pressure on the part of the bourgeoisie to sweep away outmoded obstacles to the functioning of an industrial capitalist economy. Up and down the country, liberal industrialists and opinion-makers demanded freedom of entry into any trade (*Gewerbefreiheit*), freedom of movement, and freedom of settlement. Burgeoning industry needed hands, and these freedoms were essential to ensuring that it could have them when it needed them.

Freedom of movement was vital to employers, the Essen chamber of commerce noted, for if "indigenous" workers were permitted to upset the supply of labor by using the strike weapon in labor disputes, employers must be free to reestablish the balance by drawing in new workers from outside. Moreover, according to the chamber of commerce in Breslau (Wroclaw):

> It is not enough that freedom of movement be introduced in one state. It is necessary that in general every citizen of a German state be free to apply his energy wherever in his opinion he can do so most advantageously, that industry take its workers wherever it can find them, and that the various regions transfer their labor force or temporary population surplus without hindrance and in accordance with their needs.[61]

Traditional German *Kleinstaaterei* (the profusion of small principalities, dukedoms, etc., that dotted the Central European landscape) and the privileges of towns fettered the emergence of a vibrant industrial capitalism, which demanded that the area in which Germans should be able to move freely be pushed outward toward the "national" boundaries.

Yet the labor needs of German industry took liberals even further in their calls for greater freedom of movement. So desperate were many of the factory barons for labor power that they wanted to open Germany to anyone who might wish to try their luck there. Liberal propagandists thus proposed to extend the freedom of movement to foreigners as well. By adopting laws guaranteeing the freedom of movement, wrote the liberal Berlin *National-Zeitung*,

> we shall first of all create for the German a fatherland in the matters which are closest to him. We shall retain the strength and ability which grow so abundantly in our soil, and we will attract from other nations the strength and ability which can and want to contribute in our commonwealth to our welfare, honor, and might. Through freedom of movement we shall create public spirit and national sentiment, welfare and contentment.[62]

The newspaper's editors apparently saw no contradiction in the notion that foreigners might wish to contribute to German "welfare, honor, and might"; they seem to have regarded it as a foregone conclusion that takers would be found for this proposition.

The Darmstadt chamber of commerce was even blunter about its attitude toward opening Germany to the free entry of foreigners:

> From the point of view of economic interests, which cannot be influenced by considerations of foreign policy, the extension of this freedom of movement to outsiders should not be denied under any circumstances, not even when there is no reciprocity. For the inflow of foreign capital, labor, and intelligence can only have a good influence on the development of the country, never a harmful effect.[63]

The internationalism of the German bourgeoisie with respect to labor recruitment was stimulated in part, of course, by a massive emigration – principally to the United States, to which a million and a quarter Germans had moved during the decade of the 1850s[64] – of potential workers availing themselves of the recently enhanced freedom to leave the country. Despite French fears of demographic inferiority that led them to dragoon colonial troops in order to remain militarily competitive with the Germans,[65] industrialists across the Rhine worried that their countrymen were escaping, via emigration, the great maw of factory work that they needed to keep fed.

The powerful forces – both political and technological – driving in the direction of greater freedom to move around on the part of the popular classes entered on a collision course, however, with the policing impulses of the German states. In Prussia, for example, the police had grown increasingly preoccupied with the surveillance and control of the "dangerous classes" during the first half of the nineteenth century. According to Alf Lüdtke:

> With a few exceptions, the "higher," cultivated and educated classes were seen as those "elements" which underpinned and supported the state; in

contrast, the "lower popular classes" constituted an unpredictable latent force whose menace could erupt on the streets, or in the taverns, at any moment – a ready refuge for anti-state "machinations."

Police vigilance was especially intense with respect to itinerants, vagrants, beggars, and wandering journeymen, who were most likely to suffer the indignities of harassment by the Passport and Aliens Police (*Paß- und Fremdenpolizei*).[66] There is little reason to think that the situation differed dramatically in other German states; indeed, in the South, where towns' authority to exclude the poor remained greater, surveillance of the floating population may well have been even more strict than in Prussia.

It was against this background that Saxony, Bavaria, Hanover, and Württemberg concluded the Passport Treaty of 7 February 1865.[67] The treaty abolished the requirement that travelers within these states, whether their subjects or foreigners, be equipped with a passport for entry, exit, or internal circulation, as well as any obligation to have papers visaed by the authorities. At the same time, however, in keeping with states' need to maintain their embrace of populations for policing purposes, travelers still had to be able to demonstrate satisfactorily to the authorities who they were, where they officially resided, and, "if the purpose and duration of the trip made it necessary," that they had the means to support themselves. In order to be in a position to "legitimate" themselves in this manner, members of the contracting states were permitted to request an appropriate travel document from the relevant officials; these documents were to be regarded as valid across the territories of those states. While each state retained the right to determine which officials were authorized to issue these travel documents, the parties to the treaty agreed to limit such authority to the municipality in which the applicants maintained their official residence. Foreigners who were otherwise able to legitimate themselves adequately could also receive a document for travel within the territories covered by the agreement, valid for four weeks. Those hailing from one of the other contracting states could do the same, but only under the condition that officials in the place of official residence be informed. The parties to the treaty also agreed to endeavor to develop simplified, standardized formats for their travel documents, and to recognize as valid for travel purposes those identification documents required of "specific classes of persons in order to pursue their occupations, such as the 'service books' (*Dienstbücher*) of domestic servants, the 'work books' (*Arbeitsbücher*) of itinerant journeymen and factory workers, etc., as long as they include a personal description and the signature of the bearer."

Despite these moves to liberalize passport controls on both German and foreign travelers, the itinerant poor remained subject to special restrictions. In order to travel legally in the territories of the contracting states, persons whose work required them to move about – "musicians, organ grinders, conjurers, tight-rope walkers, marionette puppeteers, those traveling with wild or trained animals, knife sharpeners, etc." – were still required to obtain travel authorization from the appropriate officials in their state of residence, and these documents were to include their state or municipal membership, description, and signature. More significantly, those seeking to find work or to enter domestic service were subject to the same requirement. The contracting states were also at liberty to retain or introduce visa requirements for these groups.

Finally, there remained two clauses devoted to special security measures with respect to passport policy. The contracting parties were free to deny passports that might be requested by those "from whom there is reason to fear that they may endanger public security." Each of the parties to the treaty, moreover, retained the right temporarily to reintroduce passport requirements "in cases of threat to public security as a result of war, unrest, or other events or for other substantial reasons."

It is hardly surprising that the contracting states would wish to reserve to themselves the authority to impose restrictions on movement when they felt the need to do so, but the continued subjection of the itinerant "dangerous classes" to special passport obligations flew in the face of liberal demands for freedom of movement and travel. Under mercantilism, foreigners had often enjoyed greater freedom to come and go than did subjects of a particular realm, typically because of efforts to restrain the departure of those with especially desirable skills. Here, however, the matter was different: special control was exercised exclusively over the lower classes, who were treated more like "foreigners" in our contemporary terms. The mentality underlying the 1865 passport treaty viewed the mobile poor as potential criminals who, as such, should always be subjected to anticipatory surveillance. The resemblance to the treatment of foreigners today, under a more fully developed interstate system rooted in the idea of the nation-state, is unmistakable. The lower classes in Germany at this point constituted something like an internal "foreign" nation.[68] Yet in consequence of its drive toward creating the necessary preconditions of capitalist industry, Prussia would soon spearhead a move to liberalize controls on movement more thoroughly, specifically exempting the "dangerous classes" as well as foreigners.

THE DECRIMINALIZATION OF TRAVEL IN THE NORTH GERMAN CONFEDERATION

Although it had been a party to the negotiations leading up to the 1865 Passport Treaty, Prussia ultimately refused to endorse the agreement.

The terms of the pact had nonetheless left the door open to "all states of the German Confederation" who had not originally signed on to accede to it at their convenience, an opportunity of which a number of other states quickly availed themselves. By the following year, however, the German Confederation was in a shambles. The Peace of Prague (1866) that concluded Prussian hostilities with Austria and France mandated that Prussia form a new confederation in the German lands. Yet the states of the south, with their traditions of local autonomy, regarded with considerable trepidation the prospect of finding themselves submerged in any federated structure led by Berlin. Indeed, a Prussian agent in Württemberg reported to his superiors in the capital that southerners were mocking the constitution of the North German Confederation that had been submitted to the constituent *Reichstag* in February 1867, saying it included "only three articles: 1. pay, 2. be a soldier, 3. keep your mouth shut." At first unable to obtain consensus on a new confederation with the southern states, Bismarck settled instead for a sort of halfway house on the road to the further consolidation of Germandom. In May 1867, the Prussian *Landtag* assented to the constitution, and the North German Confederation was born.[69]

Though largely comprising and certainly dominated by nobles, the *Reichstag* of the Confederation soon turned its attention to the concerns pressed upon it by liberals and industrialists, particularly including the matters of freedom of movement and travel. While the strongly agrarian and aristocratic composition of the North German political elite may make this seem paradoxical, it was not. Steinmetz has noted that while the Prussian-German state was controlled by groups whose social physiognomy might lead us to expect an instinctive hostility to industrial capitalism, "at almost every critical juncture these very elites sided with industry against agriculture and promoted the penetration of capitalist markets and a capitalist logic in parts of society that were still relatively traditional."[70] So it was when they turned their attention to the issue of controls on movement.

The proposed passport law for the North German Confederation was introduced into the *Reichstag* at Bismarck's behest on 18 September 1867.[71] In most respects the law followed the terms of the Passport Treaty of 1865 between Saxony, Bavaria, Hanover, and Württemberg. The bill thus proposed to abolish passport and visa requirements for subjects of the states of the Confederation as well as for foreigners, irrespective of whether they were entering, leaving, or moving about within the territory comprised by the Confederation's member-states. The law also forbade the continued use or introduction of so-called "residency cards" (*Aufenthaltskarten*) throughout the territory of the Confederation. According to the official commentary accompanying the bill, these certificates had already faded from administrative practice in most of the municipalities of Saxony and Prussia. The law intended to abolish only those documents designed purely to regulate residency; those necessary for the continued practice of a trade – even though they might be referred to as "residency cards" – were permitted to remain. The legislators' purpose here was clearly to eliminate restrictions on *residency* rather than on access to occupations, which they understood would persist in certain areas.

At the same time, the proposed law reaffirmed the right of the authorities to demand that travelers "legitimate themselves" in some reliable fashion. In furtherance of this objective, the bill provided a legal right to a passport for any subject of the Confederation who wished to request one, as long as no legal grounds stood in the way.[72] This provision was clearly intended to facilitate movement by guaranteeing subjects of the Confederation access to travel documents they might have felt would be useful, even if they were not required. Moreover, the proposed law mandated that the costs associated with the issuance of a passport should not exceed the modest sum of one *Thaler*, and could indeed be distributed gratis at the discretion of the issuing state. The bill also envisioned a standardization of the passport documents used by the various states.

It is worth noting that the right to a passport was granted exclusively to subjects of the Confederation. The failure to mention any terms upon which foreigners might gain access to German passports – though in fact they continued to do so – suggests that the interstate system of movement controls was taking more coherent shape as a framework regulating the movements of strictly demarcated bodies of citizens defined by their legal nationality. Less and less frequently would persons travel in alien territories with papers issued by another state than that of which they were nationals.

Finally, echoing the provisions of the 1865 Passport Treaty, the bill reserved to the presiding authority of the Confederation (*Bundespräsidium*) the right to reinstitute passport controls temporarily in the event that "the security of the Confederation or of an individual member state, or the public order, appears threatened by war, internal unrest, or other developments." The authors of the commentary on the bill regarded it as "inappropriate" (*unthunlich*) to attempt to list these various possible "developments" specifically, a fact that would goad the civil-libertarian proclivities of several parliamentarians when the bill came up for discussion in parliament.

The authors of the new law observed that, because some of the signatories of the 1865 Passport Treaty were now members of the North German Confederation, the Confederation needed to develop a passport policy that met with their assent. The legislators expressed the hope that a further agreement could be reached with the south German states soon after the present proposal had been adopted, resulting in a unification of passport law throughout the German lands that would soon constitute the second German Empire after 1871.

Here the most likely source of potential friction was the North German law's rejection of special passport obligations for the "dangerous classes" as had been provided for in the 1865 treaty. Despite the bill's broad similarities with that agreement, in this respect the proposed law went much further toward liberalizing passport policy than had the treaty. Aside from expanding the area in which freedom from passport requirements held sway, therefore, the most important feature of the bill lay in what it did *not* do: no groups of the population were singled out as liable to comply with special passport or visa obligations. This absence of particular restrictions on the lower orders marked the most significant departure of the 1867 law from the provisions of the earlier treaty.

The commentary on the bill spoke directly to this conflict between the two laws. First, the authors noted that the bill's stipulations did not affect statutes requiring specific occupational groups to equip themselves with documents, such as itinerant apprentices with their *Wanderbücher* or domestic servants their *Dienstbücher*. To be sure, these documents could serve the aim of regulating movement. But it was decisive, according to the authors of the bill, that these certificates had not been originally or mainly intended for this purpose. Rather, possession of such documents was "in the interest" of the bearer, for they facilitated the search for work.

This was especially so, the explanation went on, in those cases where guild organization maintained sway, and the evidence of a years-long apprenticeship provided by the *Wanderbücher* was indispensable for gaining access to the relevant artisanal market. "Likely though it therefore appears that journeymen will continue to carry *Wanderbücher*," the legislators saw no need to require them to obtain special documents authorizing their travel as such:

> It would seem completely unjustified, given the general abolition of passport requirements, if one were to make exceptions that would disadvantage precisely those classes of travelers who have previously been most harassed by the constant police control of their travel documents, leaving entirely aside for the moment the effort in time and resources demanded of the authorities themselves in the face of the very large number of itinerant journeymen and other work-seekers, and which effort is out of all proportion to the usefulness of those efforts in the individual cases.

Even if the underlying motivation was "Liberal" in the sense of creating the legal foundations of free-market capitalism, the legislators' explanation of their enterprise bespoke a "liberal," egalitarian intention in the area of freedom of movement that bore witness to the coming of that "equality" that Tocqueville had anticipated would spread across the world after his trip to America in the early decades of the nineteenth century.[73] As Tocqueville suggested, it had grown increasingly unacceptable to subject the lower classes to special legal disabilities simply as a result of their social position.

The bill's authors were particularly distressed at the possibility that the special restrictions of the 1865 passport law concerning "those seeking domestic service or [waged] work" should be extended to the entire Confederation. Still, if necessary, the authors of the law were prepared to accept that the exceptions to the general abolition of passport controls enunciated in 1865 could remain provisionally in force in the southern German states if that proved to be the price of an agreement on passport policy with them. In this respect, at least, the inhabitants of southern Germany who mocked the constitution of the North German Confederation appear to have underestimated the liberal impulses afoot in the Prussia of their day.[74]

At this point, Reichstag deputies were invited to submit proposals for changes to the bill before its actual discussion. The amendments tendered mainly concerned three issues: the wording of the guarantee that the authorities would still have the right to demand that people "legitimate themselves" and the question whether this authority was a proper subject of the passport law; the terms under which the government could reimpose passport requirements; and the precise nature of the authority of the municipalities to exclude or expel unwanted persons. With respect to this last issue, *Reichstag* representative von Kirchmann proposed that townships should have the right to exclude or expel their own members only on the basis of a specific legal authorization, or if they availed themselves of poor relief; all other rights of the municipalities were to be abolished. The socialist Wilhelm Liebknecht suggested an amendment to this amendment that would have struck the words "their own members." The point, of course, was not to penalize people for becoming poor, but to limit the power of the local community to exclude people, whether they were members of the municipality in question or not.[75]

The *Reichstag* debate over the law began on 30 September 1867.[76] Dr Friedenthal, the bill's official *rapporteur*, opened the discussion by remarking that the purpose of the proposed law was to dispose of obsolete legislation that was based on the notion "that removal from one's place of residence – that is, travel as such, [and] that taking up residence elsewhere are undertakings which, as a matter of public order, belong not in realm of the free decision of the individual, but are matters *dependent upon an official authorization* [emphasis in original] in the form of travel documents and residency cards, dependent upon unremitting police control, a shameful sort of police surveillance that must accompany the traveler without cease . . ." Friedenthal took it for granted that there could be "no differences of opinion regarding the need to dispose" of this sort of control, and that the debate could turn only on four issues: (1) whether the law provided sufficient guarantees for the freedom of movement; (2) the relation of the law to the right of the police to demand that persons "legitimate themselves," "*irrespective of whether these persons are travelers or not* [original italics]"; (3) the extent to which the law transforms the former *obligation* to carry a passport into a *right* to obtain one; and (4) the relation between this law for the entire Confederation and the laws of the individual states. While the representatives to the *Reichstag* did raise a variety of objections to the proposed law, Friedenthal was basically correct: no one ever challenged the fundamental aims of the law, and it was ultimately adopted in precisely the form in which it had first been submitted.

Noting that the passport bill before the house constituted an improvement "in the direction of greater liberty" over the Passport Treaty of 1865, Friedenthal affirmed that the law did, indeed, represent an adequate guarantee of the individual's freedom of movement. He found the renewed guarantee of the police authority to demand that people identify themselves hardly in need of further justification; it simply went without saying that the state had to have some way of "embracing" those unknown to its agents. As for the third issue, that of the bill's creation of a *right* to a passport, Friedenthal found this a "particular advantage" of the law, a right "of the greatest value for the working classes." Finally, Friedenthal framed the matter of the relation of the confederal law to those of the individual states precisely in terms of the matter of a right to a passport. This right was limited only by "legal obstacles" to the issuance of a passport. The individual states would be free to determine what these might be, but "it is certainly desirable . . . that there be no room for doubt that it is not a matter of the whim of the authorities wherein consist the legal obstacles." Friedenthal further applauded the freedom of the various states to determine for themselves which officials would be authorized to issue passports, particularly including local officials closer to the needs and problems of passport applicants. Finally, he stressed the importance of making travel documents cheap and easily accessible to the working classes, which in turn would help prevent official abuse of the provision authorizing the police to check personal identities.

In view of the bill's advantages for the working classes, a representative from Dortmund named Dr Becker declared himself unwilling to postpone "for even a day more than is absolutely necessary" the adoption of the law as written. For

> this law transforms the worker's duty (*Pflicht*), when he no longer finds work in the place where he normally resides, to seek work elsewhere, into his right and his matter of honor. It is a horrible contradiction in the existing legislation that the worker is threatened with disadvantages for his unemployment and neediness, and, when he seeks work, is subjected to a scrupulous police surveillance which, if he ignores it, puts him in danger of being punished as a vagabond and of suffering damage to his property, his honor, and his self-esteem.

Despite all the lofty talk about the worker's "honor," one senses the effusions of a would-be employer of cheap labor power behind Becker's enthusiasm for the passport law. It is not clear whether the repeated references to a male worker were simply a function of German grammar, in which the pronoun for the worker (*der Arbeiter*) is necessarily transformed into a "he" (*er*), or whether Becker was simply blind to the gender implications of the bill. Yet the vast majority of those seeking domestic service (*Dienst*, as opposed to *Arbeit*) – the other group from whom restrictions were to be lifted – were surely women.[77] In all events, Becker was eager to get his fellow parliamentarians to adopt the new passport law in order to dispense with the bureaucratic arbitrariness under which the laboring masses suffered: "Gentlemen, here we are beginning to sweep out a great Augeas's stable of police ordinances."

This the *Reichstag* proceeded to do after only relatively minor sparring. One of the highlights of the debate came when the Marxian socialist, Wilhelm Liebknecht, who rose to defend a proposed ban on expulsions from Germany, whether the person concerned was German or foreign.[78] In a role that would become common among socialists, Liebknecht sought to defend general human rights against the rights granted by nation-states only to their own subjects. He began by chiding the authoritarian practice whereby Prussia until that time had felt free to expel any non-Prussian German, without the need to justify that action on legal grounds. If the *Reichstag* did not explicitly abolish this practice, Liebknecht continued,

> we will be giving the police the right over a larger area . . . over the territory of the entire North German Confederation, to expel as "foreigners" those Germans who are not subjects of the North German Confederation – such as Austrian Germans, who despite the terms of the Peace of Nikolsburg [i.e., the Prague Treaty that ended the war with Austria after the battle of Königgrätz (1866)] still belong to Germany, Württemberger, Badenese, etc. I think that those gentlemen who call themselves the national party *par excellence* will not object if those Germans who are subjects of German states but not of the North German Confederation are assigned the same rights as those of the North German Confederation. Indeed, it is necessary to expand this right even further. A right that does not exist for all is no right . . . Gentlemen, it is necessary for us to proceed in the same fashion that England, that free country, has already taken, and to extend to foreigners

the same right that exists for Englishmen. There is no such thing as police expulsion in England; the government there does not have the right to deny someone their place of residence . . . Gentlemen, it is necessary that that be introduced here as well, that the police system, whose extensive development in the state of Prussia has done more to undermine German unity than any other institution – a system that has facilitated the politics of blood and iron to which we owe the disastrous war of last year, to which we owe the fact that Germany is now so riven and so powerless externally.

At this point in Liebknecht's stirring critique, the chamber grew restive. The president of the assembly moved to close debate on the paragraph, but this failed to carry.

Then Eduard Lasker, a member of the National Liberal party who was one of the outstanding parliamentarians of the era as well as "a constant thorn in [Bismarck's] side,"[79] rose to support Liebknecht's position. Lasker admonished the *Reichstag* that "it is a barbarity to make a distinction between foreigners and the indigenous (*Einheimischen*) in the right to hospitable residence (*in dem gastlichen Rechte des Aufenthalts*). Not only every German, but every human being has the right not to be chased away like a dog." Because the representatives of the Prussian government had repeatedly indicated that they were opposed to the practice of police expulsions, Lasker said, he felt confident that the government would endorse his view of these matters. Yet Liebknecht's amendment failed along with the one to which it was attached. Ultimately, the law was adopted essentially as originally proposed.[80]

As a result, the North German Confederation had moved to decriminalize travel – to remove from that act the suspicion and police surveillance that had previously attended it, especially for the lower classes. By abolishing passport controls and simultaneously reaffirming the right of the state authorities to be in a position to embrace all persons, whether travelers or not, movement as such now came to be legally regarded as a normal aspect of daily life. The law powerfully promoted the shift from documentary controls on movement to documentary substantiation of identity that would soon gain ground across Europe, but without yet privileging nationals over non-nationals with respect to who was subject to these regulations. In the discussion about the clause in the law reasserting the state's authority to demand that people "legitimate themselves," Count zu Eulenburg, later to be Minister of the Interior in the Empire, summarized the matter succinctly: "The purpose of this paragraph is to put travelers on an equal legal footing with all other citizens."[81]

BROADER SIGNIFICANCE OF THE 1867 LAW

The Prussian-German *ancien régime* was collapsing fast. Freedom to travel, to move about unhindered and without explicit state authorization, had been established as the law of the land. The Confederation deepened its commitment to such liberty only three weeks later when the *Reichstag* adopted a law guaranteeing freedom of settlement (*Freizügigkeit*) to its subjects.[82] The law provided for the right to settle and acquire property anywhere a person wished in the territory constituting the Confederation, irrespective of religion or lack of previous municipal or state membership, without being subjected to special disabilities by the authorities in either their place of origin or their new residence. Moreover, subjects of the Confederation were to be at liberty to practice any trade, whether sedentary or itinerant, under the same conditions as those to which the indigenous residents were subject.

Just as important as these measures was the fact that the rights of municipalities to deny residency to persons were almost entirely abolished. The law shifted this authority "outward" to the level of the constituent states of the Confederation, which were free to exclude persons – such as convicted criminals, vagabonds, and beggars – at *their* borders. Building on the earlier Prussian prohibition on the right of the municipalities to refuse entry to those they feared *might*, at some later date, become poor, municipalities throughout the Confederation were now left with the authority to exclude only the *currently* poor – and the law mandated that states could limit even this authority if they chose to do so. The connection in these laws between freedom of movement and the elimination of local restrictions on access to poor relief suggests that the fabled Bismarckian social insurance legislation of the late 1870s had as much to do with the creation of a unified national labor market as with efforts to take the wind out of the sails of a rapidly maturing socialist labor movement.

Indeed, recent research has demonstrated persuasively that "the working class was a minor player in the creation of the welfare state" in Germany.[83] This judgment seems copiously confirmed by the debate over the 1867 Passport Law, through which the German political elite "liberated" workers in search of work "in their own interest," rather than in response to their demands. Even though freedom of movement was intrinsically connected to the eventual creation of the German national welfare state, it also went hand in hand with other liberal freedoms such as the destruction of guilds and the corresponding freedom of entry into all occupations (*Gewerbefreiheit*), a connection that contributed to the hostility of artisans toward liberalism and to their later support for reactionary anti-capitalist movements.[84]

The law on passports adopted by the North German Confederation in 1867 – which was crucially bound up with broader Prussian-led efforts to institute the legal preconditions for industrial capitalism in Germany, especially including a free market in labor – came at a time when fears of

the working class were comparatively mild. Radicalism had been deci-
mated after 1848, and despite Tocqueville's prescient warnings about
the rising political salience of the "social question,"[85] socialism as an
organized movement remained in its infancy.[86] Despite the lingering
fears of revolution that hung in the air even after 1848 had been
reduced to a memory, these factors helped to provide a "window of
opportunity" through which the remarkably liberal 1867 law slipped. As
the socialist movement gathered force, however, the government in
1878 – the same year as the so-called "socialist law" that banned socialist
parties – took advantage of the provision for reimposing passport
requirements when public order was threatened, and required that all
"outsiders" (*Fremde*) and newly arrived persons in the Imperial capital be
equipped with a passport or "pass card" "until further notice."[87]

It is also worth emphasizing that the passport policy adopted in 1867
by the Prussian-led North German Confederation was considerably
more progressive than the 1865 treaty between Saxony, Bavaria,
Hamburg, and Württemberg on which it largely was based. The 1867
passport law sharply differed from the treaty in ways that reflected the
Prussian state's stronger commitment to economic liberalism. In view of
Prussia's fabled reputation for persistently reactionary political and economic attitudes, this result may surprise. In fact, however, this finding is
consistent with recent research that has demonstrated persuasively that
the political and economic impulses of the Prussian state during this
period were deeply "bourgeois" – even if those impulses were articulated
by Junker aristocrats rather than card-carrying members of the middle
classes.[88] The removal of passport restrictions on movement, and its
contribution to the creation of a larger space in which a common citizenship held sway, was in all events part of that "revolution from above"
that "cumulatively established the conditions of possibility for the development of industrial capitalism" in Germany.[89]

Yet it must always be borne in mind that the "unification of Germany"
and the creation of a Second Empire that took place under Bismarck's
tutelage did *not* result in the creation of a "German nation-state" if that
is to mean a state exclusively "of and for" all Germans. The German
Kaiserreich was both too small and too large to fill that bill. As a result of
the Prussian conflict with Austria that had come to a head at the Battle
of Königgrätz (1866), Bismarck settled for a "little-German solution"
(*kleindeutsche Lösung*) to the problem of territorial unification – a solution that excluded those parts of Austria that had belonged to the first
(Holy Roman) Empire, but included Prussian acquisitions in Poland
that had never been part of that earlier entity. From the perspective of
the territory it did include, the Empire held a variety of ethnic minori-

ties, such as Poles, Danes, Sorbs, and Alsatians, who were not "German" by most people's reckoning, perhaps least of all their own.

Moreover, the state itself lacked the centralized, uniform administrative structure that the French revolutionaries had built, completing the work of the *ancien régime*. The federated states retained substantial autonomy in a variety of matters, even including the use of military force. Municipalities, moreover, maintained significant independence in a number of policy areas, including social policy. These qualifications, however, have hardly inhibited both contemporaries and subsequent commentators from speaking of the Second Empire as the achievement (however "belated") of the "German national state," thus contributing to the notion that such a thing exists – what Steinmetz has suggestively referred to as "the nation-state effect."[90]

The "long nineteenth century" bore witness to an increasing freedom of movement for the lower orders of society, who were liberated from the feudal shackles that had once bound them to their birthplaces. The expansion of legal mobility for the popular classes generated tension in arrangements for poor relief that presumed domicile as the foundation of access to benefits, provoking the need to codify the criteria for belonging. In order to develop national markets, German economic and political elites strove to expand the limits of citizenship to the "national" level. This process presupposed the abrogation of local community rights to restrict the entry of "co-nationals" that had been rooted in their traditional obligations to provide poor relief. At the same time, it entailed a democratization of legal standing, so that the "internal foreign nation" comprising the lower classes had to be elevated to at least a legal par with their social "betters."

Nonetheless, developments in Germany had signaled a broader European shift toward greater freedom of entry and exit, even for foreigners. Under the influence of an "overwhelming consensus" during the 1860s and early 1870s that economic liberalism was the surest recipe for prosperity, as Hobsbawm has put it, "the remaining institutional barriers to the free movement of the factors of production, to free enterprise and to anything which could conceivably hamper its profitable operation, fell before a world-wide onslaught."[91] In England, the passport provisions of the 1836 Aliens Restriction Act went largely unregarded until the Aliens Act of 1905 revived them. Indeed, Lord Granville wrote in 1872 that "by the existing law of Great Britain all foreigners have the unrestricted right of entrance into and residence in this country,"[92] substantiating the view of the situation in England offered by Wilhelm Liebknecht during the *Reichstag* debate over the 1867 passport law.

Similarly, in France, with the exception of the period of the Paris Commune, the once-severe passport controls on internal movement had become "entombed in desuetude," although the persistence of the *livret* until the end of the nineteenth century surely discriminated against the movements of many a humble work-seeker.[93] The enforcement of passport controls on those entering and exiting the country had similarly been allowed to lapse, not to be rejuvenated until the Great War.[94]

These developments came together under the ideological aegis of economic liberalism, which however held no strong brief for the sanctity of national borders. The result of this extraordinary conjuncture was that passport requirements fell away throughout Western Europe, useless paper barriers to a world in prosperous motion. In the course of defending the widening right to freedom of movement in nineteenth-century Europe, an Italian legal commentator, Giovanni Bolis, wrote in 1871 that "the surest thermometer of the freedom of a people is to be found in an examination of its legislation concerning passports." Bolis strongly advocated the elimination of international passports "not merely as a homage to the civility of the times . . . but as a measure of great importance for economic relations, favoring commerce, industry, and progress, facilitating the relations among the various countries, and liberating travelers from harassment and hindrances."[95] Bolis's remarks constitute a quintessential statement of the liberal attitude toward freedom of movement that came to prevail in Europe around this time.

Yet states' insistence that they be able to embrace mobile populations resulted in a heightened preoccupation with identification documents that allowed governments and police forces to establish who (and "what") a person was when they wished to do so. With democratization, identification of all became more important than controlling movements as such.

CHAPTER 4

TOWARD THE "CRUSTACEAN TYPE NATION": THE PROLIFERATION OF IDENTIFICATION DOCUMENTS FROM THE LATE NINETEENTH CENTURY TO THE FIRST WORLD WAR

Despite the generally liberal attitude toward freedom of movement that carried the day in Europe during the late nineteenth century, governments became increasingly oriented to making distinctions between their own citizens/subjects and others, a distinction that could be made only on the basis of documents. At first this concern was typically directed at specific groups of undesirable outsiders, but it gradually spread and became a general trait of ever more socially integrated "national" societies. Thus despite the fact that the period from the late nineteenth century until the First World War has been frequently viewed as an unexampled era of free movement in the modern age, the period also saw the spread of various kinds of identification documents that sharpened the line between national and alien and thereby contributed to what has aptly been called the "naturalization of nativism."[1]

In the United States, for example, which had been more or less open to free movement for the white population, the development of passports and identification documents grew dramatically toward the end of the nineteenth century. As elsewhere, the ultimate result would be to promote the institutionalization of documentary controls designed to regulate movement and to distinguish clearly between nationals and others. As the preferred destination of enormous numbers of migrants from around the world during this period, the posture of the United States played a crucial role in the shift toward more rigorous and bureaucratic mechanisms for regulating movement.

PASSPORT CONTROLS AND STATE DEVELOPMENT IN THE UNITED STATES

The United States' experience with passports, and with immigration controls more generally, reflected the weak, diffuse character of the

American state itself before the late nineteenth century. There has never been much concern about the issue of emigration from the United States, as there had been from mercantilist European countries. And although the opposition to immigration in nineteenth-century America was greater than is widely believed, restraints on entry into the United States during most of the century tended to be haphazard and indirect. The Alien Act of 1798, the first serious breach in the policy of openness to European immigrants, aimed to complicate the settlement of foreign radicals on American soil. Arising in the context of the French Revolution and its aftershocks, the Act was a response to fears of alien subversion – especially from French and Irish sources – that drew its inspiration from the first Aliens Bill in England in 1793.[2] Yet the law had little impact on the course of immigration to the United States.

The first effort to deal with immigration as a *national* concern in the United States emerged in 1819, when Congress adopted legislation (modeled on the British Passenger Acts) to restrict the number of persons that could be carried in transatlantic passage. Although the backers of the measure indicated that their purpose was to improve overcrowded conditions on the passenger ships, the law had restrictive effects that may have been unintentional but not necessarily undesirable. Perhaps more important in the long run, at the same time that the federal government assumed greater responsibility for supervising the commerce in passengers, it also instituted its first official statistics on immigration. As Zolberg has pointed out, the advent of federal immigration record-keeping "constituted both a symbolic extension of the domain of state concern and a foundation for the potential exercise of further regulation when circumstances changed."[3] The law thus laid some of the essential early groundwork for the bureaucratic administration of immigration regulation in the United States. The ability of the state to count would-be immigrants would prove to be a critical feature of its capacity to restrict their entry, especially when immigrants' national origins came to play a key role in determining their eligibility for admission.

Still, before the Civil War much of the regulation of immigration remained within the purview of the individual states of the Union. In addition to the federal limitations on passenger numbers relative to deck space on boats, a number of states imposed requirements that shipmasters and ship owners post bonds against the possibility that their passengers would fall on the public purse after their arrival. By driving up the costs of passage, these measures impinged upon the business of those involved in passenger-carrying enterprises, leading shippers to challenge these laws in the courts as a restraint of trade. In response to these legal challenges, in which ship owners insisted that they should not be forced to assume responsibility for their human cargo, "the

Supreme Court in 1837 upheld state provisions requiring the master of a ship to submit a detailed report on the passengers, ruling that the states had a right to know who was coming within their boundaries."[4] In the process, the Court also effectively endorsed the continued primacy of the states over the federal government in determining immigration laws. A decade later, however, the Supreme Court reversed this holding in the 1848 *Passenger Cases*, in which it found that states' head taxes on passengers was an unconstitutional infringement on the federal prerogative of regulating foreign commerce.[5]

The federal government further strengthened its jurisdiction over migration matters in 1856, when Congress asserted the exclusive right to issue passports and mandated that they should be issued only to American citizens. Before that time, no federal statute governed the granting of passports. While the Department of State typically assumed this responsibility, the individual states and even municipalities had frequently distributed them as well. Despite the issuance of Department of State circulars informing applicants that passports issued by lower-level authorities would not be recognized by foreign governments, the lack of any legal provision for the granting of passports led to "impositions . . . upon the illiterate and unwary by the fabrication of worthless passports."[6]

The issuance of passports – essentially, documents attesting citizenship – by state and local authorities before 1856 reflects the accuracy of the holding that, during the antebellum period, the central government of the United States had "only a token administrative presence in most of the nation and [its] sovereignty was interpreted by the central administration as contingent on the consent of the individual states."[7] The law mandating exclusive federal control over the issuance of passports was adopted amid increasingly grave sectional tensions that led to intensified efforts to establish the dominance of central government authority.[8] While the assertion of that control may have suggested growing state coherence, however, the failure of North and South to reconcile their respective social systems soon plunged the United States into its bloodiest and most destructive conflagration.

The Civil War was a war of political and economic unification as well as a "war to save the Union" (Lincoln),[9] and it is thus not entirely surprising to find that developments analogous to those afoot in Germany were taking place almost simultaneously in the Reconstruction-era United States. A year after the North German Confederation moved to "decriminalize travel" and create a more coherent space of free movement within its borders, an 1868 decision of the US Supreme Court struck down a Nevada tax on every person leaving the state by means of public transportation. The justices' ruling derived from the argument that the right to travel from state to state was a right of national citizenship[10] – a status just then being conferred upon the country's former slave population by the Fourteenth Amendment. The Supreme Court's holding helped insure the right of Americans to move freely throughout the country. Within only a decade or so after the Supreme Court widened the basis of American citizenship and affirmed that that status afforded its bearers freedom of movement across US territory, however, the government would begin to restrict free access to the country to many who arrived on its shores – a process that coincided loosely with the "closing of the frontier."[11]

After the Civil War, business elements hungry for labor power developed a growing appetite for overseas sources of labor, in part to combat strikes staged by burgeoning trade unions. The unions were dominated by whites who represented the dominant Anglo-German as well as Irish stock, and sought to protect the interests of these white ethnic workers. Employers on the West Coast, for their part, increasingly warmed to the prospect of recruiting non-whites who were generally thought to be able to survive on less than native white workers. As the war came to an end, European immigration exploded, reaching its nineteenth-century zenith in 1882 as transportation improved and transatlantic passage became cheaper.[12] Yet immigrants from a less familiar source began to arrive in growing numbers on the newly conquered Western flank of the spreading American republic, provoking the ire of various native whites.

PAPER WALLS: PASSPORTS AND CHINESE EXCLUSION

Around the time of the Civil War, political developments and a series of violent upheavals in China had made it both more appealing and more possible to leave that country, developments that fueled interest in emigration to the western United States. Against this background the United States and the Chinese imperial government concluded the Burlingame Treaty of 1868, under which the Chinese were permitted to immigrate freely into the country without, however, any corresponding right to become naturalized American citizens. Because they were barred from inclusion in the US body politic, the Chinese admitted under the Treaty were, in effect, early versions of what came to be known as "guestworkers" during the post-Second World War era in Europe. Yet despite the legal disabilities involved, Chinese streamed into the country in substantial numbers in the ensuing years.[13]

Within a mere fifteen years, however, the stance of the American government toward Chinese immigration – and indeed toward immigration generally – would begin to shift dramatically. In 1880, the Chinese and American governments signed another treaty granting the United States the right to limit the entry of Chinese whenever such immigration "affects or threatens to affect" American interests. The United States thus reversed the terms of a treaty allowing the untrammeled influx of Chinese labor that it had so eagerly sought little more than a decade before. Two years later, the United States adopted the first of the Chinese Exclusion Acts, barring the importation of Chinese contract labor for ten years. Congress subsequently renewed the law several times and extended it to other Asian groups; the statutory exclusion of the Chinese only came to an end with the American extension of a wartime courtesy to its Chinese ally during the Second World War.[14]

The State Department objected to the Chinese exclusion law as an abrogation of the Burlingame Treaty and as an irritant in Chinese–American affairs. Such protests on the part of ministries of foreign relations were, in fact, typical during this period, because anti-immigrant measures undermined established notions of reciprocity among nations and of the treatment that states expected for their nationals abroad.[15] With rising anti-Chinese violence in the Western United States, however, the State Department reversed its position with the reasoning "that violating the [Burlingame] treaty would offend China less than allowing its subjects to be lynched." In the same year, the US government adopted the Immigration Act of 1882, which extended earlier state laws to exclude convicts, lunatics, idiots, and persons likely to become public charges.[16] While the prohibition on the entry of these groups was anything but novel, the federal effort to restrict a particular racial/national group was a notable departure: "In making a distinction based on race and nationality, the act augured a significant new era in federal legislation and American attitudes toward immigrants."[17]

Here I want to focus on the administrative implementation of the Chinese Exclusion Act, for it constituted the first serious attempt in American history specifically to exclude members of a particular group whose relevant characteristics were knowable only on the basis of documents.[18] In order to make sense of the various documentary requirements associated with the enforcement of the exclusion law, it must be borne in mind that the 1882 law barred only newly entering laborers; those who had entered the US at least ninety days before the Act took effect were permitted to remain. In addition, while the Chinese were not allowed to naturalize, court decisions had recognized as American citizens those who were born on US soil.[19] Moreover, the Act exempted other groups such as merchants, teachers, students, and travelers. Because the Chinese had previously been welcomed into the United States and many were in the country legally, the new law made it critical that they be able to establish that they had a right to remain in the United States or to reenter if they left – conditions that could only be met by recourse to documents. In order to sort out the eligibles from the ineligibles, the measure thus mandated "an elaborate system of registration, certification and identification."[20]

First among these provisions was that Chinese laborers legitimately in the United States under the terms of the Act who wished to leave the country were required to obtain a certificate of identification – also known as a "return certificate" – from the collector of the port prior to their departure. The collectors of the ports, not immigration officers *per se*, were thus authorized to distribute the document that established Chinese residents' right to reenter the country, and to determine whether any Chinese were entering the country legally under the terms of the law: in short, they assumed the duties of immigration inspectors. In addition, all Chinese from the exempt categories, other than diplomatic personnel, were required to have in their possession a certificate from the Chinese government upon entering the country – a "Canton" or Section Six certificate, which derived its name from the relevant provision in the 1882 law. The various Chinese Exclusion Acts did not specify whether women and children were admissible. Some judges held that their status was determined by their own qualifications, so that they were required to have a Section Six certificate of their own, whereas other judges maintained that the status of women and children followed that of the husband or father. The dispute was not finally resolved until 1900, when the Supreme Court upheld the latter position, ascribing to the wives and children of Chinese men the same immigration status as the husband/father. When the Chinese challenged the documentary requirements imposed upon them, the ensuing disputes were settled in the courts – often in favor of the Chinese rather than the customs officials who enforced the law, a fact that tended to mitigate its severity.[21]

Chinese objections to the certificate requirements notwithstanding, California politicians insisted that the administration of the Exclusion Act was having all the inhibitory power of a large-gauge sieve and demanded a more vigorous enforcement of its provisions. These demands resulted in the passage in 1884 of an amendment that tightened the documentary requirements imposed upon the Chinese. In an effort to preclude the frequent claims of laborers that they had left the country before the advent of the "return certificates," the new law mandated an end to exceptions concerning the stricture that all returning laborers originally in the country legitimately had to have such a certificate or be denied reentry. When the Chinese challenged this clause, however, the Supreme Court ruled that laborers should be readmitted who could prove by means other than the certificate of identification that they resided in the United States lawfully under the terms of the Act.

In addition to the tighter restrictions on laborers, the 1884 law also sought to firm up the definition of and the documentary controls on exempt categories of Chinese:

[T]he word 'merchant' was defined to exclude hucksters, peddlers, and fishermen engaged in drying and shipping fish; the traveler's certificate must state where he proposed to travel and his financial standing; the certificates of identification from the Chinese Government must be verified as to facts and visaed by the United States diplomatic officer at the port of departure, [in order] to be *prima facie* evidence of right of re-entry . . .[22]

This last procedure constituted an early version of that system of "remote control" – involving passports and visas stamped at the emigrants' point of departure by consular officials of the destination country – that Aristide Zolberg has appropriately characterized as a decisive feature of immigration regulation after the Great War. For all Zolberg's perspicacity about the dynamics of Chinese exclusion and the development of "remote border control" during the 1920s, however, he overlooks the fact that the latter was first experimented with in the effort to exclude the Chinese, not Europeans – the main target after the First World War.

Despite the greater stringency of documentary requirements and despite official findings that the exclusion law had led to a significant drop in the number of Chinese in the United States, further efforts to keep them out arose in the late 1880s. On 13 September 1888 Congress adopted a law denying reentry into the country of Chinese laborers who had returned to visit China unless they had a wife, child, or parent in the United States, or owned at least $1000 of property. Shortly thereafter, when a project to draft a new treaty relating to Chinese immigration floundered, the Scott Act excluded any Chinese laborer then outside the United States who had not returned to the country before the passage of the Act, prohibited the issuance of any more certificates under the terms of the 1882 law, and voided all those previously issued. Thus no Chinese laborer who left the United States would have the right to return any longer, and some 20 000 certificates guaranteeing Chinese reentry into the US were nullified. Net arrivals of Chinese fell sharply during the following year.[23]

The Chinese quickly mounted legal challenges to these restrictions, however. Just one week after the passage of the Scott Act, a Chinese laborer named Chae Chan Ping returned to San Francisco from a visit to China and requested reentry on presentation of his certificate of identification. In consequence of the new law, he was refused admission into the country. Chae Chan Ping challenged the constitutionality of the law, asserting that Congress had no authority to exclude aliens. The case went all the way to the Supreme Court, which upheld the constitutionality of the Act, though not on the customary grounds that Congress had the authority to regulate foreign commerce. Instead, the Court held that the Constitution granted Congress a variety of powers that made it sovereign in the land, and "any independent nation must have 'jurisdiction over its own territory,' including the power to exclude aliens, if it were to be truly sovereign."[24] This holding contrasted sharply with Lord Granville's view, stated only fifteen years earlier, that aliens were free to enter the United Kingdom at will, as well as with the general climate of relatively free movement that had taken hold in Europe during this period.

The severe strictures of the Scott Act notwithstanding, agitation against the Chinese – especially among politicians from the Pacific coast states – continued unabated. The exclusionists complained that the appropriations and machinery for identifying and deporting Chinese were inadequate, and during the run-up to the 1892 presidential election California Congressman Thomas Geary proposed a new law designed to strengthen the measures precluding or eliminating the Chinese from American society. Among the provisions of his proposed law was one that required Chinese residents to register themselves and to obtain an identification certificate including a photograph to forestall misuse and falsification. As ultimately adopted, the law called for all Chinese laborers to obtain certificates within one year, and, if arrested, imposed upon the Chinese themselves the burden of demonstrating their legitimate presence in the country.

The Chinese Minister in Washington and the Consul-General in San Francisco, as well as Chinese representatives in Peking, protested vehemently against the law. These objections were joined by those of the Chinese Consolidated Benevolent Association in San Francisco – perhaps better known as the Chinese Six Companies – the major organization representing the interests of Chinese in the United States, which held that the Act was unconstitutional and advised the Chinese not to comply with its registration provisions. As the period within which registration was to have been completed approached its close, Representative McCreary of Kentucky noted that so far only 13 242 out of 106 668 Chinese had actually registered, and proposed an extension of the registration period. Defending his bill, Congressman Geary replied that "it was impossible to identify Chinamen," and California Senator White insisted that the Chinese had to be photographed as well as registered. Their California colleague, Representative Maguire, said the Geary law was "not a deportation but a registration law, merely a passport system . . ." To these sorts of objections McCreary responded that it was unnecessary further to violate the treaty with China by requiring the Chinese "to be tagged, marked, and photographed."

In the end, however, the registration system was adopted largely as originally proposed, and the federal government expanded the facilities for registration and sent officers directly to encampments of Chinese to expedite the process. Mary Coolidge, a thoughtful and diligent early student of

Chinese immigration to the United States, concluded: "Thus, at last, was set in operation at great expense, a system of registration which the officials in charge of the execution of every act since 1882, had declared to be indispensable to effective administration" of Chinese exclusion.[25] Indeed, the various identification certificates inspired by the exclusion laws, which functioned as the equivalent of passports for those wishing to gain entry into the United States during the period in which the exclusion laws were in effect, continued to play an important role in the administration of Chinese exclusion for years to come.

THE "NATIONALIZATION" OF IMMIGRATION RESTRICTION IN THE UNITED STATES

During the same period when the law had come to impose strict documentary surveillance on the Chinese in response to the wishes of political interests in the Western states of the country, the regulation of immigration was becoming more and more clearly understood as a mandate of the federal government in the United States. Hearings by joint congressional committees to determine the goals of US immigration policy had led to recommendations aiming "not to restrict immigration, but to sift it, to separate the desirable from the undesirable immigrants, and to permit only those to land on our shores who have certain physical and moral qualities."[26] In pursuit of this objective, immigration regulation came to focus on those who might be a burden on the public purse and those regarded as "unassimilable" or otherwise unworthy of inclusion in the American civic body.

Against this background, Congress adopted the Immigration Act of 1891, which placed the regulation of immigration under the authority of the Secretary of the Treasury, created a new Superintendent of Immigration within the Treasury Department, strengthened the enforcement provisions of earlier laws, and installed twenty-four border inspection stations. All of these measures contributed to the bureaucratic institutionalization of immigration control, which for the first time had become national in character as a consequence of this legislation. Yet for the time being, Chinese immigration continued to be regulated by the Exclusion Acts, whereas that from Europe was governed by the Superintendent of Immigration – a fact that, ironically, allowed the Chinese more leeway to challenge their treatment in the courts.[27]

In keeping with the recommendations of the congressional inquiries into the aims of American immigration policy, the administrative structures called forth by the 1891 law were designed to enable the government to distinguish between those who were thought to be good candidates for American citizenship, and those who were not. These priorities promoted a process whereby all immigration would be administered by the same bureaucracy (even if different groups of potential immigrants were subjected to different policies). With the increasing prevalence of eugenics and other race-conscious approaches to population management, the ranks of those held to be unworthy of admission into or citizenship in the United States expanded beyond the Chinese to include a variety of groups regarded as impure, unclean, idiotic, non-white, or incapable of understanding the principles of republicanism. The proliferation of the categories of excludables pushed in the direction of a more uniform administration of immigration control, and in the early 1900s the separate administration of Asian and European immigrant streams disappeared as the drift toward the "nationalization" of immigration regulation became consolidated institutionally.

In 1903, the work of the Commissioner General of Immigration in the Treasury Department was transferred to a full-fledged Bureau of Immigration in the newly created Department of Commerce and Labor, and Chinese immigration fell under its purview along with that of Europeans. The exclusion of the Chinese was rendered permanent in 1904, a harbinger of things to come for other Asian and European national groups – as long as the necessary documents could be created and imposed. In 1907, the "Gentlemen's Agreement" closed off the access of Japanese laborers to the United States when the Japanese government agreed to stop issuing them passports, a policy later extended to Japanese women who were to travel to the United States as "picture brides" of future husbands whom they knew only as a photograph. The situation was more complicated with Filipinos, subjects but not citizens of the United States after acquisition of the islands from Spain. As US "nationals" – persons "owing allegiance, whether citizens or not, to the United States" – they could not be subjected to restrictive immigration laws. Ironically, however, the acquisition of overseas possessions such as the Philippines forced the US government to expand access to passports to a variety of non-citizen "nationals," reversing the general trend toward distribution of those documents exclusively to citizens.[28]

Along with the growing worries about the racially inferior, concerns also spread that various categories of persons would render the American stock less wholesome in political, moral, or medical terms. The latter fear soon helped give birth to the Public Health Service and to legislation excluding those with contagious illnesses. US restrictions on the admission of the medically dubious stimulated the development overseas of both governmental and steamship company efforts to insure that would-be emigrants would pass muster when they arrived in American ports.[29] Gradually, many of the activities associated with US immigrant inspection would be transferred abroad, as control of immigration moved from the territorial borders of the United States to the emigrant-sending countries themselves – a development that would dramatically enhance the capacity of states to restrict the influx of outsiders.

SOVEREIGNTY AND DEPENDENCE: THE ITALIAN PASSPORT LAW OF 1901

The installation of the medical inspection facilities of one country on the territory of another was just one example of the way in which any strong conception of state sovereignty had to be modified in the course of achieving states' monopolization of the legitimate means of movement. Just as there were often "external" determinants of emigrant health inspection, and indeed of citizenship laws that might be thought to be at the very heart of state sovereignty,[30] passport requirements might be imposed in one state as a result of the restrictions laid down by another. Such was the case with the Italian passport law of 1901.

The passport law of 1901, which remained the major legislation on passports until 1967, appeared to be a departure from the widespread warm feelings toward the freedom of movement in Europe at that time. Certainly its detractors regarded its requirement that transoceanic travelers be in possession of a passport before purchasing their steamer tickets as the reintroduction of a noxious restraint on exit. The provision smacked of supposedly outmoded restraints on emigration typical of the pre-liberal period, and liberal and leftist parliamentarians strongly opposed it. The opponents of the law presumably knew that big landowners tended to oppose emigration because they feared that depopulation would drive up the wages they had to pay.[31]

In fact, however, the legislation arose not from an urge to choke off exit, but rather from a desire to insure that Italian emigrants would not be denied *entry* into American ports (North and South, though principally the former). This intention could not have been made clearer than by the decree's requirement that passports be delivered within twenty-four hours of a legitimate request, a provision reiterated in the law on emigration adopted the same day. This "epoch-making" law sought to provide protection for emigrants from the various commercial interests involved in the emigrant trade, and enhanced the role of the state in migration processes by creating a General Commission for Emigration intended to guide outflows and offer assistance to those departing.[32] The Italian state strode vigorously toward supervision of migration matters during this period, though their chief concern was with facilitating emigration, not restricting immigration.

Because of its potential impact on the fate of the much-discussed Italian emigration, the passport law provoked sharp controversy in

Parliament. The law's backers argued that too many Italian would-be emigrants had been turned back in the preceding years upon their arrival on American shores. In the debate on the proposed legislation, one supporter of the bill, Eugenio Valli, told the chamber that more than 1200 Italian emigrants had been refused entry into American ports during 1899–1900. In order to forestall repetition of these denials, Valli urged the house to mandate that, in addition to a passport, departing emigrants be required to have a medical certificate attesting to their state of health. "In the United States," Valli explained, "if they believe or suspect that there is a danger that the Italian emigrant . . . is likely to become a public charge, they will throw him out with the most remorseless brutality."[33] Presumably these unsuccessful emigres had not been inspected by American examiners before their departure.

According to other supporters of the passport requirement for transatlantic migrants, the immigration officials on the other side of the ocean were more interested in the passport as a testament of the bearer's "good conduct" than in the migrant's physical condition. As one leading proponent put it, possession of this implicit seal of approval of the sending government would greatly smooth admission to the United States, where the authorities were said to believe that the Italian immigration "concealed an infiltration of dangerous and delinquent elements."[34] Although they were hardly alone in this respect, the Italians were indeed frequently suspected by American immigration officials of carrying either political or medical contagion, as well as of being "likely to become a public charge."[35]

The adoption of the 1901 law thus reflected not so much the reawakening of slumbering authoritarian habits as it did the ruling elite's acceptance of Italy's peripheral position in the Atlantic economy and of its vulnerability to class-based movements of social protest. Faced with persistent problems of unemployment in the Mezzogiorno and of relative underdevelopment more generally, the Parliament sought to ensure that those embarked on a search for work overseas would succeed in finding what they were looking for. In addition, the Italian political leadership saw emigration as an opportunity to rid itself of some of its political malcontents. In 1896, several months after the disastrous defeat of the Italian army at Adowa (Adua) in Abyssinia, the Southern Italian economist and later prime minister, Francesco Nitti, had famously averred that emigration was a "powerful safety valve against class hatreds." Nitti knew whereof he spoke; rates of emigration from Italy during the pre-First World War period have been shown to correlate with a decline in votes for socialist parties.[36]

Some also saw the scattering of Italians throughout the world as promoting an oddly imperialist sort of nation-building. After the inglorious setback to colonial ambitions that was dealt to the Italians at Adowa, they argued that the peaceful overseas migration of Italians would extend the limits of Italy anywhere they went. But the more fervent nationalists, who insisted that conquest was the only way of dealing with excess population that was "worthy of a free and noble people," remained unsatisfied. These elements finally had their day when Italy invaded Tripoli in 1911, securing for the Italians vast expanses of desert over which they never exercised adequate control.[37] As a result of Italy's inability to subdue these areas, they failed to serve as an outlet for the overpopulated areas of the peninsula. Without extensive overseas colonies to populate, the emigration traffic remained in the more familiar streams of North and South America, and the numbers of emigrants swelled during the early twentieth century.

Discussions about how to manage the departure of so many Italians without fatally weakening the state led, in 1912, to the adoption of a new law on citizenship that stopped just short of recognizing dual nationality. Instead of adopting this approach to holding onto its progeny – a step that would have violated the posture toward dual citizenship of the United States, in particular – the new citizenship law facilitated the rapid resumption of citizenship by expatriates. Yet despite the decision not to accept dual nationality, the law went on to insist that those who became naturalized citizens elsewhere did not thereby escape their military service obligations in Italy, thus ignoring one of the principal reasons states might have for denying recognition of dual citizenship: the possibility of conflicting military loyalties and obligations.[38]

Ironically, if the liberal objections to the passport law as a restraint on movement had carried the day, they might well have had the counterproductive effect of limiting the access of Italy's seafaring jobseekers to lands of opportunity. The law's opponents were nonetheless correct in claiming that, even if the law was not presently intended to restrict departures, it could be used to that end at some later time. The coming of the Great War would prove to be that later time; when that conflagration broke out, Italy's troop needs would lead it to use passport controls to ensure that its able-bodied sons could not simply flee the colors unhindered.

THE SPREAD OF IDENTIFICATION DOCUMENTS FOR FOREIGNERS IN FRANCE

During the same years that the United States was developing a "national" (i.e., "nationwide") approach to immigration questions that was also increasingly "nationalist" (i.e., antagonistic to other nations),[39] France of the Third Republic was taking steps to distinguish more sharply between its own nationals and others. While these distinctions did not immediately lead to restrictions on the access of the latter to French territory, the creation of a bureaucratic machinery for determining who was a Frenchman and who was not could and would later be used to facilitate exclusions. The documents that would be used to separate the national from the non-national emerged from a broader debate over the criteria of French nationality, in which the two major issues were the search for sources of new military recruits and associated resentment against the fact that foreigners on French soil escaped military obligations. One major result of this debate was the adoption of the 1889 law on French citizenship, which extended French nationality to the children of immigrants born on French soil.[40]

Yet the emergence of an embryonic "social citizenship" also played a role in promoting identification documents that would divide the French from the non-French. Whereas health care and social insurance laws of the Second Empire had made no distinction between national and foreigner, most of the social welfare laws of the Third Republic mandated that the benefits should be reserved for French natives.[41] In view of the large resident population of foreigners, means would have to be developed to implement these discriminatory policies, as well as to determine who was a French person more generally for purposes of assessing their obligations for military service.

The relative openness of the borders beginning in the 1860s had resulted in the influx of considerable numbers of non-Frenchmen. In view of their exemption from military service, some argued in the French parliament that these persons had special advantages in the labor market relative to indigenous workers. Starting in 1884, demands arose for a special tax on foreigners that would amount to a sort of "compensation" for the disadvantages suffered by native hands. This proposal failed in the face of complaints from the Foreign Ministry of precisely the sort raised by the State Department in response to the Chinese Exclusion Acts. The Ministry objected that such a tax would violate the freedom of movement clauses inscribed in treaties between France and a variety of other countries, and that therefore "such measures would have led to France's exclusion from the international 'community of nations.'"[42]

In the event, the parliament devised a means for circumventing the possibility that France would be driven out of the "community of nations" as a result of discriminatory taxation of foreigners. Instead of levying a direct tax, the government would require all foreigners wishing to establish a residence in France to register themselves in the town hall of the place where they resided. Upon doing so, they would receive a registration card – but only for a fee. In order to divert the suspicions of neighboring governments that they were trying to marginalize foreigners, the representative who proposed this scheme emphasized the matter of identification rather than that of taxation.[43]

As a result of this project, which found expression in a decree of 2 October 1888, the system of "anthropometric" identification devised by Alphonse Bertillon during the preceding decade to track recidivist criminals was extended to the entire resident foreign population of France. Bertillon believed that individual stigmata were essential for identification and could be used to construct behavioral typologies, and *bertillonage* came to be an essential element of identification systems of various kinds, along with Galton's nearly simultaneous invention of fingerprinting. Still, we should not overestimate the effectiveness of these measures: governmental officials failed to implement them due to lack of understanding of their requirements, lack of resources to handle the task, or simple lack of interest, and immigrants themselves were slow to fulfill the new registration demands out of unawareness or a dearth of concern to carry out their requirements.[44]

The 1888 decree was directed at all foreigners without distinction, but precisely its generality led to objections among those who sought to control more rigorously the access of foreigners to the French labor market. These protests underlay the passage of the "Law concerning the Sojourn of Foreigners in France and the Protection of National Labor" of 8 August 1893, which mandated registration by all foreigners wishing to exercise an income-generating occupation. In order to register, the immigrant – who was presumed by the law to be male – had to present a valid piece of identification, normally a birth certificate. Those from countries that failed to establish a person's civil identity (*état civil*) had to adduce a proof of identity validated by the consular officials of their country. Wives who, though not engaged in commercial activities directly, assisted their spouses in such businesses, were required to sign a personal declaration to this effect. In short, the law aimed to afford the French state a better "embrace" of those who, depending on economic circumstances, might be deemed less deserving of income-producing work than French nationals. Non-wage-earning foreigners such as students and *rentiers* remained subject to the 1888 decree. The statute of 1893 distinguished for the first time in French law between "working" and "non-working" immigrants, and thus helped to create the now-familiar image of the "immigrant worker."[45]

The trouble with the 1893 law was that it imposed controls only on those who sought a fixed residence in France and wished to pursue an occupation on that basis. In other words, it left out those who practiced an ambulatory *métier*. Gradually, the parliament – notably including future prime minister Georges Clemenceau – directed its attention to this suspect group. As a result, a 1912 law focused on the control of "nomads" (itinerant persons and groups) and the vagaries of their existence. While the law ignored the question of nationality and theoretically applied to all "nomads," it was in fact directed at foreigners, according to a contemporary analyst, for most of the "nomads" then circulating in France were of foreign origin. Whatever their nationality, such persons were now required to carry the "*carnet des nomades*," an "anthropometric identity document" that included fingerprints and photographs. The point was to insure that these wanderers would have a precise and "immutable" identity, even if this necessitated imposing a new one upon them. The authorities were free to refuse to issue these documents to those requiring them, however, giving the government "the possibility of denying individuals not only the right to reside but also the right to enter, on the grounds that their presence is deemed dangerous." Here the mobile non-national, the inscrutable outsider within, increasingly replaces the itinerant dangerous classes – the internal "foreign" enemy of old, which in Germany had been liberated from these restrictions by the North German law of 1867 – as the object of routine suspicion. By 1917, identification cards would become mandatory for all foreigners, and passport controls on their entry were reintroduced.[46]

The development and distribution of various forms of documentary identification helped to constitute people of different countries as mutually exclusive "nationals" who shared a common interest in the fate of their state – an interest that might well put them at odds with the nationals of other states. In late nineteenth-century Germany, this process grew to a considerable degree out of the struggles over the fate of estate-based agriculture in the German east, where a beleaguered aristocracy drew on impoverished Slavic workers that came to be perceived as a threat to the purity of Germandom.

THE RESURRECTION OF PASSPORT CONTROLS IN LATE NINETEENTH-CENTURY GERMANY

Although the liberal North German law of 1867 remained the fundamental statute regarding passport controls in Germany until after the Second World War, its provisions with respect to population movements into Germany were already being abrogated in the late 1870s.[47] In early 1879, the Imperial government imposed passport requirements on those coming from Russia in order, it said, to forestall the importation of a plague that had broken out there. Travelers returning to Germany from Russia were now required to have in their possession a passport that had been visaed within three days of their departure by the German embassy in Saint Petersburg or by a German consular official, and visaed again upon their arrival at the German border.[48]

The reintroduction of passport requirements in order to protect the German population from a serious medical threat would seem to have been reasonable enough. Yet only a few months later, the order was revised and the requirement was dropped that visa applicants demonstrate that they had not been in any of the areas (thought to be) contaminated by the plague during the preceding twenty days. In other words, *all* travelers from Russia were now required to have a passport visaed by German authorities in Russia and at the borders of the Empire.[49] A further revision of the law in December 1880 softened its strictures somewhat by repealing the visa obligation for subjects of the Empire, as well as for those from countries that permitted Germans to enter their territories without visas.[50] Nearly fifteen years later, yet another update of the law abolished visa requirements entirely on those returning from Russia, but left the passport requirement intact.[51]

These various revisions of the original February 1879 ordinance suggest that the German restrictions on entrants from Russia were not entirely related to the plague. The influx of Russian-Polish labor probably played a role as well. Despite the insistence of agricultural (and some industrial) employers that they needed labor, Bismarck – citing the "threat to the state potentially posed by a Polonization of a large segment of the Prussian population" – ordered the expulsion from Germany of some 40 000 Polish workers in 1885, and Poles were excluded from Germany for the next five years.[52] The demand for labor continued unabated, however, and after Bismarck's fall in 1890 the importation of Polish workers was resumed under strict conditions.[53] In 1893, no less a figure than Max Weber called for the "absolute exclusion of the Russian-Polish workers from the German east," a position widely held among political leaders despite the interests of agricultural and other employers. In the absence of such restrictions, Weber famously feared that Germany was "threatened by a Slavic flood that would entail a cultural retrogression of several epochs."[54]

Despite the obvious ethnocentrism in Weber's remarks, it is worth recalling that he also viewed the importation of the Poles as a "means of struggle in the anticipated class struggle in this area, directed against the growing self-consciousness of the workers." In effect, Weber saw the Poles as "scabs" in the contest between agricultural workers and employers.[55] In this respect the position of the Poles in eastern Germany paralleled quite closely that of the Chinese in California a few years earlier: both groups were used by employers as instruments in the ripening class struggle, and both became the object of restrictive measures based on their alleged "racial" characteristics despite employer interests in their continued presence. "Racial" concerns would increasingly trump economic rationality as pseudo-scientific theories of eugenics moved to the fore in Germany and elsewhere in the coming years.

The imposition of passport controls on those coming from Russia was in all likelihood part of the inchoate efforts to regulate the flow of Polish migrant labor. During this period, it was not unknown for foremen on agricultural estates seeking to hamper the mobility of foreign workers to "require that the workers give them their passports and luggage."[56] This sort of usage would help explain why after 1894 passports were required for those entering Germany from Russia even though visas were not; in these cases, the passport was being used simply as an identification document rather than as a border-crossing authorization. In any event, the sustained controversy over the importation of Polish workers ultimately led to the imposition in 1908 of a *Legitimationszwang* mandating that all foreign workers carry an identification card. These documents were an essential aspect of "a system of surveillance of foreigners as complete and total as feasible, as well as [of] an extensive bureaucracy for their supervision and control" in the form of the German Farm Workers Agency (*Deutsche Feldarbeiterzentrale*), first established in 1905. Still, the degree of effectiveness of these restrictions should not be overestimated, for they were frequently skirted by employers and workers alike when this served their interests.[57]

Alternatively, the continued existence of passport requirements for travelers from Russia may have been a way of punishing that country for its continued insistence upon passport controls as a requirement of entry into its territories, in contradiction to the more open-handed practice then established in most of western and central Europe.[58] Yet as we have seen, a countertrend – a drift toward the "nationalization" of European states, that is, their stricter distribution of positions and benefits to their own nationals – had clearly been underway during these years. Toward the end of the century, this nationalizing process found explicit expression in a Prussian decree strictly prohibiting the relevant authorities from issuing passports to foreigners other than in exceptional cases, a departure from a practice still quite common at that point. "Close examination [of the applicant's nationality] is necessary," the order insisted, "because unfortunate negotiations with foreign governments may have to take place that often result in Germany having to take in the passport-holder simply because he or she has a German passport."[59] The international system of states comprising mutually exclusive bodies of citizens was taking firmer shape, not least because governments increasingly had the capacity to get documents into people's hands identifying them as belonging to one country or another. Individual states, moreover, were less and less willing to extend their protections to non-nationals, giving rise to a system in which passports would be granted only by the officials of those states and only to their own nationals.

Still, on the very eve of the First World War, a German student of the passport system wrote:

> Because in recent times the position of foreigners has grown much different from before . . . most modern states have, with but a few exceptions, abolished their passport laws or at least neutralized them through non-enforcement . . . [Foreigners] are no longer viewed by states with suspicion and mistrust but rather, in recognition of the tremendous value that can be derived from trade and exchange, welcomed with open arms and, for this reason, hindrances are removed from their path to the greatest extent possible.[60]

It seems clear from the evidence we have examined so far in this chapter that this assessment cannot have been an entirely accurate picture of the foreigner's situation. Yet these remarks suggest the enormous influence that economic liberalism still held in the minds of many Europeans. It was this latter set of ideas that had undergirded the unprecedented trend toward the relaxation of passport controls in late nineteenth-century Europe. Only the Great War would definitively reverse that trend.

THE FIRST WORLD WAR AND THE "TEMPORARY" REIMPOSITION OF PASSPORT CONTROLS

The booming of the guns of August 1914 brought to a sudden close the era during which governments viewed foreigners without "suspicion and mistrust" and they were free to traverse borders relatively unmolested. As was typical of wartime, the conflagration generated hostility toward those who might bear the *patrie* ill-will, and a renewed preoccupation with controlling their movements. Mobilization for war stiffens the backs of states and, like the threat of a hanging, concentrates their minds; administration becomes focused on one single and overriding aim. The achievement of that aim during the First World War led to the consolidation of views about foreigners and methods for restricting their movements that would prove to be an enduring part of our world. It was not only foreigners that were affected, however, even if they bore the brunt of the new restrictions: the nationals of the various countries were subjected to intensified documentary surveillance during the Great War as well.

In pursuit of the objective of greater control over the movements alike of the national and the alien, passport controls were reintroduced across the continent. At first, reflecting the persistence of the view that such controls were acceptable only during time of war, the newly reinstituted passport requirements were typically thought to be provisional

measures, responses to a state of emergency. That the war would ultimately have the effect of bringing an end to the *laissez faire* era in
international migration would not have been predicted by many contemporaries.[61]

Thus, for example, French passport restrictions from the revolutionary period that had been "allowed to lapse" were restored in the face of
the crisis.[62] In addition, French lawmakers used the crisis to demarcate
further between the French citizen and the foreigner via documents.
Despite official protests from the French trade union confederation CGT
that some of the newly adopted fingerprinted identification cards treated
the citizen like "a convict," war-inspired xenophobia allowed the government to strengthen the documentary identification requirements for
foreigners. In consequence of two decrees promulgated in April 1917,
identification cards became mandatory for all foreigners above the age of
fifteen living in France. The cards were to include the bearer's nationality, civil status, occupation, photograph, and signature, and special color
codes were employed to mark out wage earners in agriculture and industry.[63] The foreigner – and especially the "immigrant worker" – was
becoming more and more intelligible by the documents he or she carried.

In Britain, the Aliens Restriction Act 1914 sharply enhanced the
power of the government, "when a state of war exists," to prohibit or
impose restrictions on the landing or embarkation of aliens in the
United Kingdom. The law made no explicit mention of passport
requirements, which in any event had already been rejuvenated in 1905
in response to the threat of a large-scale influx of East European Jews,
and only after long years of opposition to an Aliens Bill by the stalwartly
Mancunian Liberals.[64] Still, the law put the onus of proving that a person
is not an alien on that person, making documentary evidence of one's
nationality largely unavoidable, particularly if one did not look or sound
"British." It also provided for the possibility of requiring aliens to live, or
of prohibiting them from living, in certain areas, and of registering with
the authorities their place of domicile, change of abode, or movement
within the UK. Finally, the Act made provision for the appointment of
immigration officers to carry out the order, an expansion of immigration bureaucracy that helped strengthen the momentum for keeping
passport controls in place after the war.[65]

The German government, too, adopted new passport controls under
the emergency clauses of the liberal 1867 law – but now, rather than apply-
ing only to those coming from Russia, they applied to everyone. Already
on 31 July 1914, Germany implemented "temporary" passport restrictions
on anyone entering the Empire from abroad. In the interest of permitting
the return of eager or otherwise mobilized soldiers, the requirement was
relaxed for those who could produce papers demonstrating that they were

German subjects, stateless former Germans, or permanent residents of the *Reich* who had only been abroad temporarily. This provision presumably was implemented for the good reason that these people might very well not have had passports when they originally left Germany. Meanwhile, in order to avoid the flight of unwilling cannon fodder, those owing military service were to be eligible for passports for exit from Germany only with the approval of their commanding officers. At the same time, foreigners in any area of the Empire declared to be in a state of war were required to have a passport giving a proper account of their person. In the absence of a passport, other satisfactory documents were to be accepted, again presumably because the new regulations might have caught them with their papers down.[66]

Before the year was out, Germany strengthened these regulations further. Now, anyone who wished to enter *or leave* the territory of the Empire (excluding Alsace-Lorraine) was to be in possession of a passport. Foreigners *anywhere* in that territory, not just in war zones, also were required to have a passport or other acceptable document. All such passports, moreover, had to include a personal description, photograph, and signature of the bearer, along with an official certification that the "bearer is actually the person represented in the photograph." Finally, *foreign* passports for purposes of *entry* into the Empire had to have a visa from German diplomatic or consular authorities. At least during this early phase of the war, the Germans were nearly as concerned about controlling the movements of German nationals – in part, no doubt, in order to keep the soldiery fresh with recruits – as they were about keeping watch on those of foreigners.[67]

The next step in securing the territory of the *patrie* at war, taken in mid-1916, added to the passport requirements that a visa (*Sichtvermerk*) from German authorities was to be required from everyone, German or foreign, entering or leaving the territory of the Empire as well as of certain occupied areas.[68] In addition to complicating the task of departing from German territory, this proviso fortified the "remote control" of the German military and consular bureaucracy over those wishing to enter from abroad, effectively extending outward the borders of the Empire.

An accompanying order detailed, with stereotypically German precision, by and to whom German passports could be issued, the information they were to include, a standard passport form, the acceptable form of a *foreign* passport (which was supposed to conform to all the criteria of a German passport, including photograph, etc.), the form of a personal identity document (*Personalausweis*) acceptable in place of a passport, and the terms and conditions for the issuance of visas, depending on whether these were for exit from, entry into, or transit through German territory. The order reaffirmed the late nineteenth-century stricture that German passports could be issued only to German nationals, a status that was to be appropriately recorded. Notably, if the passport bearer had previously been stateless or of non-German nationality, such prior nationality or lack thereof and the date of naturalization to German citizenship were to be duly indicated in the passport.[69] Clearly, the German authorities thought it was best to be aware of the possibility that someone might have divided loyalties, even despite having undergone the rigors of naturalization.

The Italians' first step concerning documentary controls on movement after the outbreak of hostilities was not to issue new passports, but rather to recall those already in circulation among their citizens. By a decree of 6 August 1914, the government suspended the right of emigration of those obliged to do military service, annulling all passports in their possession. Like the German passport regulations, this order indicated the close connection between passport controls and efforts to insure that military recruits for the defense of the *patrie* would not be wanting.[70] Given the over-representation in the poorly paid and worse-fed infantry of Southerners with only a weak sense of national loyalties, it was hardly surprising that the Italian government would expect conscripts to abscond if given the chance.

In an effort to forestall such insubordination, the government tightened the passport requirements for Italians going abroad to work in May 1915. Now, those bound *anywhere*, not just across the Atlantic, had to have a passport in order to leave, and in order to get one they had to present a work contract to the officials of the Royal Commissariat of Emigration. This, too, was intended as a "transitory" restriction, and would be abandoned once peace returned and Italy resumed its position as labor supplier to the more developed world.[71]

On the same day, the Italian government imposed passport requirements on foreigners wishing to enter the Kingdom, reversing many years of an open-door policy. They made up for lost time, however, by immediately requiring not just passports but visas issued by Italian diplomatic or consular authorities in the place of departure as well. The severe law went on to require foreigners to present themselves to public security officials within twenty-four hours of their arrival to explain the circumstances of their sojourn in Italy, as well as any military obligations which they might owe to the state of which they were nationals. A copy of this written declaration was to be sent to district officials responsible for public security; the declarants received a certificate attesting that they had fulfilled the requirements of the law. The papers necessary for moving around within Italy as a foreigner began to multiply. In addition, the law made residents of Italy part of the apparatus for keeping watch over foreigners. Anyone, citizen or foreigner, sheltering a foreigner had to submit to police officials a list of such persons within five days of their arrival, and within twenty-four hours to inform those officials of their departure and "the direction they have taken." In an indication of the growing reliance on modern technology to control movement, the Italians, like the Germans, demanded that such passports include a photograph and a signature authenticated by the issuing authority.[72]

Yet the fact that each government felt the need to state such requirements also reflected the incoherence of the passport system of the time and the uncertain status of these documents in international law. The Germans' insistence that the passports of those entering the Empire conform to German standards could not make them do so. Only after the Second World War would serious intergovernmental efforts be undertaken to standardize passport requirements in order to insure that those wishing to enter a particular country would have documents meeting its stipulations.

The year 1916 intensified the Italian concern with documentary controls on movement, yet all three of the regulations issued concerned Italians rather than foreigners. A decree of 16 March temporarily suspended the issuance of passports for travel abroad, whether for work or any other purpose.[73] Three months later, another required a passport of every Italian citizen entering or leaving the kingdom. While this decree again made passports available for going abroad, such passports had to include a visa from the district public security office. Visas from an Italian embassy or legation were also necessary for entering the Kingdom, and these had to indicate both the length of the visa's validity and the precise location at which the person would enter Italian territory. Subjects of Austria-Hungary who were Italian nationals were required to have a special passport described in the decree.[74] Finally, an order of 27 August revived *internal* passports, a document last addressed in statute in the law on public security of 1889. In order to be valid, these passes, too, now had to have photographs and to conform to the new model attached to the decree.[75]

Clearly, the opponents of the 1901 law had been right to fear that passport controls on Italians broader than those envisaged by that legislation might someday return. What is striking about the wartime Italian laws is that, despite having reversed a long-standing policy of undocumented entry to foreigners, most of the wartime restrictive legislation actually concerned Italians wishing to leave the country. Italy's traditional experience as a country of emigration suggests that, when the exigencies of war demanded stepped-up military recruitment, retaining Italians who might have sought to shirk their soldierly obligations in favor of seeking work abroad was a larger problem for the government than that of keeping out foreigners. Indeed, some 290 000 soldiers –

about six percent of the total – faced courts martial in Italy between May 1915 and September 1919, usually for desertion.[76]

"TEMPORARY" PASSPORT CONTROLS BECOME PERMANENT

The generalized anxiety about borders that existed during the war did not subside with its end. Instead, the "temporary" measures implemented to control access to and departure from the territories of European states persisted into the shallow, fragile peace that was the interwar period. Although based on the liberal 1867 law of the North German Confederation abolishing passport requirements, an order of June 1919 reiterated and rendered permanent the wartime requirement that anyone crossing the borders of the *Reich* in either direction be in possession of a passport with visa, and reaffirmed the paragraph insisting that all foreigners in the territory of the Empire carry a passport.[77]

In Britain, similarly, the wartime restrictions on aliens won greater permanence with the Aliens Order 1920, which extended the validity of previous restrictions beyond the war's end. These restrictions, according to the Order, "should continue in force . . . not only in the [wartime] circumstances aforesaid, but at any time." Henceforward, *anyone* entering or leaving the UK was required to have "either a valid passport furnished with a photograph of himself or some other document satisfactorily establishing his national status and identity." The passport became the backbone of the system of documentary substantiation of identity used to register and keep watch over the movements of aliens in the UK. As in Italy during the war, foreigners in the UK were now subject to extensive reporting and documentary requirements, and keepers of inns in which aliens might happen to stay were drawn into the apparatus of surveillance over foreigners. The Order also mandated the maintenance of a "central register of aliens" under the direction of the Secretary of State.[78]

The Italians remained the anomaly. A decree of May 1919 reaffirmed the wartime requirement that emigrants have a passport in order to leave, whatever their destination.[79] According to a study of emigration restrictions by the International Labor Office, moreover, Italians intending to depart for work in countries that required passports had to show a work contract before receiving their travel documents.[80] Again, however, what might have appeared to be – and, when necessary, could be transformed into – restrictions are better understood from the point of view of Italy's continued interest in exporting workers. As passport controls remained in force across Europe and in the United States after the war, the obligation that Italian emigrants have a passport and, where required, a work contract in order to get it were clearly efforts to *facilitate* rather than limit emigration. The passport obligations for foreigners entering Italy during the war years were never abolished, but this matter appears to have been of considerably less import to the Italian government than that of insuring that would-be emigrant workers be in a position to enter their destination countries, at least until the Fascists took power in the early 1920s.

THE UNITED STATES AND THE END OF THE *LAISSEZ FAIRE* ERA IN MIGRATION

In the aftermath of the First World War, "the laissez-faire era in international labor migration had come to a close."[81] An important cause of this caesura was the erection of rigid barriers to entry into the United States, for it, too, allowed initially temporary, wartime passport restrictions on aliens to persist into the postwar period, at the same time that it extended the range of national groups who were denied entry into the country. The United States government first responded to the renewal of European restrictions on movement with an executive order on 15 December 1915, requiring all persons leaving the United States for a foreign country to have a passport visaed by American officials before departure – a prudent enough measure in view of the fact that such documents had once again come to be required in many destination countries.[82]

Then, in early 1917, the US Congress adopted a law – over repeated vetoes by President Wilson – that excluded adult immigrants unable to pass a simple literacy test, which had the effect of excluding large numbers of people from areas of Europe that offered their inhabitants little schooling. In addition, the law prohibited entry by those from a "barred zone" in the Pacific; with Chinese, Japanese, and Korean immigration largely forbidden, the main targets of this legislation were Asian Indians who were technically "Aryans" or "Caucasians," and who were thus excluded on geographical rather than ethnoracial grounds.[83]

Finally, on 22 May 1918 – with the war nearly at an end – Congress adopted "An Act to prevent in time of war departure from or entry into the United States contrary to the public safety," which authorized the American President to impose specific restrictions on aliens wishing to enter or leave the country. The Act thus gave statutory foundation to the passport requirements adopted in December 1915. On 8 August 1918, President Wilson gave the law teeth with an executive order mandating that "hostile aliens must obtain permits for all departures from, and entries into, the United States."[84] At the end of 1919, Congress passed a revised version of the 1918 law that addressed only the issue of *entry* into the United States and dropped any mention of the proviso that the country find itself "in time of war."[85] As a result of these laws, the putatively "temporary" measures designed to ferret out "hostile aliens" were transmuted into weapons in the fight against "the undesirable, the enemy of law and order, the breeder of revolution, and the advocate of anarchy . . ." Passport controls came to play an important role at this point; one indication of this fact is that the various regional sections of the 1918 report of the Commissioner General of Immigration included only one separate discussion of "passport matters," whereas by 1919 all of the regions did so.[86] With Asians from the "barred zone" almost entirely excluded, literacy tests required, and documentary restrictions in place, the stage was set for more thoroughgoing measures of exclusion.

Yet in one region that constituted a significant source of immigrant flows, namely Mexico, restrictionism failed to carry the day, although not for lack of official attention. It should be recalled here that US involvement in the First World War was sparked to a considerable extent by the "Zimmermann telegram," which was published in the American press on 1 March 1917, and instructed the German minister in Mexico City to offer German support to Mexican efforts to recover Texas, New Mexico, and Arizona in the event of war between Germany and the United States.[87] With fears of alien infiltration from the south on the rise, beginning in 1917 border control measures along the Mexican frontier grew feverish. In a letter to the Commissioner General of Immigration dated 5 February 1918, however, the assiduous Supervising Inspector of the Immigration Bureau responsible for the border, Frank Berkshire, informed his boss that his resources were inadequate to patrol the border effectively, and that the cooperation of other government agencies and the military, while willing, was too uncoordinated to be of use. Berkshire thus proposed the creation of a separate, permanent organization, "similar perhaps to the Northwest Mounted Police of Canada," numbering 2000–3000 men and charged specifically and exclusively with the task of controlling movements across the border.[88]

Apparently Berkshire failed to receive the immediate help he had requested, however, for he soon felt compelled to inform his superiors that the efforts of his subordinates to control the border had been largely unavailing. Indeed, to the extent that they accomplished anything at all, they had exercised control over the wrong people. In the 1918 report of the Commissioner General of Immigration, Berkshire wrote in the section of his summary concerning "Passport Matters" that the number of agents detailed to monitor the border was simply not sufficient to be effective. Berkshire noted that passport controls, however meticulously carried out, could be undertaken only at the "regular immigration ports of entry," which left many miles of "remote and unfrequented points" easy targets for the movements of enemies. Accordingly, Berkshire concluded:

It is logical to assume that the most dangerous of the enemy's agents have sought, and will continue to seek, these points to avoid attracting attention. In the main, therefore, the passport regulations as now enforced discommode thousands of loyal, or in any event, not unfriendly persons whose legitimate business or innocent pleasures naturally take them through the regular channels, while the frontier elsewhere is inadequately guarded.[89]

In essence, Berkshire was pointing to the much greater difficulty of using documents to control a land border than to restrict the entry of passengers on steamships (or, later, airplanes). A few years later, as the futility of paper barriers in the face of so much open country came to be recognized, his pleas for more manpower to control the lengthy Mexican frontier would be answered with the creation of the Border Patrol in 1924. Despite its preoccupation nowadays with controlling the movements of Mexican immigrants, the Patrol initially focused on restricting the entry of Europeans and Asians whose immigration had been circumscribed by the various acts of the preceding years. With the late nineteenth-century foreclosure of cheap immigrant labor from across the Pacific and the growing restrictions on European immigrants, Mexico had come to serve as a critical source of labor in Southwestern agriculture and industry – a role it continues to play today. The new Border Patrol, gradually retooled to regulate the influx of countless brown-skinned peasants, would ultimately come to play an important if ambiguous role in regulating the flow of Mexican labor into the United States, gingerly negotiating the conflicting pressures of labor-hungry agricultural interests on the one hand, and domestic political groups bent on restriction on the other.[90]

The creation of the Border Patrol took place in the context of a much broader restrictionist thrust on the part of the American government that would soon entail the projection of state power far beyond the territorial borders of the country. In 1921, the United States adopted the first "national origins" quota, restricting immigration to a small percentage of those nationalities represented in the US population in the 1910 census. Realizing subsequently that large numbers of Southern and Eastern Europeans had entered the country by that time, the defenders of white America returned to the ramparts three years later to pass another law that took as a baseline the 1890 census, when the "Nordic" stock of the country was more predominant.[91] But restriction of incoming persons along these lines was easier said than done. Because the 1921 law had mandated a quota system without adequate provision for its implementation, hundreds of excess visas were issued abroad to steamship passengers making their way to the US. As a result, steamer captains would seek "to bring their passengers into the United States at the earliest possible moment after the opening of the new quota month. Midnight ship racing into New York Harbor in order to cross the entrance line before quotas were exhausted became a monthly event, and much distress and many deportations usually followed."[92] This arrangement simply would not do.

The Immigration Act of 1924 thus provided that American consuls abroad be charged with the task of keeping control of the quotas themselves and distributing immigration visas accordingly. At the same time, various other qualifications – including police checks, medical inspections, financial responsibility determinations, and political interviews – could be established long before the intending immigrant reached the country. As many who have taken the tour of Ellis Island National Park will know, the stated purpose of this approach was to avoid situations in which eager but impecunious emigrants might sell off all their worldly possessions in order to purchase a steamship ticket, only to be told upon arrival that they were inadmissible for any number of reasons. In contrast to this interpretation, Zolberg has characterized this set of procedures as a form of "remote border control," a major innovation in immigration policy implementation that "proved remarkably effective from the time of [its] institutionalization in the 1920s until well into [the] 1970s . . . [and] which by any reasonable standard must be reckoned as a remarkable administrative achievement."[93]

While both interpretations of the new requirement may be correct without contradiction, for our purposes it is essential to see that the system worked because of the development of documentary requirements that powerfully supported the claims of states to monopolize the legitimate means of movement. The passport requirements on foreigners left intact after the First World War provided the essential administrative basis for the implementation of the restrictionary immigration laws of the 1920s. How else was the immigration officer at Ellis Island to know whether a would-be immigrant belonged to one of the nationalities whose immigration was to be restricted under that legislation?

It is true that the newly permanent passport controls that persisted after the First World War generally applied not just to foreigners, but to both citizens and aliens. This was a necessary outcome of the desire to control borders against unwanted entrants, however, and aliens had increasingly come to be seen as lacking any *prima facie* claim to access to the territory of a state other than their own. In the absence of telltale markers such as language or skin color – which are themselves inconclusive as indicators of one's national identity, of course, but which nonetheless frequently have been taken as such – a person's nationality simply cannot be determined without recourse to documents. As an ascribed status, it cannot be read off a person's appearance.

The (re)imposition of passport controls by numerous West European countries and the United States during the First World War and their persistence after the war was an essential aspect of that "*révolution identificatoire*"[94] that vastly enhanced the ability of governments to identify their citizens, to distinguish them from non-citizens, and thus to construct themselves as "nation-states." With the general rise of the protectionist state out of the fires of the First World War, [95] the countries of the North Atlantic world became caught up in a general trend toward nationalist self-defense against foreigners. Documents such as passports and identification cards that help determine "who is in" and "who is out" of the nation here took center stage, and thus became an enduring and omnipresent part of our world.

These documents were an essential element of that burgeoning "infrastructural" power to "grasp" individuals that distinguishes modern states from their predecessors.[96] Specific historical forces such as the development of welfare states and the rise of labor movements seeking to control access to jobs and social benefits certainly played their part in promoting immigration controls and the sharpening of states' capacities to distinguish between "them" and "us."[97] Yet there were specifically political factors involved as well, particularly the advance of processes of democratization that increasingly brought the individual members of national states into closer relationship with states across the North Atlantic world. The tighter connection between citizens and states as a result of democratization led to an intensified preoccupation with determining who is "in" and who is "out" when it came to enjoying the benefits – both political and economic – of membership in those states.[98] This is one of the ways that democratization promoted bureaucratization, a dynamic that Weber noted long ago. In the process, passports became essential to the bureaucratic administration of modern mass migration, just as identity cards have become something like the "currency" of domestic administration, marking out eligibles from ineligibles in the areas of voting, social services, and much more besides.

CHAPTER 5

FROM NATIONAL TO POSTNATIONAL? PASSPORTS AND CONSTRAINTS ON MOVEMENT FROM THE INTERWAR TO THE POSTWAR ERA

The growing importance of national belonging resulted in a profusion of bureaucratic techniques for administering the boundaries of the nation, in both territorial and membership terms, in the period up to and immediately after the First World War. At the same time, the number of states that understood themselves in national terms was increasing as a product of the collapse of the Austro-Hungarian, Ottoman, and Russian Empires: the era witnessed the end of dynastic states in Europe and the elimination of the "easy-going nations" of the past in favor of what Karl Polanyi called the "crustacean type of nation," which crabbily distinguished between "us" and "them."

The rapidly improving technological possibilities for movement thus confronted intensified controls on ingress into the territories of European states, although restrictions on departure had increasingly become the province of authoritarian states alone. Egidio Reale, the leading contemporary analyst of the new passport regime, describes its impact with a variant of the Rip Van Winkle story: a man awakes during the interwar period from a slumber of some years to find that he can talk on the telephone to friends in London, Paris, Tokyo, or New York, hear stock market quotations or concerts from around the globe, fly across the oceans – but not traverse earthly borders without stringent bureaucratic formalities in the course of which his nationality would be scrutinized closely.[1]

Yet the unprecedented difficulty of international migration that flowed from the successful state monopolization of the legitimate means of movement in the post-First World War era had ironic consequences as well. In a world of nation-states, in which the population of the globe is theoretically divided up into mutually exclusive bodies of citizens, international migration is an anomaly with which the state system has some awkwardness coping. Those who lack the attributes of citizenship in a country, and especially those who find themselves without the documents attesting to their legal identity and status, face special problems in navigating the system. After the First World War, as huge population flows were set in motion by political and social change, forces associated with the League of Nations – an organization that both ratified and sought to transcend the notion of a world comprising nation-states – felt compelled by circumstances to attempt to deal with the reality that many in the game of international musical chairs had ended up without a seat in the turbulent aftermath of the war.

With millions of people on the move in response to the transformations that were taking place, and often seeking to escape violent conflict, the limitations of a system that presupposed mutually exclusive citizenries all of whom were distributed uniquely to one state or another became apparent almost immediately in the interwar era. The most obvious challenge to such a system was the emergence of that "most symptomatic group in contemporary politics," the stateless, whose plight "is not that they are not equal before the law, but that no law exists for them; not that they are oppressed but that nobody wants even to oppress them."[2] The efforts to alleviate some of the problems encountered by these wanderers among worlds led to the creation of the first international refugee regime, a coordinated if not entirely effective effort on the part of numerous states to clear away the difficulties faced by many stateless migrants during this period. Prominent among these efforts were attempts to reduce the barriers to migration that the stateless confronted, not least by providing them with travel documents that would be recognized by potential receiving states.[3]

Despite the innovation of the burgeoning refugee regime and its (limited) contribution to resolving the various problems of forced migrants, the period would culminate in dramatic movements of refugees occasioned by the Nazis' project to attain European (and indeed global) dominion. The biological racism at the root of Nazi ideology underwrote a kind of national imperialism. The ultimate aim of Nazi policy was to eliminate elements of the German population that were "alien to the blood" (*art-* or *blutsfremd*) – especially Jews – or "life unworthy of life" (*lebensunwertes Leben*, such as homosexuals and Gypsies), as well as to subjugate, enslave, and exterminate groups outside German borders that were deemed inferior in the racial hierarchy, such as Slavs. It is not difficult to see that the achievement of this racial-imperialist program demanded a great deal of classification and identification of particular population groups. Identity documents and the imposition of visible marks of group affiliation – a reversal of earlier trends away from "writing on the body" against the will of those written upon – were crucial to the Nazis' goals of creating a purified master race that ruled arbitrarily over or extirpated non-Aryans. The hardening of passport controls on movement that issued from the First World War would also contribute to the miseries faced by the many victim groups that the Nazis singled out for "special treatment" during their assault on Western civilization, although the extent to which immigration restrictions in the democratic countries resulted in disaster for the Jews has recently been the subject of renewed debate.

THE EMERGENCE OF THE INTERNATIONAL REFUGEE REGIME IN THE EARLY INTERWAR PERIOD

In the tempest of revolution and imperial collapse that followed the First World War, millions were set adrift as multinational empires were transformed into nation-states across much of Europe. At the same time, populations that fell under the sway of authoritarian states found that their chances for departure were undermined, whether in the interest of strengthening military forces or to prevent the enemies of a regime from propagandizing against it abroad. This pattern testifies to the truth of the observation that a concomitant of the nation-building processes of this period was that "prohibitions against exit were associated with the creation of internal conditions that produced a desire to leave and with expulsion."[4] This apparently contradictory set of circumstances characterized especially well the situation in Russia after the Bolshevik revolution.

Among the groups impelled to leave their countries of origin following the First World War, the refugees from Russia were surely the most prominent in the eyes of those concerned with migration issues. Subjects of the new Communist regime left the Soviet Union *en masse* during the civil war and the associated famines of 1919–22; the demographer Eugene Kulischer estimated the total out-migration from that country alone in the early interwar period at 1.75 million. This figure included a variety of ethnically non-Russian groups such as Germans, Poles, Rumanians, Lithuanians, Letts, Karelians, and Greeks; the "Russian emigration" proper he estimated at some 900 000.[5]

In the unlikely event that these unfortunates had managed to secure satisfactory travel documents before departing, the Soviets soon took long-distance vengeance on those who left the USSR for their presumed antipathy toward the regime. A decree of 15 December 1922 denationalized the vast majority of Russian refugees, rendering them stateless and invalidating their travel documents. In other words, by manipulating the legal status of its subjects, the Bolsheviks could punish from afar those who, by voting with their feet, brought discredit on the Soviet experiment. During the same year of 1922, the regime began strictly to prohibit emigration. This stance on the part of the Soviet government helped to stabilize the Russian refugee problem in Europe, although migrants continued to leave for the Far East until 1935.[6] Here, indeed, was the textbook combination of restrictions on departure and the production of a desire to leave that was most typical of the authoritarian states of this period.

The ascendancy to power of the Fascists in Italy in late 1922 had similar consequences, if on a much smaller scale. Soon after assuming the reins, Mussolini began rattling sabers and promoting the use of force in politics. In January of the following year, Mussolini created the Fascist Militia – a largely symbolic force, perhaps, but a private army for *il Duce* – "to defend the Fascist revolution." Within two months, the regime tightened passport requirements for those wishing to leave the country who were liable for military service.[7] The new regulations bespoke the Fascists' inclination to reverse the policy of Italian governments before the First World War, which were oriented toward facilitating emigration as a safety valve for class conflict and the tensions generated by economic underdevelopment. The Fascist posture concerning emigration was articulated by Dino Grandi, an Undersecretary of Foreign Affairs, in 1927:

> Why should Italy still serve as a kind of human fish pond, to feed countries suffering from demographic impoverishment? And why should Italian mothers continue to bear sons to serve as soldiers for other nations? Fascism will cease to encourage emigration, which saps the vital forces of race and State.[8]

By the late 1920s, the Fascists had promulgated a law against "abusive emigration" and were withdrawing passports from suspected anti-fascists. Still, Italian exile communities flourished in France; the aforementioned Egidio Reale, a socialist, was part of that emigration. The Fascist regime sought to spy on them in part by magnanimously offering to renew their travel documents abroad, an opportunity many of them had the good sense to decline. Ironically, the strictures against departure and the use of internal exile as a means of dealing with regime opponents had the result that Italian fascism proved to be the incubator of one of the most enduring critiques of the country's political and economic problems, Carlo Levi's majestic *Christ Stopped at Eboli.*[9] Despite a brief return after 1929 to the old stance of allowing jobseekers to leave in search of work during hard times, these policies put an end to large-scale emigration until after the Second World War, when Italy became the semi-periphery of a European regional economy dominated by Germany.[10]

In addition to the flows of emigres from the Soviet Union and Fascist Italy, major refugee problems developed in the area of the former Ottoman Empire as Turkey sought to turn itself into a modern, Western-oriented nation-state under the leadership of Mustafa Kemal (Atatürk). The old system of "millets," which had guaranteed autonomous self-government under Ottoman tutelage to the religious communities under its rule (Muslim, Christian, and Jewish), would have to give way in the face of growing nationalist sentiment.[11] The Greeks, who had gained independence from their Muslim overlords already in 1829, took up arms against the declining Empire in pursuit of the restoration of a greater Greece straddling the Aegean. These designs inevitably drew in Bulgaria and Serbia, who also contended for land in Macedonia, with the overall result that the Balkans became engulfed in wars lasting for a decade after 1912. For the Armenians, many of whom had enjoyed prestigious positions under Ottoman rule, the conflicts in the region had the positive result that they received an independent homeland (which became a Soviet republic after November 1920) – which they had lacked, and which might have helped protect them, when the Turks carried out a genocidal onslaught against them in 1915.

As in the contest of the late 1990s over Kosovo between Serbia and the region's ethnic Albanian inhabitants, these armed conflicts gave rise to substantial refugee movements. After a Turkish assault on Smyrna (Izmir) in September 1922, for example, over a million Anatolian Greek and Armenian refugees poured into Greece within a few weeks. In the interest of creating more ethnically homogeneous citizenries on their respective soils – a project already promoted on the Turkish side, of course, by the genocide against the Armenians – the Greeks and Turks soon organized a massive exchange of populations involving some 1.5 million people. Overall, some two million persons became refugees in the Balkans in the course of the great "unmixing of populations" that took place in the aftermath of the conflicts associated with the decline of the Ottoman Empire.[12]

In conjunction with the demise of the Dual Monarchy and the redrawing of boundaries in Austria-Hungary, the collapse of the Ottoman Empire and the revolutionary transformation of the Russian Empire gave birth to a number of new states that – against all evidence – understood themselves as ethnically homogeneous nation-states. The obvious absurdity of such claims in the "belt of mixed populations" in Central, Eastern, and Southern Europe resulted in the Minority Treaties of the early interwar period, which sought to insure certain rights to the various ethnic groups in the region who failed to achieve recognition as "state peoples" and who were correspondingly "submerged" under others who were fortunate enough to do so. In Arendt's view, the "real significance of the Minority Treaties lies . . . in the fact that they were guaranteed by an international body, the League of Nations"; because "the nation had conquered the state," it was now widely held that non-nationals could not enjoy the rights of citizens, and such rights as they had would have to be vouched for by some superordinate body. The thoroughgoing achievement of the nation-state ideal for some peoples generated a situation in which those who failed in their bid for national states were compelled to rely for their rights on a supranational organization, the League of Nations.[13] The League thus appears as sort of *deus ex machina* that arose almost of necessity from the triumph of the nation-state system, and that might help save it from its intrinsic conundrums and excesses.

These excesses were particularly apparent in the realm of migration. Many of the migrants forced to leave their homes by the often violent processes of nation-state-building faced substantial constraints on their movements as a result of the general antipathies toward foreigners and the documentary requirements that had been imposed on travelers throughout Europe during and after the war. Already in 1920, the League of Nations convened an international conference in Paris to deal with the difficulties created by the new passport regime and issued a number of recommendations designed to reduce the unwonted peacetime restrictions on movement. The 1921 conference of the Inter-Parliamentary Union in Stockholm expressed its condemnation of the passport system and called for greater freedom of movement. The pleas of the participants in these meetings, and those of later such conferences, fell largely on deaf ears, however. The passport regime had become broadly institutionalized, complicating the movements of hundreds of thousands of would-be travelers, emigrants, and refugees who lacked the documentation necessary to establish their identity – or who had been stripped of the legal nationality they needed to acquire the proper papers.[14]

The League of Nations nonetheless persisted in its efforts to smooth documentary formalities for immobilized refugees. At the height of the Russian refugee crisis in early 1922, the League of Nations' High Commissioner for Refugees, the Norwegian explorer-cum-humanitarian Frijdtof Nansen, called attention to the problem of travel documents for refugees in a report to the Council of the League. Then, in July, Nansen convened in Geneva a conference attended by representatives of sixteen governments to deal with this matter. The participants joined in the "Arrangement of 5 July 1922" to create an identification and travel document for Russian refugees that would find international acceptance, which became known simply as the "Nansen passport." According to this (non-binding) agreement, participating governments could issue the document without thereby committing themselves to granting citizenship rights to the bearer. Governments agreed to recognize the documents as valid, but at the same time they were not required to admit their bearers. The Arrangement was a considerable success; by September 1923, a total of thirty-one governments around the world had acceded to its terms, and by the end of the decade more than fifty would do so.[15]

Initially, before the documents were extended to other groups, Nansen passports stated that the bearer was a Russian national, were valid for one year, and would become invalid if the bearer acquired another nationality. Despite the fact that many of the recipients of these certificates were in fact stateless, particularly after the Soviet denationalization decree of December 1922, the designation *"personne d'origine russe"* was included not only because the recipients were former Russian nationals but also because "one would not have dared to tell the Russian emigre that he was without nationality or of doubtful nationality." Moreover, later attempts to provide uniform identity cards to all stateless persons were "bitterly contested" by holders of Nansen passports because they would thus have lost the distinctive mark of their status as refugees of Russian origin.[16]

Yet the demands of the refugee crisis in early interwar Europe led ineluctably to the extension of the Nansen passport to other groups. The Armenians – formerly subjects of the Ottomans, the Czarist Empire, the short-lived independent Armenian Republic, or Soviet Armenia, but now scattered throughout Europe and Asia Minor – frequently found themselves similarly ill-positioned to present the passports and identification documents demanded of them in their places of would-be refuge. In May 1924, accordingly, the League of Nations reached another "Arrangement" granting the Armenians access to Nansen passports. Nearly forty governments assented to this expansion of international authority to issue travel documents to the stateless.[17]

Despite its obvious usefulness to the Russians and Armenians who received it, the Nansen passport had serious shortcomings. Chief among these was the fact that the certificates offered their bearers no guarantee of (re)admission to the country that had issued the document. In certain respects this made it rather easy for governments to distribute Nansen passports; by supplying these documents to would-be travelers, they could facilitate the *departure* and international travel of refugees without assuming any responsibility to take them in at a later time. In 1926, an intergovernmental conference with participants from twenty-five countries took an important step toward ameliorating this deficiency by agreeing to revise the original arrangement to the effect that Nansen passport-holders would henceforth have the right to have a return visa stamped on the certificate. Presumably because this new provision came dangerously close to granting these refugees rights of access to territory that were now typically reserved for citizens; however, only about half of the governments that had acceded to the original Arrangement endorsed the new agreement.[18]

Two years later, the League of Nations took a further step toward giving certain elements of a kind of supranational citizenship to bearers of Nansen passports. A new "Arrangement" of 30 June 1928 gave the High Commissioner for Refugees the authority to perform certain consular functions on behalf of refugees, including certifying their identity and civil status, attesting to their character, and recommending them to government and educational authorities. These arrangements were eventually codified into international law in the 1933 Convention on Refugees. On the same day, the League also further expanded the list of groups that could be granted Nansen documents. The groups affected were principally some 19 000 Assyrians and other Christian minorities from formerly Ottoman territories. Only thirteen states signed this accord, however.[19]

Despite its shortcomings, the Nansen passport was a notable achievement in a period that apotheosized the nation-state. The historian Michael Marrus has referred to this period as "the Nansen era," and described the significance of the Nansen passport as follows:

> For the first time it permitted determination of the juridical status of stateless persons through a specific international agreement; at a time when governments and bureaucracies increasingly defined the standing of their citizens, it nevertheless allowed an international agency, the High Commission, to act for those whom their countries of origin had rejected.[20]

A recent analyst of the origins of modern refugee arrangements has written simply: "The beginning of international refugee law can properly be dated to the creation of the Nansen passport system."[21] Indeed, the Nansen passport represented the first step toward resolving at the supranational level the internal contradictions of a system of movement controls rooted in national membership. These contradictions were the underside of the Wilsonian idea of national self-determination that gave birth to both a number of new nation-states and to the group of "stateless persons" that so typified the interwar scene in Europe.

The persistence of strictures on movement across national borders also derived, however, from economic policies that dramatically reversed the economic liberalism that had underwritten the late nineteenth-century period of relatively unencumbered movement. During the interwar period, free trade gave way to protectionism, the constraints of which helped bring on the Great Depression of the 1930s. Writing about the era of the "national economy" that characterized the interwar period, Hobsbawm has described the results as follows:

> For a few years the world economy itself appeared to be on the verge of collapse, as the rivers of international migration dried to trickles, high walls of exchange controls inhibited international payments, international commerce contracted, and even international investment showed momentary signs of collapse. As even the British abandoned Free Trade in 1931, it seemed clear that states were retreating as far as they could into a protectionism so defensive that it came close to a policy of autarchy, mitigated by bilateral agreements.[22]

The devotion to liberal economic policies that had lifted the fortunes of free movement during the nineteenth century had now been abandoned. Karl Polanyi trenchantly summed up the situation in these terms:

> [P]rotectionism everywhere was producing the hard shell of the emerging unit of social life. The new entity was cast in the national mold, but had otherwise only little resemblance to its predecessors, the easygoing nations of the past. The new crustacean type of nation expressed its identity through national token currencies safeguarded by a type of sovereignty more jealous and absolute than anything known before.[23]

Currencies within, passports without.

Or within, if the country was of the totalitarian variety. Whereas the labor needs of industry had resulted in occasional acute shortages of labor until 1932, the famine that resulted from the disastrous collectivization policy of the First Five Year Plan (1928–33) confronted the regime with the potentially uncontrolled migration of starving peasants to already overcrowded cities by the end of that year. The Bolsheviks decided that something had to be done. In a bureaucratic effort to regulate domestic migration flows, Stalin (re)introduced the internal passport, which soon became "one of the main levers of social and political control in the USSR."[24]

Actually, the 27 December 1932 law inaugurating the passport system was the centerpiece in a broader effort by the regime to stanch the influx of peasants into the cities. These included a tightening up of the system of registration for residents of urban areas, with which the passport system was intimately tied; a law strengthening punishment for absenteeism, such that workers absent for as little as a day were to be fired, evicted from enterprise housing, and deprived of their ration cards; decrees designed to reduce the number of workers receiving rations, diminish abuses of the rationing system, and connect the distribution of rations directly to work and the enterprises; and, in the spring of 1933, a directive barring collective farm workers from leaving rural areas for work in the towns.[25] This remarkable series of decrees made it increasingly impossible for Soviet citizens to find food or housing unless they were properly registered and domiciled – which registration, in turn, was vital for receiving a passport for movement within the USSR. Because these documents constituted the backbone of a system of controls that linked employment, residence, and access to goods, the internal passport would come to constitute an essential part of the everyday life of the Soviet citizen, "the heart of police power"[26] in the Soviet Union.

Even in democratic societies, however, the strains of global economic collapse threatened to reverse the achievement of unified national spaces of free movement. Less well-known than the immigration restriction bills of the 1920s is the fact that, in the 1930s, patrols were set up at the California borders to keep out hungry escapees from the misery of the Dust Bowl, who were "deported" immediately if they seemed likely to become burdens on the public purse. It took until 1941 for the Supreme Court to invalidate the law authorizing these expulsions, at which time the court reaffirmed the right to domestic travel as a right of citizenship.[27] In the same year, the United States introduced what would become the permanent requirement that its departing citizens have a passport in their possession, at least for travel outside the Western Hemisphere. As on previous occasions, the obligation initially was conceived as a provisional, wartime measure, and rested on a presidential proclamation of a national emergency.[28] The immediate emergency that gave occasion for such a proclamation, of course, was Nazism.

PASSPORTS, IDENTITY PAPERS, AND THE NAZI PERSECUTION OF THE JEWS

The National Socialists' approach to dealing with their Jewish "problem" was a complex mixture of the "reactionary" and the "modern."[29] On the reactionary side, they reintroduced measures for the control of population movements and for the identification of persons that were throwbacks to earlier ages and practices since superseded and left behind by more democratic governments. And in an era in which national citizenship had become the *sine qua non* of access to rights, the Nazis adopted such reactionary measures as stripping their internal enemies of their citizenship in order to deprive them of protection and leave them vulnerable to the persecutions that one could visit upon the rightless, especially on those lacking a "homeland" state to which they might appeal for aid.

The "modernist" side of the pincers involved, among other things, the use of the most advanced techniques of population registration and documentary controls on movement to keep track of real or putative enemies and to mobilize the population to achieve the regime's ends.

For example, the Nazi government began to construct the administrative machinery for identifying and monitoring the whereabouts of Jews with a special census of German Jews carried out in conjunction with the general census of June 1933. This extraordinary count, which aimed to establish "an overview of the biological and social situation of German Jewry," determined that there were at that time exactly 16 258 Jews in Germany who had been born outside the country but who had subsequently acquired German citizenship. More broadly, 115 000 foreign or foreign-born Jews lived in Germany in mid-1933, a figure representing twenty-three percent of the total Jewish population.[30]

It was against this background that the regime began to undertake measures to marginalize non-German Jews, such as the denationalization law of 14 July 1933. The "Law on the Retraction of Naturalizations and the Derecognition of German Citizenship" empowered the regime to denationalize anyone who had acquired German citizenship between the end of the war in 1918 and the day Hitler took power as Reichskanzler in late January 1933. It was probably not coincidental that this measure, which took aim at naturalizations carried out by the Weimar government much reviled by the Nazis, was adopted on Bastille Day (14 July) 1933. The implementing order for the law made clear that "East European Jews" were one of its central targets. These recently immigrated groups, many of whom had come fleeing pogroms in Poland and elsewhere, were the object of a good part of the regime's earliest "special treatment." Yet of the *Ostjuden* who had entered Germany during the Weimar period, as we have seen, relatively few had acquired citizenship. As a result, "the Nazis were to discover that even they could not revoke the citizenship of those who were not citizens."[31] Soon enough, of course, the Nazis would see to it that no Jews could ever be citizens with the Nuremberg laws of 1935.[32]

The 1933 special census of Jews in Germany, however, was only the beginning of the Nazis' effort to invoke the most sophisticated statistical and administrative means to pursue its program of racial domination. The dozen years of existence of the "thousand-year *Reich*" would generate a proliferation of censuses, statistical investigations, registers of foreigners, identity cards, and residence lists that ultimately constituted the administrative foundation for the deportations to Auschwitz and the other death camps. Over time, these diverse methods of "embracing" (*erfassen*) the German population, and especially certain "negatively privileged status groups" within it, became intimately linked to the passport system. The reinforcement of "external" forms of identification by "internal" had important ramifications for many Jews who sought to leave Germany to escape Nazi oppression.

Despite the regime's outspoken antipathy toward Bolshevism, the first major move by the National Socialist government in the direction of a firmer embrace of the German population bore remarkable similarities to that taken only two-and-a-half years earlier by the Soviets. On 1 June 1935, the regime reintroduced a type of internal passport known as the "work-book." The immediate purpose of the work-book was to permit the more effective allocation of labor by the regime. Initially, possession of this document applied only to the practitioners of skilled occupations in which labor shortages existed, but it quickly spread to other areas as well. Together with the registry based upon all work-books issued, the little booklet documented the working life of the bearer, changes of job, periods of unemployment, and any alleged breaches of work contracts. Through the work-book system, not just the unemployed, but all Germans could theoretically be put under surveillance in the interest of the well-planned insertion of labor power where the regime wanted it most. The government later extended this system, refined to keep track of changes of address, to the entire population immediately before the Second World War in the form of the "people's registry" (*Volkskartei*).[33]

Around the same time, a number of German states required that beggars and vagabonds be in possession of a Vagrants' Registration Book (*Wanderbuch*), a certificate containing a record of the bearer's encounters with charities and official agencies responsible for the itinerant poor. (Because "tramping" was regarded as a way of life appropriate only to men, Registration Books were not issued to women.) Although these documents had been in existence for a long time, they did not become a requirement until the Third Reich. Failure to produce the necessary documents upon the request of the police could result in arrest, which in turn might land the offender in a charitable asylum, a work-house, or a concentration camp. As in the case of the work-book, the aim of these restrictions was to insure that the state would have untrammeled access to the labor-power of the unemployed and "work-shy," as well as providing the authorities with greater opportunities to check into a person's possible criminal background. Despite pressures to create a nationwide registry of the homeless population, this never came about, and the effectiveness of the Registration Books as a means of surveillance was correspondingly limited. After the outbreak of the war in September 1939, however, their issuance was suspended entirely, as vagrancy was simply declared illegal.[34] As the strictures on internal movement grew more severe, the documentary controls on movement beyond the boundaries of the Third Reich became more repressive as well.

The Nazis gave official expression to the intimate connection between internal and external types of registration and documentary controls on movement with the "Law on Passports, the Foreigner Police, and Residential Registration, as well as on Personal Identity Documents" of 11 May 1937. The decree gave to the Interior Minister a free hand to reorganize these administrative areas, collectively referred to as the "systems of personal identity documents" (*Ausweiswesen*). Among the prerogatives handed to the Interior Minister was the authority to abolish once and for all the 1867 law of the North German Confederation that had eliminated passport requirements other than as a temporary, emergency measure, as well as the series of laws from the First World War and the Weimar period that had been instituted under its terms.[35] The unceremonious demise of this notable legacy of the late nineteenth-century era of relatively free movement heralded developments that would help generate both a massive upsurge of refugees and a project for controlling movement that ended all movement.

In order to achieve the desired "seamless overview" of the German population and its peregrinations, the regime implemented the Order on Residential Registration (*Reichsmeldeordnung*) of 6 January 1938. This was the jewel in the crown of thorns created by the Nazis to track the population, and again bore remarkable similarities to the measures taken in connection with the introduction of the internal passport in the Soviet Union during late 1932. The Führer justified the law on the basis of its contribution "to the protection of the *Volksgenossen* from criminals and to facilitating the struggle of the security police against them." In the interest of more complete compliance with its regulations, the Order made it easier to fulfill them and eliminated any fees for doing so. At the same time, penalties for failure to comply were stiffened, including jail terms. The registration forms of all non-Germans were automatically forwarded to the aliens authorities. The Order obliged the staff of hospitals, youth hostels, and hotels to report their patients and guests within twenty-four hours to the proper officials.[36]

Though these registration requirements were hardly novel, they were now carried through with an unprecedented thoroughness. Whereas before 1938 residential registration requirements had been spotty across the country and evading them was a "popular sport," the *Reichsmeldeordnung* created the foundation for the "most complete possible embrace (*Erfassung*)" of the entire population.[37] Access to the Jewish population would especially be facilitated. According to one observer professionally concerned with such matters, the *Reichsmeldeordnung* would henceforth make it "possible to track completely both the external and the internal movements of the Jews (*Glaubensjuden*)."[38] The noose was tightening.

Measures such as these were at the heart of the Nazis' efforts to embrace the German population and to monitor the movements of those deemed enemies by them, especially Jews. The essence of these efforts was the requirement that some form of documentation be produced in order to fulfill satisfactorily the reporting obligations. The police chief of Hamburg, where these measures had been carried out most effectively before their adoption as the *Reich* standard, described the benefits of the system this way:

> The principal advantage of the Hamburg registration system consists in the so-called personal identification obligation (*Ausweiszwang*). This means that all persons wishing to register themselves and their dependents must identify themselves through official documents. Accordingly, the registry, which can be kept current by way of regular updates from the local registry offices (*Standesämter*), can be used without further ado for administrative purposes such as the issuance of passports, driver's licenses, residence permits . . . etc.[39]

The *Reichsmeldeordnung* thus facilitated a nationwide, homogeneous approach to insuring that all persons had been captured in the official web of identification apparatuses.

Not coincidentally, an order of July 1938 required Jews by the end of that fateful year to acquire an identification card (*Kennkarte*) indicating their Jewishness. When they did so, a black mark was to be added to their cards in the files of the "people's registry."[40] In a further indication of the direction things were taking, the other group required by the July 1938 law to have an identification card in their possession were men liable for military service.[41] Shortly thereafter, the Foreigners' Police Order (*Ausländerpolizeiverordnung*) generously stated that foreigners were welcome in the territory of the *Reich* as long as they demonstrated that they were "worthy of the hospitality accorded them." The Order authorized the expulsion, by force if necessary, of all foreigners from German territory; there were no means of legal redress for an expulsion order mandated under its terms.[42] This directive above all affected the Jews who, after all, had either never acquired citizenship or had been stripped of their citizenship in consequence of the Nuremberg laws. The Nazi effort to expel these "enemies of the people" was intensifying.

These developments occurred in the immediate aftermath of the League of Nations conference in Evian, France that had been convened in early July 1938 to address the growing problem of refugees from Germany and Austria and their difficulties in finding safe havens of settlement. The problem of emigration from German-dominated areas became more severe after the *Anschluss* of Austria in March, not least as a result of the enthusiasm of *Untersturmführer* Adolf Eichmann, who had been developing plans for large-scale expulsion of Jews since at least mid-1937. The Nazis' efforts to push the Jews out of their domains soon led to the creation of a Central Office for Jewish Emigration under Eichmann's direction.[43] But the Nazis' plans to expel the Jews were not necessarily consistent with an international system that reserved the right to admit only those whom they chose to admit, a fact that may ulti-mately have helped to push the Nazis toward extermination as the "final solution" of the "Jewish problem."

Although all of the delegations to the Evian conference expressed their commitment to humanitarian assistance, only the Dominican Republic made a concrete offer of admissions: its representatives hoped that they could find agricultural settlers for some of the more unpromis-ing areas of their country. Otherwise, the governmental representatives at the conference mainly bemoaned the degree to which their countries had been "saturated" with refugees and pointed to ongoing problems of unemployment and economic malaise in the course of drawing sharp limits around their ability to accept more refugees. The conference's main accomplishment was the creation of the Intergovernmental Committee on Refugees (IGCR), an organization that came into being largely because the United States did not wish to work under the aegis of an organization – the League of Nations – that it had never joined. The results of the conference were generally regarded as a disappointment.[44]

Soon after the Evian conference, the problem of refugees from German-controlled Europe would worsen dramatically. The *Reich* expanded its reach on 1 October by its occupation of the Sudetenland, in the frontier territory of Czechoslovakia. This extension of Nazi rule also had the effect of bringing more Jews under German domination, of course, and thousands of the country's Jews sought to flee their new overlords. At the Evian conference, a Swiss police official had objected to the surge of Jewish immigration into Switzerland from Austria after the *Anschluss*, to which the Swiss government had responded by impos-ing a visa requirement on holders of Austrian passports. After discussions with the German government, the Third Reich on 5 October required all German Jews to turn in the passports in their possession, which the regime then returned to them stamped with a red "J." In addi-tion to the special identity cards Jews were required to carry within Germany, their travel documents now marked them clearly as Jews when they sought to traverse international boundaries. Ironically, by putting potential receiving governments on notice that the bearers of these pass-ports were "undesirables," this move may well have inhibited the Nazis' increasingly strenuous efforts to expel Jews from the Reich.[45]

Indeed, as of the autumn of 1938, only an estimated one third of the roughly 500 000 Jews counted in Germany (*Altreich*) as of mid-1933 had left the country, despite a growing catalog of laws designed to exclude Jews from German society and make their lives there more unpleasant. Yet the pressure on Jews to leave intensified further after *Kristallnacht*, the "night of broken glass," on 9 November 1938. After this outbreak of violence and destruction, it became increasingly difficult to sustain the belief that the Nazis would be content merely to marginalize and stig-matize the Jewish population, and large numbers of Jews now sought to leave German-controlled Europe.

Did the red "J" make it more difficult for Jews to find refuge outside Hitler's Europe? Over the last twenty years or so, it has become a com-monplace that many Jews were condemned to death by the immigration barriers and documentary identification requirements raised by many countries of Europe and North America during the preceding period, and by the unwillingness of most countries to admit Jews as refugees, as suggested by the results of the Evian conference. This view is perhaps most prominently associated with the work of the historian David Wyman, but it has become widely influential. According to the now standard view, the immigration restrictions that emerged from the First World War and their strict enforcement during the 1930s in an effort to protect national labor markets during the depression consigned many Jews to their deaths because they were unable to find a refuge from Nazi persecution.[46]

More recently, William Rubinstein has argued vigorously that the notion of "paper walls" surrounding the Western democracies – and the broader claim that the democracies could have rescued more Jews in various ways, such as by bombing Auschwitz – is an ahistorical myth. Rubinstein insists that the "paper walls" argument is misguided for a sim-ple reason. According to him, relatively few Jews left Germany before *Kristallnacht* in November 1938 because they believed that this was one of those periodic outbursts of anti-Semitism that would soon "blow over." But, in contrast to the claims of the critics of Western policies toward the Jews, those who did leave Germany found refuge in the Western countries without great difficulty. What must be understood, in Rubinstein's view, is that after the beginning of the war in September 1939, the obstacle Jews confronted was no longer that of *getting into* other countries, but rather that of *getting out* of Nazi-controlled Europe.

In order to appreciate Rubinstein's argument,

> it is imperative that the Jews of the Nazi Reich must, at all times, be distin-guished from the 7.5 million Jews of continental Europe who came under Nazi rule between the outbreak of the war and V-E Day. *The Jews of conti-nental Europe, apart from Germany, were not refugees, either before or after 1939,* were not subject to Nazi rule prior to the coming of the war, or imagined that they would ever be, let alone that they would be murdered in history's greatest genocide."[47]

In short, the fundamental distinction is that between *refugees* (from Germany, Austria, and the Sudetenland before September 1939) and *prisoners*. For the Jewish prisoners of the Third Reich after 1939, Rubinstein argues, the only "rescue" from which they might have bene-fited would have come about through the Allies' swifter prosecution and conclusion of the war against the Nazis. Contrary to the view of critics such as Wyman, Rubinstein insists, the Allies did as much as they could (or nearly so) to provide aid and succor to those Jews who actually chose to flee while they still had the chance to do so.

While there is much that is appealing about Rubinstein's interpretation, there are also flaws in his argument that render suspect his overall conclusions. For example, Rubinstein ignores the fact that, during the first years of the Third Reich, the problem of refugees from Nazism became sufficiently serious that the League of Nations moved to intervene. First, already in 1933 the League created the position of High Commissioner for Refugees from Germany, a post first held by an American, James G. McDonald, from 1933 to 1935. As a result of German opposition to the office's activities, however, the High Commissioner was relegated to a separate institution based in Lausanne rather than in Geneva, where the League was headquartered. During McDonald's tenure, the League debated for years whether it should extend the Nansen passport system to refugees from Germany. In the course of these discussions, it became apparent that France and Britain were loathe to annoy Germany, which they wished to appease, and the idea was eventually shelved. With the issue of travel documents for refugees hung up in fruitless wrangling, McDonald concentrated his efforts on securing the admission of refugees. He ultimately facilitated the placement of approximately two thirds of the 80 000 refugees who left Germany between 1933 and 1935. While that record is not unimpressive, according to these figures some 27 000 would-be refugees ended up without a place to go.[48]

McDonald's successor from 1936 to 1939, a Briton named Neill Malcolm, pressed the matter of travel documents, however, with the result that the League adopted an "Arrangement" in July 1936 authorizing governments to issue travel documents to Germans and stateless persons coming from Germany who lacked the protection of the German government. These provisions applied primarily to Jews who had been denationalized in the aftermath of the adoption of the Nuremberg laws. This provisional agreement was transformed into a "Convention on the Status of Refugees Coming From Germany" in February 1938. In due course, these arrangements were extended to refugees from Austria and Czechoslovakia as these countries acceded to or fell under Nazi rule. Clearly, contrary to Rubinstein's reading of the situation, those in the League of Nations concerned with refugee matters believed that there was a problem regarding would-be refugees' access to travel documents that would facilitate their movement across international space, as well as their access to places of refuge more generally.

Despite this evidence that German and stateless Jews coming from Germany and elsewhere confronted serious difficulties in departing from or finding refuge outside Hitler's domains, Rubinstein rejects the view that German Jews were ultimately condemned to death at German hands by the "paper walls" that kept them out. It is true, as Wyman showed, that between 1933 and 1945 the quotas for immigrants from Germany (and Austria) were never filled – before 1937 they never exceeded a quarter of the allotment. It is also true that this fact may be attributable in part to anti-Semitic attitudes on the part of the consular officials evaluating the visa applications of Jews in continental Europe. But in order to evaluate satisfactorily whether other countries took in Jewish refugees when they presented themselves as asylum seekers, it is necessary to consider whether the quotas may have been under-filled because Jews did not seek to take refuge abroad. On the basis of this kind of evidence, Rubinstein argues that the reason the immigration quotas to the United States from Germany and Austria remained unfilled before 1939 was that very many Jews failed to "read the hand-writing on the wall" and chose not to leave Germany for the United States in large numbers until after *Kristallnacht* in November 1938.[49]

Perhaps the most sensible conclusion to draw from this debate is this: like many other groups, Jews confronted significant barriers to admission into countries of potential safe haven during the 1930s, and the "paper walls" that had been erected during the early interwar period complicated the negotiation of international space for all of them. With the development of new bureaucratic apparatuses since the First World War, states had become much more effective at identifying possible interlopers and using documentary restrictions to keep out those they did not wish to admit. And surely anti-Semitism played some role in keeping Jews out of potential receiving countries. But this does not in itself justify the claim that the Allied states could have done a great deal more than they actually did to "rescue" Jews from the Nazis.

During 1939, the apparatus for "embracing" the population of the Reich moved into high gear. In order to facilitate the identification of "racial enemies," after 1 January, all Jews whose given names did not appear in the "Catalog of Jewish First Names" were required to rein-scribe at the Registry Office (*Standesamt*) with the name "Israel" or "Sarah."[50] In February of 1939, as noted previously, the regime ordered the expansion of the "people's registry," which henceforth was to include an entry for each and every person in the population. According to the bureaucratic administrators charged with keeping the registry, its purpose was to enable the Nazi regime to mobilize the entire population in the event of war.[51] Then, in May, the Third Reich carried out a census that constituted "the capstone in the 'embrace' of the Jews." In addition to the census form itself, a supplementary card introduced at the behest of the *Wehrmacht* and the security forces under Reinhard

Heydrich was to be filled out as well. The purpose of the card was to give the security forces a clearer overview of the Jewish population and the army a better picture of the training of its potential inductees.[52]

The Reich Statistical Office, which carried out the census, thus performed vital services in fulfilling what Heydrich, after assuming the position of *Reichsprotektor* in Czechoslovakia, bombastically (but not altogether inaccurately) described as "the fighting tasks in the administrative sector." Heydrich understood that the precondition for what he called the "task of achieving the idea" was not merely "a superficial seeing, but rather a thorough grappling with (*Befassen*) and grasp (*Erfassen*) of things."[53] To achieve these aims, the tasks of counting, identifying, registering, and tracking became central activities of the German occupying forces wherever they went.

After the conquest of Poland in early September 1939, the Nazi regime stiffened the existing regulations of the *Reichsmeldeordnung* concerning identification and registration and extended them to its newly acquired territories. The justification was the usual one that "precise surveillance of persons' movements" was essential to the defense of the "fatherland in danger."[54] Those taking occupancy of or leaving a dwelling now had to report their movements within three days, rather than the previous peacetime requirement of one week; foreigners as well as stateless persons, who before had been on the same legal footing as Germans in this respect, had to register their assumption of new quarters or their departure from old ones within twenty-four hours. In response to Gestapo allegations of noncompliance by the so-called "Polish-Jewish criminal and political criminal element," the penalties for transgression of these regulations were stiffened. Thenceforward, according to a letter from the chief of the province of Upper Silesia, those in the occupied Eastern territories who failed to report themselves to the proper authorities, or who made false declarations when doing so, were to be sent to a concentration camp.[55]

With the occupation of Poland in September 1939, of course, the Nazis assumed control over a Jewish population of several million, as well as of a Slavic people that they regarded as racially inferior. At this point, their plans for population engineering and ethnic resettlement of the Eastern territories remained uncertain. The ultimate fate of the Jews – that is, the meaning the Nazis would give to the notion of a "final solution" of the Jewish question – remained indeterminate. Christopher Browning has argued that, between the seizure of Poland in 1939 and the invasion of the Soviet Union in 1941, the Nazis' plans for the Jews focused on two chief projects: their resettlement to the Lublin Reservation (the region between the Bug and the Vistula rivers) or the seemingly even more bizarre "Madagascar Plan," under which the Jews of Europe would be eliminated by shipping them to the remote island off the African coast.

Yet these undertakings were caught up in a broad project for the racial reorganization of eastern Europe, and accordingly at times the resolution of the "Jewish problem" had to take a back seat to the displacement of the Poles or the settlement of ethnic Germans in their stead. As a result of the "frustration that had built up over the bottlenecks of demographic engineering in eastern Europe" since the conquest of Poland, the Madagascar plan came to seem particularly appealing. But the implementation of that plan required the defeat not just of France – which the Germans achieved by the summer of 1940 – but also of Great Britain, and it soon became apparent that this was not going to happen very quickly. "The greater the frustration, the lower the threshold to systematic mass murder," Browning writes. "Thus the Madagascar Plan was an important psychological step toward the Final Solution." By the time of Operation Barbarossa (the invasion of the USSR) in mid-1941, the Nazis' frustration about the Jewish question had reached boiling point. As they overran more territories with large Jewish populations, their tendency to equate "Jewish" and "Bolshevik" facilitated their treatment of Jews in the same manner that they treated Bolsheviks: summarily. The *Einsatzgruppen* were unleashed, and by October plans had been adopted to deport Jews to death camps equipped with poison gas facilities. During the same month, Jewish emigration from Germany was finally forbidden. The extermination of European Jewry had begun.[56]

The Nazis had by this time simplified the process of identifying and "embracing" the Jews by reverting to one of the oldest methods of anti-Jewish discrimination – the requirement that they were a distinguishing mark, the Yellow Badge. First introduced in the Government General of Poland in late 1939, a decree of 1 September 1941, mandated that the Yellow Badge was henceforth to be worn by all Jews above the age of six in Germany, the Polish provinces, and the Protectorate of Bohemia and Moravia. This measure was in part a response to the fact that, as a French police official pointed out, travel restrictions on Jews and "Negroes" introduced by the Nazis in France could only be fully enforced against the latter because of their relatively easy identification on the basis of skin pigmentation. The badge facilitated the isolation and segregation of Jews "as well as strict control of their movements and activities."[57]

The imposition of the badge met with significant resistance not only in the Western occupied countries, especially in France, Holland, and Belgium, but also in Czechoslovakia. Even in Germany, where the order requiring Jews to wear the badge was widely welcomed by the "Aryan" population, it also generated considerable consternation, especially among practicing Christians. The severe penalties for transgressions of the requirements, however, resulted in more thorough compliance with the regulations in the East. With the identification and segregation of Jews made easier by this distinguishing mark, the deportations from Germany to the East began on 16 September 1941.[58] The thoroughly "modern" project of a systematic extermination of European Jewry, which depended to a great extent on the mobilization of advanced administrative means, also relied for its implementation on some of the most "reactionary" methods of discriminating between "us" and "them."[59]

Just as there was opposition to the Jewish star, the Nazis' more modern attempts to achieve a firm grasp on the Jewish population met with resistance as well. Despite their efforts, the Nazis were unable to achieve full compliance with the requirements regarding identification papers and registration with the authorities. In 1942, *Reichsführer-SS* Himmler complained that significant portions of the population failed to carry official documents with photographs, such as passports and identity cards, as they were required to do by law. In response, he announced his intention to undertake a renewed campaign to remind the populace of these requirements.[60]

Beyond noncompliance with such regulations, resistance to the German occupation in other countries sometimes focused directly on its bureaucratic methods. For example, cases of arson and raids on the offices responsible for population registration swelled during 1943 and 1944 in the Netherlands. In January 1944, Himmler received a letter from a high official of the occupation regime there reporting that attempts to update the population registry had resulted in the distribution of critical leaflets, attacks on registry officials, and the pronouncement of death sentences against them.[61] It was not lost on occupied and terrorized populations that the systems of identification and registration were vital to the implementation of the Nazis' designs for mastery of Europe and its racial purification.

Passports, identification cards, population registries, and visible distinguishing marks intended to keep watch on and control the movements of Germany's population came to constitute an interlocking if not flawless system of registration and tracking. These mechanisms facilitated the task of locating and monitoring Jews, with the ultimate result that they were available for extermination. All this supports Rubinstein's notion that, after September 1939, the Jews of Europe were *prisoners* of Hitler's regime. In a dramatized version of the last days of Adolf Eichmann, playwright Heinar Kipphardt has the Israeli prison warden ask Adolf Eichmann, "as an expert," what the Jews could have done to avoid the fate the Nazis had planned for them. Eichmann's response:

> Disappear, disappear. Our vulnerable point was if they had disappeared before we had been able to register (*erfassen*) and concentrate them. Our

commandos were terribly understaffed, and even if the police in the various countries had helped us with all their strength, the Jews had at least a fifty-fifty chance. Massive flight would have been a catastrophe for us.[62]

As we have seen, especially after 1937, the Nazis did their best to avert such a "catastrophe."

In order to carry out their "final solution" – whether that entailed expulsion, as at first, or extermination – the Nazis needed, and did their utmost to build up, a massive administrative machinery for identifying and "embracing" the population. These identification mechanisms helped both to keep the war machine fed with recruits and to identify and separate off enemies of the *Volk*, particularly the Jews. Documents such as identity cards and passports were essential elements of this system, and while it is not clear that Jews suffered disproportionately from the "paper walls" erected by the countries of the North Atlantic world after the First World War, their negotiation of international space was hardly facilitated by those barriers, either. These facts would not be forgotten in postwar German debates about passport controls, nor in broader European efforts to reduce the stringency of documentary controls on movement.

LOOSENING UP: PASSPORT CONTROLS AND REGIONAL INTEGRATION
IN POSTWAR EUROPE

The close of the Second World War confronted those involved in the regulation and facilitation of movement with a daunting task.[63] The number of Europeans displaced by the Second World War has been estimated at approximately 30 million, of whom some 11 million found themselves outside their countries of origin at war's end. Postwar conflicts in Eastern and Southern Europe, in turn, generated further flows of refugees. A considerable number of these massive groups of migrants were settled relatively expeditiously. This was mainly because of the dynamics of the largest flow: millions of ethnic Germans, whether old settlers or new, who were retreating with the German armies or expelled from several countries in Eastern Europe were accommodated in one of the two states then taking shape in the Allied-occupied zones of Germany. Yet many others, not least about two million subjects of the Soviet regime who often had little sympathy for Communism and hence little desire to return to Stalin's domains, remained outside their home countries and in need of assistance to negotiate their way across international space.

Already during the Second World War, international efforts were undertaken to facilitate the movements of the enormous wave of refugees uprooted by the conflict. Earlier exertions led by the American and British governments were consolidated in 1943 under the aegis of the United Nations Relief and Rehabilitation Administration (UNRRA). That agency, however, fell prey to the bickering among the Second World War allies that would soon come to be known as the Cold War. Although UNRRA certainly helped in the process of repatriating many displaced persons after the war, a considerable portion of the responsibility was handled, however unwillingly, by the Allied military forces. According to Michael Marrus, the Allied command repatriated 5.25 million displaced persons to Western European countries during May and June 1945 alone, a rate of more than 80 000 per day.[64] The documentary obligations that DPs had to fulfill are likely to have been relatively minimal in a situation of this magnitude.

Soon thereafter, the International Refugee Organization (IRO) was established in 1946 to minister to the needs of "the last million" European refugees, and was scheduled to go out of existence in 1951 upon completion of that task. Like the UNRRA, the IRO became entangled in Cold War disputes reflecting divergent foreign policy strategies of the two superpowers that would profoundly shape subsequent international responses to refugee problems. The IRO was succeeded after the creation of the United Nations in 1949 by the UN High Commissioner's Office for Refugees (UNHCR).

Despite the fact that two major refugee crises outside Europe had arisen since V-E Day – some 14 million persons set in motion by the partition of India and Pakistan in 1947, and several hundred thousand Palestinians associated with the creation of the state of Israel in 1948 – UNHCR was at first exclusively concerned with displaced Europeans. A separate institution, the UN Relief for Palestinian Refugees, was created to deal with the latter crisis, and *ad hoc* arrangements were developed to deal with other refugee crises elsewhere. Gradually, however, UNHCR came to regard the rest of the (non-Palestinian) world as its mandate. In its founding charter, UNHCR took over the novel notion adopted by the IRO that individual refugees had rights irrespective of their nationality, a feature that constituted a major shift from the prewar approach that treated refugees in terms of their membership in national groups. At the same time, in order to reduce the range of its jurisdiction, UNHCR was relieved of responsibility for the stateless.[65] Under the terms of the Refugee Convention of 1951, contracting states are enjoined to issue travel documents to refugees and asylum-seekers in their territories who might find themselves in need of such documents. In certain circumstances, the International Committee of the Red Cross (ICRC) may issue an emergency one-way travel document for humanitarian purposes, although foreign-country immigration officials are not obliged to recognize such documents.[66]

Efforts to reduce the severity of the passport regime inherited from the interwar period were being made at the national level as well during this time. Even before the war had officially ended, Belgium and Luxembourg had exchanged notes aimed at reducing passport controls. By 1950, the Netherlands joined this effort and nationals of the three countries were given the right to travel among them with only a national identity card. In mid-1954, Denmark, Sweden, Norway, and Finland agreed that their nationals could travel without passports or other travel documents when traveling among those countries, and that such persons no longer needed to be in possession of a residence permit when residing in a Scandinavian country other than their own. These arrangements were extended by a 1957 Convention that provided for the elimination of passport controls at the internal frontiers of these Scandinavian countries (which thus implicitly extended the freedom of movement to non-nationals traveling among these countries).[67] These agreements had wider influence, encouraging the Tourism Committee of the Organization for European Economic Cooperation (forerunner of the OECD) to conclude "that the final goal, the pure and simple abolition of passports, is not merely a utopian aim."[68]

In the interim, one of the main objectives of the advocates of liberalized movement in Europe was the creation of a European passport. The proponents of a European passport have had to fight tooth and nail against the tribunes of national sovereignty, however. The Secretary-General of the Council of Europe, a strong supporter of the idea of a European passport as a symbol of a unified continent, inquired of Europe's national governments in the early 1950s as to their position concerning the possibility of creating such a document. The replies he received indicated that those governments were not yet prepared to forgo their national passports, but would prefer to see simply a standardization of national passports. Accordingly, the Council's Committee of Experts on Passports and Visas abandoned the broader aim of a European passport for the time being, and instead submitted proposals to the Committee of Ministers toward the more limited end of standardization in March 1952.[69] As late as the mid-1980s, the CDU government of West Germany felt compelled to defend the incipient introduction of the European passport by reminding the *Bundestag* that it would remain "legally a national passport."[70]

Similarly, the advocates of passportless travel within Europe have struggled mightily against the surveillance preoccupations of the police bureaucracies. In response to the negative replies of the member governments to the Council of Europe's inquiries regarding the creation of a European passport, the Council asked its Legal Committee to assess the effectiveness of the existing system of passport controls. In its 1953 report, the Legal Committee suggested that the passport control systems of the various states were largely ineffective in achieving control over the entry of undesirable persons into their territories and the exit of those of their nationals whose departure they wished to hinder, and that these purposes could be achieved by other available means in any case. The Legal Committee also found the system to be a source of considerable inconvenience. In view of the delays entailed by passport controls at the frontiers of European countries, it concluded that "despite the remarkable technical achievements of the twentieth century, the journey from Paris to London by rail and sea could be done in less time at the beginning of the century than in 1953."[71]

The preoccupation with surveillance that was inspired by the notion of national sovereignty was strikingly in evidence in the debates over the first passport law of the fledgling Federal Republic of Germany (FRG). First, the adoption of the new law was a symbolically important element of the broader quest for sovereignty of the new German state. The proposal for a new passport law had been occasioned by the early 1950 notification by the Allied occupying powers, under whose authority such matters had remained since the end of the war, that they were prepared to restore this prerogative to the West German government. The Allies nonetheless reserved to themselves the right to deny the issuance of a passport to those included in the blacklists they were keeping. Although these reservations were a matter of particular concern to Communists, against whom the blacklists were primarily directed, a number of *Bundestag* deputies and the Interior Minister himself noted that this infringement on the authority of the Federal Republic constituted "a limitation of our sovereignty which is, over the longer term, incompatible with partnership on an equal footing."[72] The adherents of this view regarded control over the distribution of passports as a central attribute of national independence, akin to the authority to issue a unique currency. Then as now, state-builders see the authority to issue one's own passport as a vital element of sovereignty.

Against the background of the emerging Cold War, the achievement of the sovereignty of a West German state also entailed the hardening of the separation between the Federal Republic and the German Democratic Republic (GDR), a development that many Germans were reluctant to countenance. The Communists of Western Germany were particularly loathe to let the two states drift apart, hoping that some settlement could be achieved under conditions more favorable to Communist aims. Despite its basic commitment to German unity, however, Konrad Adenauer's Christian Democrat Union (CDU) had instead chosen to wait out the Cold War until such time as a more congenial government came to power in East Berlin and paved the way for reunification under non-Communist auspices. In the meanwhile, the CDU adopted a strategy whereby it accepted the deepening division of the two Germanys while trying to avoid conceding the sovereign legitimacy of the East German regime. The Hallstein Doctrine, which punished foreign governments that established diplomatic relations with the GDR, reflected this fundamental aspect of early West German foreign policy.

This basic approach to "intra-German" affairs found expression in the new passport law in several ways. First, the law's backers insisted that East Germans were not required to have passports to enter the territory of the Federal Republic from the GDR, because they were not aliens: the FRG never conceded the existence of a separate East German citizenship. Similarly, West Germans were not obliged to have a passport to enter the territory of the GDR (though the GDR might require them for entry), because it was not held to be "foreign territory." The fundamental reason for these provisions, according to the government, was that the frontier between the two states was "not an external border, but merely a demarcation line of the occupying powers."[73] In view of the fact that no peace treaty had been signed to conclude the Second World War, this posture was on solid legal ground.

Second, the government had initially proposed that all persons crossing a border in either direction between the Federal Republic and a foreign country – that is, countries other than the GDR – have a visa in order to do so. Critics of the government's version, including the powerful *Industrie- und Handelstag* (analogous to the American Chamber of Commerce), challenged the need for a visa requirement for Germans. Ultimately, the Government was able to get agreement only on the notion that the Interior Minister was authorized to require, at his discretion, a visa requirement for foreigners entering and leaving the Federal Republic. This arrangement helped to sustain the notion that "Germans" East and West remained part of one coherent space of free movement, while consolidating more securely the dividing line between "Germans" and foreigners.[74]

The issue of the passport's enhancement of the state's surveillance capabilities also occupied a prominent place in the debates over the 1952 law. Again, this was a matter of special concern to the Communists in the *Bundestag*. Communist deputies pointed particularly to the paragraph that gave the government the authority, when it deemed "public security or the constitutional democratic order" threatened, to mandate special conditions for entry or exit from the FRG, as well as the clause permitting it routinely to deny passports to those who "endanger the internal or external security of the Federal Republic." According to the Communists, these clauses would be used principally against them, as could be seen in past abuse of such laws. A Social Democratic deputy reinforced these claims, asserting that these provisions aimed chiefly at restricting the freedoms of Communists even as leading Nazi functionaries had been permitted to come and go as they pleased.[75] The Communists had good reason for their fears: the United States government had just adopted a clause denying passports to Communists in section 6 of the Internal Security Act (also known as the Subversive Activities Control Act, or McCarran Act) of 1950.[76]

In addition to the restrictions motivated by Cold War concerns, the government's proposed law included bizarre throwbacks to restrictions on movement typical of the early nineteenth century. Its initial section 11 proposed penalties, including a possible one-year jail term, for those who diverged from the route or destination prescribed in a German visa. The aforementioned Social Democrat pilloried the absurd circumstances to which such a clause could give rise with a small tale about a German vacationer in Switzerland who, deciding along the way to go to Geneva rather than Zurich, as well as to make a little side trip to Chamonix in France, would have twice violated the law as first submitted.[77] The final version of the law imposed these penalties only on foreigners crossing the borders of the Federal Republic, or temporarily resident within them.

There was something odd about the government's preoccupation with the surveillance of travelers. In the course of his remarks introducing the proposed law, the West German Interior Minister – the same official who was to be responsible for its implementation – delivered himself of a quite radical critique of passport controls. Anticipating the above-described findings of the Legal Committee of the Council of Europe, the minister averred:

> All the experts essentially recognize that the really dangerous people almost always find a way to get in and out. Passport requirements, and especially visa requirements, thus result in a heavy burden on the movement of the broad mass of innocent travelers. An enormous – and largely useless – administrative effort is expended trying to get a few wrongdoers by issuing millions of passports and visas to innocent people.[78]

Yet the Interior Minister went on to defend the law as necessary to the security of the Federal Republic and successfully shepherded it through the *Bundestag*. Apparently no amount of sense could persuade the law's supporters that passports were of marginal value (at considerable cost) in enhancing public security. The German Interior Minister's remarks concerning the inefficacy of passport controls for the "really dangerous people" recall the despondency of US Immigration Service inspector Frank Berkshire when called upon to implement passport controls along a largely unguarded 2000-mile border in the period after the First World War:[79] passports can only regulate the movements of those who are prepared to subject themselves to passport checks. Those who know how to avoid border checkpoints will not need to furnish themselves with the legitimate "means of movement." Even if the Interior Minister's actions belied his words, it is difficult to imagine anyone in a similar position of responsibility dismissing the usefulness of passports in today's pervasive atmosphere of "crisis" in immigration matters.

An earlier immigration "crisis" already loomed on the horizon for Great Britain after the close of the war, rooted in the privileged rights of access of British colonial subjects to the imperial center. The process of freeing colonies that were increasingly regarded as anomalous and untenable gathered steam on the heels of a war that had been fought at least in part against the idea of domination by foreigners. With the British Nationality Act of 1948, each of the countries of the Commonwealth was to set its own citizenship laws, although citizens of Commonwealth countries were to enjoy a shared status of British subjecthood (also known as Commonwealth citizenship). While each of the Commonwealth states was permitted to continue the long standing practice of establishing its own citizenship and immigration policies with respect to other member states, the UK itself remained open to all comers from its overseas dominions: "it was the only one-way street in the commonwealth."[80]

In addition, although the Republic of Ireland was not a member of the Commonwealth, it concluded arrangements for a passport union with the UK that allowed for passportless travel between the two countries of their respective nationals. Finally, in order to ease access to the UK to travelers from the countries of northwest Europe, the government adopted in 1960 a facility known as the British Visitor's Card. The card, which was printed in England for the British Travel Association, was distributed free of charge to travel agencies in the countries with which the United Kingdom had concluded an agreement for the document's use. These travel agencies would provide the would-be traveler with a Visitor's Card upon request. Agreements to use the Visitor's Card were made with Luxembourg, the Netherlands, Belgium, France, Switzerland, and the Federal Republic of Germany. The laxity of these arrangements, which gave the authority to issue a passport-like travel document to people with an economic incentive to encourage travel, must have made the UK's borders seem dangerously vulnerable to many concerned with such matters.[81]

Efforts to end this vulnerability came first in the form of the Commonwealth Immigration Act of 1962. Under the Act, the rights of British subjects to enter the UK were substantially limited. It mandated that citizens of the Republic of Ireland, British Protected Persons, and many Commonwealth citizens became subject to immigration controls. As a result of the legislation, only three categories of persons were entitled to enter the United Kingdom freely: persons born in the United

Kingdom; persons holding a United Kingdom passport who were also citizens of the United Kingdom and colonies; and, finally, Commonwealth citizens who held such a passport issued in the United Kingdom or the Republic of Ireland. The purpose here was clearly to stanch what had been a steady inflow of non-white migrant labor from the Caribbean and the Indian subcontinent during the 1950s.[82] This legislation is especially peculiar in that – as a consequence of the crazy-quilt and jerry-built pattern of allegiances and privileges characteristic of the Commonwealth – it makes possession of a passport in certain cases the foundation for the applicability or not of immigration laws, rather than immigration laws the basis for the obligation to carry a passport. Underlying this set of dispensations was the notion of British subjecthood with close ties to the metropolis (viz., Commonwealth citizens who hold a UK passport *issued in the UK or Ireland*).

This principle became the foundation for an extraordinary set of immigration proposals occasioned by the prospect of the immigration of several thousand UK passport holders from Kenya in 1967–68. The Kenyan government had announced plans to "Kenyanize" the country's economic life, sending the considerable Asian population into a panic and into the arms of Great Britain, of which they were nationals. In response to the impending arrival of 7000 of these unfortunates, the Secretary of State for Home Affairs proposed on 22 February 1968, to introduce a bill to bring "under immigration control *citizens of the United Kingdom* holding United Kingdom passports *who have no substantial connection with this country*." This was an inventive but ominous oxymoron that would have made refugees of these Commonwealth citizens, for they had acquired their UK passports perfectly legitimately in the course of the negotiations over Kenyan independence in 1963. Those agreements had exempted the Asian Kenyans who were UK nationals from the terms of the Commonwealth Immigrants Act of 1962.

The Home Affairs secretary was looking down the road, perhaps, at over a million people potentially able to enter the UK free of immigration controls, but he seems to have grasped the relative novelty, at least in a putatively democratic country, of what he was doing. In the course of his remarks introducing the bill to the House of Commons, the Secretary asserted: "This is a unique situation. There has been no precedent for it, as far as I know. This will be the first occasion on which legislation of this sort has been proposed." It was not exactly the first time such a thing had been proposed, of course. An order of 25 November 1941 had stripped of their German citizenship all Jews domiciled abroad and confiscated their property in Germany, making refugees of them as well.[83]

The precarious situation of the Kenyan Asians of British nationality became especially clear when the government of India, a likely alternative destination, made clear that it would refuse them admission, "not by way of retaliation but to emphasize [to the UK government] the urgent necessity of allowing persons their rights of citizenship irrespective of the country of origin." The International Commission of Jurists called the Act "racist" and characterized by "unprecedented discrimination by creating a category of British citizens deprived of the right to enter the territory of a country of which they are nationals." The outcry forced the British to back off from parts of this scheme and led them to provide vouchers permitting repatriation to the UK to British Overseas Citizens, British Subjects (without citizenship), and British Protected Persons who were not dual nationals.[84]

Still, the episode made dramatically clear the extreme explosiveness of the racial politics of passports in the decolonizing United Kingdom, as well as the broader problem of who among the varieties of British subjects was to have unrestricted access to the territory of the UK. The British government addressed the matter of access to its territory in the Immigration Act of 1971, a comprehensive statute that introduced the categories of "patrial" and "non-patrial" and abolished the distinction between aliens and Commonwealth citizens that had previously governed entry and settlement in Great Britain. Thenceforth, only "patrials" had the right to enter Britain, although there were some substantial exceptions, such as citizens of member-countries of the EEC. The law had significant racial implications, because "patrials" were defined in such a way as to include the progeny of white people who migrated from Britain to most of its overseas possessions while excluding many whose Commonwealth citizenship would once have given them access to British soil. Non-patrials wishing to gain entry to Britain were required "to obtain a work permit issued by the Department of Employment for a specific job with a specific employer for a specific period of time." "Non-patrials," in other words, were transformed into guest workers. Despite the fact that the law actually expanded the number of those eligible for admission to Great Britain, its main target was to limit the access of non-whites to the territory.[85] Subsequent experience suggests that the law has not been very successful in achieving this aim.

The issues that provoked a postwar revision of Italian passport law concerned not so much getting in but – as usual in Italy – getting out. The law as proposed had, in fact, nothing whatever to do with entry into Italy by foreigners. Instead, the statute aimed to modernize various aspects of Italian passport legislation and to bring that legislation into conformity with clauses of the postwar Italian Constitution guaranteeing the freedom of citizens to leave and return to Italy. In particular, the law sought to remove from the realm of administrative discretion both the matter of the issuance of passports to particular persons and that of determining where they could go once supplied with a passport.

With respect to the latter issue, the 1967 law provided that passports were to be valid for all countries whose government Italy recognized, eliminating the potential for arbitrariness (and the extra work) involved in having to list the acceptable countries in each case. This provision excluded only four countries from the choice of possible destinations for Italians: China, [North] Korea, Vietnam, and the German Democratic Republic. The first three spots blacked out on the map are likely to have been included in deference to the foreign policy wishes of the United States; the presence there of the GDR probably reflected the Italian government's reluctance to violate the Hallstein Doctrine, which, as noted earlier, called for retaliation by the West German government against any country that established diplomatic relations with East Berlin. In this as in other respects, the passport law eventually adopted in late 1967 derived from Italy's status as a semiperipheral labor exporter, especially to Germany and the United States.

At the same time, references in discussion of the law to the "rapid progress of tourism" suggest that Italy's own "economic miracle" was taking hold, drawing more Italians into the widening stream of pilgrims to the wonders of the world.[86] The 1967 law only rationalized practices that had been going on *de facto* throughout the postwar period, for Italian labor had been a critical factor in the postwar economic booms in France and Germany. The freedom of Italian workers to take up employment in the more developed parts of Europe, undergirded by a deepening commitment to free labor mobility in the countries of the European Communities, surely contributed to economic improvements at home as well. In this respect, changes in Italian passport policies simply reflected broader trends toward easier mobility that were afoot in the European Community.

The drive toward greater freedom of movement in postwar Europe has been intimately connected with the effort to create a common market, and especially with the desire of the various states to "have recourse to manpower available in the territory of any other Contracting Party."[87] In 1957, article 48 of the treaty creating the European Economic Community proposed to eliminate controls on movement within the Community for nationals of its member states. Numerous agreements toward this end have been adopted in the intervening period in the form of bi- or multilateral arrangements as well as by supranational organizations such as the Council of Europe, the European Coal and Steel Community, the EEC, and the European Union. The so-called

Schengen Accords of 1985, mandating passportless travel for European Community nationals between France, Germany, and the Benelux countries, were the instruments ultimately designed to achieve the goal of unrestricted, passportless travel within Europe. Other countries have joined the accords in the meantime. Yet France, in particular, has been persistently skittish about giving up its national passport and reluctant about implementing the agreements.

The Federal Republic of Germany, by contrast, has generally been in the forefront of support for the project of European unification. Yet the West German government's enthusiasm for introducing the European passport, a matter debated in the legislature in the mid-1980s, may have had as much to do with the license it provided for introducing machine-readable control documents as with its value as a symbol of European unity. The government's desire to use this technology, along with the intimate relationship between new legislation on passports and personal identity cards, provoked a donnybrook debate in the *Bundestag*. Much of the controversy resulted from the presence in German politics of a new force that was disinclined to ignore the centrality of personal identification documents to the functioning of Nazism, namely the Greens. Accordingly, a good deal of the discussion swirled around the increasingly salient issue in German politics of "data protection" (*Datenschutz*), for the Greens' deputies harshly criticized the extent to which the personal information gathered in the course of issuing passports could be used for surveillance purposes by the government. In addition, more fundamental doubts were once again raised about the effectiveness of passport controls in controlling undesirables, among whom terrorists were uppermost in the minds of the more conservative deputies.[88]

In the end, however, those eager to stamp out the "terrorist threat" got their way, and the Federal Republic adopted machine-readable and (allegedly) unfalsifiable passports. A notable intermingling of domestic and international pressures underlay the adoption of the law. Personal identity cards had become increasingly acceptable as a substitute for a passport in intra-European travel, and the West German government had already moved toward introducing (putatively) non-falsifiable, machine-readable versions of those cards. In consequence, the government was loathe to forgo the "gain in security" thus achieved by allowing the passport to remain at a lower technological standard. If it had done so, a German traveler exiting from the Federal Republic would have been able to leave the country with a document regarded by the authorities as less reliable than the identity cards.[89]

From our current vantage point, perhaps the most striking feature of the law and the debate over its adoption was that, like the 1967 Italian passport legislation, it had virtually nothing to do with immigration. The similarity between the two pieces of legislation stops there, however. As noted previously, the Italian regulations, reflecting Italy's subordinate position in the regional and global economic system, were primarily concerned with facilitating departure. The German law, in contrast, expressed a long-standing (if hardly unbroken) preoccupation with surveillance and internal security.

Despite the lack of concern about immigration in the 1985–86 debates over the new West German passport law, worries about the vulnerability of the outer boundaries of the European Community have risen with the loosening of its internal borders. In late 1986, for example, the British Home Secretary, expressing fears obviously rooted in the UK's own experience with these matters, proposed the tightening of the Community's external controls as internal controls are relaxed. The Community responded by announcing the creation of a working group to explore these issues.[90] To be sure, as one commentator has put it: "The European communities have been instrumental in eroding the stringent passport control which has gripped Europe for the last fifty years."[91] But this has scarcely meant the end of passport and similar controls on cross-border movements in Europe.

Accordingly, one of the most important consequences of regional integration in Europe has been a heightened attentiveness to racial distinctions, at least on the part of the guardians of national borders. If travelers are not routinely required to produce documents demonstrating their nationality, and the continent is perceived by many of its inhabitants, however anachronistically, as "white," visible markers thought to signal membership grow in importance as reasons for suspecting that a person may be liable to movement controls as a non-national of the Community's member states. Skin color, hair, and the other stigmata of racial identity unavoidably move to the fore as means of identifying outsiders.

This background must be borne in mind if one is to evaluate satisfactorily the contemporary concern that states may be "losing control" of their borders.[92] These claims generally rest on two principal arguments: that liberal states are hamstrung by humanitarian concerns such as pressures for family reunification and the growing unpalatability of restrictive measures such as deportation, and that states lack the administrative capacity to control inflows of people.[93] While the arguments about humanitarian concerns certainly have some validity, this is hardly tantamount to saying that states lack the means to interdict unwanted immigrants or to use those means when they wish to do so.

With the loosening of the internal borders in the European Community as a result of the Schengen accords, for example, worries about the vulnerability of its outer boundaries have risen sharply and corresponding measures have been taken. Indeed, migration scholar Anthony Richmond has recently argued that "the most economically developed and affluent countries are banding together to protect their privileged position in much the same way that Afrikaners and others of European descent sought to maintain their dominance in South Africa" – not least with a variety of documentary controls on movement.[94] Much of the recent concern about unwanted immigration within the European Union has been focused on Italy as the perceived "weak link" in the Schengen countries' defenses against undesirables. In response, Italy recently adopted a new immigration law designed to tighten documentary requirements, penalize both illegal immigrants and migrant smugglers, and make deportations of illegals more swift and certain.[95] The continuing importance of national identity in determining access to the advantages offered by particular nation-states is amply revealed by the fact that those same European states that have been relaxing border controls internally remain preoccupied with excluding non-nationals of the member-states.

Moreover, even if they no longer need passports to traverse intra-Community frontiers, nationals of the European Union's member states still require documentation (typically the national ID card) to demonstrate their nationality, precisely because nationality is an ascribed status that *cannot be established without reference to documents*. Because the member countries of the Community are eager to deny access to their territories to non-nationals of its member states, the necessity of being able to establish one's nationality remains in force. Indeed, the persistently *disqualifying*, rights-*limiting* character of a passport as a marker of nationality has led to the growing phenomenon today of people *destroying* their documents in a desperate attempt to gain access, via the asylum process, to countries that have otherwise closed off access to people of their nationality.[96]

If anything, the documentary controls and other bureaucratic defenses that states have erected against unwanted migration are constantly being strengthened and rationalized. In this respect, the activities of the International Civil Aviation Organization – an agency formed in 1944 to facilitate air travel and that now includes some 182 member-countries – are of considerable importance. Country representatives to the ICAO meet regularly to try to standardize travel documents and upgrade them technologically. The organization has been particularly eager to encourage its member states to adopt machine-readable passports and visas, which contribute to "speeding up clearance operations, increasing security and providing additional safeguards against alteration or counterfeiting of identity information." By 1991, some 35 million of these ICAO-designed documents were in circulation among a number of states, "and their use is spreading rapidly."[97] There is little evidence that states are prepared to abandon documentary requirements of some kind, precisely because such restrictions can be used flexibly to regulate movement in response to fluctuating political and economic exigencies.

The existence of migration controls profoundly influences the likelihood, and thus the actual incidence, of migratory movements, though this broad structural feature of the international system tends to disappear in discussions of immigration control focused on short-term analyses of immigration flows. In a rejoinder to those who have argued that states are losing control of immigration, Brubaker has written:

> In global perspective, the very institution of citizenship, tying particular persons to particular states by virtue of the morally arbitrary accidents of birth, serves as a powerful instrument of social closure and a profoundly illiberal determinant of life chances. True, states are open at the margins to citizens of other states – but only at the margins. Seen from the outside, the prosperous and peaceful states of the world remain powerfully exclusionary.[98]

The monopolization by states of the legitimate means of movement has hardly disintegrated, and there seems little doubt that migratory movements would grow dramatically if it were to do so.[99]

While it may be true that advancing international human rights norms increasingly commit countries to granting the same civil and social (though not political) rights to those merely resident in their territories as those accorded their full citizens,[100] this development does not necessarily signal the "decline of citizenship"[101] for most people. These arguments primarily concern the access to rights only of immigrants, not of the main stock of the populations that constitute and replenish the bodies of citizens that constitute states. Such arguments therefore tend to overstate the significance of what are, in fact, relatively marginal phenomena. From this point of view, it seems quite exaggerated to claim that, "in terms of its translation into rights and privileges, [national citizenship] is no longer a significant construction."[102]

Even if this were true, it would not necessarily be a desirable development. For all the evil that nationalism has caused in the world, the original promise of the nation-state – that is, before what Arendt called the "conquest of the state by the nation"[103] – was to give birth to a broad community of at least putative legal, political, and eventually even social equality.[104] The contemporary erosion of "Fordist" welfare regimes at the same time that states are said to be "losing control" of their borders suggests that the deterioration of reasonably well-bounded "communities of character" may go hand in hand with a decline in the sense of "mutual aid."

Michael Walzer has noted that "to tear down the walls of the state is not . . . to create a world without walls, but rather to create a thousand petty fortresses."[105] One might argue that this is precisely what we observe today with the spread of gated communities – "fortified enclaves" that recall the walled cities of post-Carolingian Europe – across the United States, in Latin America, and elsewhere.[106] The state monopolization of the legitimate means of movement may be giving way to the return of the private regulation of movement, rooted in the ownership of property within well-fortified and privately policed enclaves. This appears to be the drift of developments; there are now estimated to be some 20 000 gated communities in the United States, up from a near-zero figure only thirty-five years ago.[107] If it is, passports – a product of the political rather than the economic determination of community membership – may give way to money as the relevant form of "identification" that permits access to specified territories. Should this scenario come to pass, we would indeed be witnessing the advent of "post-national membership."

CONCLUSION:
A TYPOLOGY OF "PAPERS"

I have tried to demonstrate in the preceding pages that identification documents such as passports have played a crucial role in modern states' efforts to generate and sustain their "embrace" of individuals and to use this embrace to expropriate the legitimate "means of movement." We have witnessed over the last two centuries a shift in the "reach" of documentary controls on movement from relatively small-scale spaces (municipalities) in dynastic states to "national" spaces and, more recently, to the "suprastate" level of the European Union. The documents involved have been critical to state-building activities in that they identify who is "in" and who is "out" in membership terms, and thus help distinguish who may make legitimate claims to the rights and benefits of membership. Here I explicate in greater detail the nature of the different types of such documents and analyze their relationship to states' assertion of a monopoly on the right to regulate people's movements.

Such documents come in three basic varieties. Clearly, (external) passports and internal passports or "passes" are not the same thing, although the former appears to have evolved out of the latter to a significant degree. External or international passports, most familiar today to those from "liberal-democratic" countries, are documents associated with movement across international state boundaries. They ordinarily constitute *prima facie* evidence of the bearer's nationality. In contrast, internal passports or passes are designed to regulate movements *within* the jurisdiction of a state. The identification card, common to societies on the European continent and to those that have endured colonial domination by Europeans, constitutes a "mixed" type, lying between the other two in terms of its role in control over movement and in securing citizen access to privileges and benefits.

The legal implications of the differences between "internal" and "external" passports are far-reaching. The right to *leave* and *return to* one's country is a prerogative that has come to be widely accepted in international human rights law, even if that law is often ignored in practice. The very enunciation of such "rights," it should be noted, indicates the extent to which states and the state system have expropriated and monopolized the legitimate means of movement in our time. In contrast to the widely . recognized right to leave and return, the right to move *within* one's country is a matter of the domestic law of sovereign states, subject only to the relatively weak and largely unenforceable strictures that may be imposed by human rights norms and conventions. Despite the emergence of a greater propensity to intervene militarily in the internal affairs of states in recent years, it remains true that "once a population is incorporated into complete citizenship, a nation-state is given almost complete authority to subordinate the population: It can expropriate, kill, and starve, with relatively little fear of external intervention."[1] Needless to say, this authority extends to nation-states' control over the movements of persons within their borders as well.

Most familiar to and accepted by people today is the right of states to control *entry*, a prerogative that has come to be understood as one of the quintessential features of sovereignty. It is important to note, however, that the widespread recognition of this prerogative is a fairly recent development. Recall that in his survey of the international legal opinion prevailing during the period immediately preceding the First World War, a German analyst of the international passport system, Werner Bertelsmann, was unable to muster any consensus for the view that states had an unequivocal right to bar foreigners from entry into their territory.[2]

Still, although they have come to be governed by different bodies of law, passports and passes share the function of regulating the movements of people within and across delimited spaces, thereby affirming states' control over bounded territories and enhancing their embrace of populations. Identification cards, by contrast, are not normally, or at least not primarily, used to regulate movement, but simply to establish the identity of the bearer for purposes of state administration and of gaining access to benefits distributed by the state. Let us examine each of these documents in turn.

INTERNATIONAL PASSPORTS

The contemporary international passport is primarily an expression of the attempt by modern nation-states to assert their exclusive monopoly over the legal means of movement. But the passport cannot be reduced exclusively to a mechanism of state control, even if this is certainly its principal function today. For in addition to enhancing bureaucratic domination over persons and territories, the passport vouchsafes the issuing state's guarantee of aid and succor to its bearer while in the jurisdiction of other states. Possession of a passport thus constitutes *ipso facto* evidence of a legitimate claim on the resources and services of the embassies or consulates of the issuing state – not to mention, in extreme cases, on its military power.

For the traveler, the modern passport also functions as a *laissez passer*, bearing witness to the document's partial origins in diplomatic practice. Passports issued by the United States, for example, carry the following inscription:

> The Secretary of State of the United States of America hereby requests all whom it may concern to permit the citizen/national of the United States named herein to pass without delay or hindrance and in case of need to give all lawful aid and protection.

Individual travelers have thus been transformed into quasi-diplomatic representatives of particular countries, simply because the issuing state has usurped the capacity to authorize movement and thus "embraced" the traveler as a citizen-member of the nation-state.

These ambiguities of passports indicate that these documents cannot be regarded merely as a means of governmental control. To use again the words of the United States passport, the "passport is a valuable citizenship and identity document. It should be carefully safeguarded. Its loss could cause [the bearer] unnecessary travel complications . . ." Modern passports, like their predecessors such as safe-conducts and *laissez passers*, facilitate movement into and out of spaces controlled by others than one's own sovereign. The ambiguous significance of the passport is suggested nicely by the fact that, in the United States, passports are *issued* by the Department of State (our "Foreign Ministry"), while passports are inspected upon entry by the Immigration and Naturalization Service, a branch of the Justice Department.

Despite these ambiguities, state control over individual movement is clearly the predominant purpose of passports today. The functions performed by the passport in contemporary interstate travel may be described as follows.

Departure

Routine travel across international borders involves a three-part process. First, the individual must depart his or her state of origin. Permission to leave one's country is by no means a foregone conclusion for people from many lands, despite the widespread recognition of such a right in international law.[3] Subjects of a state cannot automatically assume that they have the right to travel abroad, a situation both manifested and exacerbated by the fact that most states now require passports for departure from their domains. Because passports are also normally required for entry into other countries, the right to a passport from one's own government is virtually synonymous with the right to travel abroad. For example, a 1967 decision by the Supreme Court of India holding that Indian citizens have a constitutional right to travel abroad also held that, in consequence, the government had no prerogative to withhold a passport from any citizen who requested one, for such withholding would have nullified the basic right.[4] Consistent with this sort of ruling, most citizens of democratic states, at least, have come to assume that they will be able to acquire a passport on demand.

These considerations point to the usual connection between access to a passport and national citizenship. A recent German study of passport law put the matter as follows:

> Each state may issue passports only to those who stand in a close factual relationship to it. As a rule, therefore, passports are issued primarily to citizens of the state in question. Only in exceptional cases are travel documents issued to foreigners who happen to be within the state's territory.[5]

This presumed connection between citizenship and possession of a state's passport is, of course, the basis for the colloquial reference to the latter as an indication of possession of the former.

Formal citizenship is not necessarily the foundation of a claim to a passport for travel, however. As indicated by the inscription in the United States passport quoted above, states may elect to offer passports for interstate travel to their non-citizen *nationals* (e.g., "denizens" such as resident aliens, refugees, asylees, or non-citizen populations over which states hold dominion). In principle, states may elect to give passports to anyone they choose, restricted only by the terms of international law and agreements and by their own legal determinations concerning to whom they want to extend their protections while those persons are abroad. According to a leading expert on international migration law, in fact:

> [S]tate practice in the issuance of passports is so varied . . . that it is impossible to establish a connection in international law between the issuance of a passport and the acquisition or tenure of nationality. The problem is not merely that very many states issue travel documents of various kinds to travelers of foreign nationality but that some [s]tates issue passports, in the strict sense of the term, to aliens of defined classes.[6]

The widespread deviations from the standard assumption of a connection between citizenship and access to a passport invalidate this assumption, even though the principal function of a passport in international law is to demonstrate the identity and nationality of the bearer.

Because states and the state system have monopolized the power to regulate international movement, persons must possess a passport regardless of its origins of issuance; this situation creates anomalies for those who have difficulty in claiming affiliation with a particular state.

Conversely, states may choose *not* to grant passports to particular persons, irrespective of their legal status (citizens, denizens, etc.). States that curtail free departure and return generally deny their subjects many of the other rights we associate with modern citizenship and human rights norms. In 1982, for example, the apartheid-era South African courts ruled that access to a passport was a privilege rather than a right for both blacks and whites, and that the government could revoke any passport without cause or appeal.[7] Yet even nominally democratic states have been known to refuse to grant documents for international travel to certain groups of their citizens. As noted earlier, for example, the State Department gained the authority under the terms of the Internal Security Act of 1950 to deny passports for international travel to members of the Communist Party.[8] These examples indicate states' interest in monopolizing the authority to grant legal passage for political or ideological reasons.

Beyond the passport itself, a number of countries insist that the international voyager acquire an exit visa as evidence of the state's acquiescence in the traveler's (emigrant's?) departure. Rulers' fears of "brain drain" often underlie such restrictions. As a result, less developed countries in particular have frequently argued that they must retain control over the departure of their subjects in order to be able to take advantage of the expenditures on education and training from which those subjects have benefited.[9] Restrictive exit policies are frequently to be found, as Zolberg has noted, in countries that impose extraordinary tasks on their populations in either political or economic terms: "it is nearly impossible to secure compliance with drastic state demands if people are able to vote with their feet."[10] Exit visa requirements make this form of voting more difficult.

Freedom of movement and citizenship rights may thus diverge in significant and unexpected ways. Modern states have frequently denied their citizens the right freely to travel abroad, and the capacity of states to deny untrammeled travel is effected by those states' control over the distribution of passports and related documents, which have become essential prerequisites for admission into many countries.

Entry

Having successfully departed the country of origin, the traveler must gain access to a destination country. In an international state system that still regards sovereignty as its most fundamental principle, no traveler can presume that receiving states will grant access to their soil.[11] At a time when substantial but unknown numbers of people become "immigrants" simply by overstaying the legally prescribed duration of their stay, limiting ingress into the territory is the best way for states to avoid entering into a series of potentially costly obligations to non-nationals.[12] Passport and visa controls are crucial mechanisms for this purpose, the "first line of defense" against the entry of undesirables. Indeed, the fundamental purpose of passports from the point of view of international law is to provide to the admitting state a *prima facie* guarantee that another state is prepared to accept an alien that the destination state may choose not to admit or to expel.[13]

For the entry portion of the process of international travel, an entry visa may be required in addition to the passport. In such cases, the passport plays primarily the role of a certificate of identification, assuring the receiving government that would-be entrants are who they say they are. If required, the visa is the document of record authorizing entry. Passports have come to be more or less universally required for admission to a foreign territory, but they may not suffice in themselves for gaining such admission. In other words, they may be necessary but not sufficient conditions for legally crossing international borders.

Just as possession of citizenship in certain countries may present barriers to international movement, the *lack* of a nationality – the condition of statelessness – may also pose severe problems for anyone wishing to navigate the international state system and its strictures on individual movement. In a world in which the legitimacy of the nation-state remains quite strong, the lack of a nationality may indeed be a calamity, and has led the United Nations to adopt conventions intended to reduce the prevalence of statelessness. Dowty dourly concludes, however, that "these efforts have not stirred a broad response."[14] The loss by the stateless of a community to guarantee their rights has had particularly profound ramifications for their ability to gain entry into states typically defined since the early twentieth century in ethnonational terms and requiring documents to regulate who may enter.

Return

Finally, the traveler wishing to return to his or her country of origin will need a passport as unambiguous evidence of eligibility for readmission. As a matter of international law, states are required to admit their own citizens (and only them). This requirement has relatively little to do with the rights of persons as such, however. Rather, the doctrine of "restricted returnability" entails that states must admit their own citizens to avoid a situation in which the state whose national a person is might frustrate the legitimate efforts of another state to expel unwanted aliens. From the point of view of the individual, the ever more widely recognized right to return to one's own country flows not from rights inhering in the individual, but rather from the exigencies of sovereignty in the international state system. Just as the passport constitutes *prima facie* evidence that the issuing country will take in the bearer if he or she is denied entry into or expelled from the destination country, the document constitutes *prima facie* evidence of a claim to return to the issuing country.

In the end, therefore, passports are necessary *and sufficient* not for gaining entry to another country but only for returning to one's country of origin. Assuming that the document is deemed to be genuine, the passport indicates that the bearer has an incontestable right to enter the territory controlled by its issuing state. This unexpected fact explains the panic that grips international travelers abroad when they discover that they have lost their passport in some distant land. Beyond the fact that the lack of a passport is likely to complicate travel to any third countries, the ill-fated tourist fears especially that return to his or her place of origin may be difficult or even impossible in the absence of a passport. A lifeline has been cut, and the traveler is adrift in a world in which states have monopolized the authority to grant passage.

The external or international passport thus proves to be a document of considerable ambiguity. As the documentary expression of modern states' efforts to monopolize the means of legitimate movement, the passport concentrates in itself the enormous increase in modern states' control over individual existence that has evolved since the nineteenth century. At the same time, bearers of these documents are ensured that they may avail themselves of the protections that states may provide in an uncertain and potentially hostile world. Modern international passports thus join together diplomatic functions with mechanisms of state control. Their spread and more vigorous enforcement during and after the First World War – as nationalist fervor reached its height, opportunities for mass travel expanded, and nation-states consolidated their control over territories and populations – indicate that the control function predominates. Still, if passports were intended purely for purposes of state control, they would hardly command such a high price on many of the world's black markets.[15] In contrast, states' control over movement is the more or less exclusive function of internal passports.

INTERNAL PASSPORTS

The internal passport or "pass" has few similarities to the international passport, with its connotations of access to foreign territories and to the protections of the issuing state while in those other jurisdictions. Internal passports lack the ambiguity characteristic of the latter as documents that both enhance state control and afford their bearers various rights and immunities. Instead, the internal passport may be a state's principal means for discriminating among its subjects in terms of rights and privileges. In particular, passes may be used to regulate the movements of certain groups of subjects, to restrict their entry into certain areas, and to deny them the freedom to depart their places of residence (or of authorized presence, as in the South African mines and urban areas during the apartheid period). In the Soviet Union, internal passports in combination with the *propiska* system of housing registration restricted the movement and domicile of Soviet subjects, especially inhibiting their freedom to take up residence in certain urban areas and constraining the departure of collective farmers from the countryside.[16]

As modern states have expanded their administrative capacity to embrace the populations resident in their jurisdictions, controls on internal movement (and on residence) have sometimes been strengthened as well. Nowadays, the use of internal passports to control movement within state boundaries bespeaks illegitimate, authoritarian governments lording it over subdued or terrorized populations. Internal passports and passes constitute a reversion to practices generally abandoned by democratic nation-states by the twentieth century. Such states have generally dropped requirements that internal movement be specifically authorized in favor of a requirement that all persons be in a position to identify themselves to the authorities when the latter demand that they do so. The identity card has thus assumed much greater importance in such countries than internal travel documents *per se*.

IDENTITY CARDS

Identity cards confront us with a documentary "gray zone." They, rather than internal passports authorizing movement *per se*, may be used by the authorities to enforce intermittent checks on movement. Those required to have such documents (often after the age of sixteen) must produce them on the demand of the organs of social order, and failure to do so is likely to be a punishable offense. Even in democratic states, such identity checks may be used to control access to certain areas, although the degree to which such regulation is admissible may be subject to legal dispute. Yet such identity documents may also be necessary for gaining access to certain rights of democratic participation (e.g., voting), public services (e.g., medical care), and transfer payments ("welfare"). Internal identification documents that may be used by states to control movement therefore frequently share some of the features of international passports, enabling their bearers to obtain access to the benefits associated with citizenship in a particular state.

Modern democratic states typically require some kind of identification card that is used to regulate movement only sporadically, but that may be crucial for acquiring certain benefits of membership (e.g., the *Personalausweis* in Germany; the *carte d'identité* in France; the driver's license or social security card in the United States, although technically speaking these are not "ID cards"). In contrast, authoritarian states often impose pass controls on movement for significant elements of the population and enforce those controls more regularly and stringently; the connection of such documents to the provision of social services or the acquisition of the benefits of citizenship is dwarfed by their use for purposes of social control. It would perhaps be most useful to think of internal identity documents as reflecting, together with external and internal passports, points on a continuum defined by the efforts of modern states to grasp their populations and monopolize control over legitimate movement. What all of these documents share in common, however, is the use of pieces of paper to construct and sustain enduring identities for administrative purposes – that is, to enhance states' embrace of individuals.

Ultimately, passports and identity documents reveal a massive illiberality, a presumption of their bearers' guilt when called upon to identify themselves. The use of such documents by states indicates their fundamental suspicion that people will lie when asked who or what they are, and that some independent means of confirming these matters must be available if states are to sustain themselves as going concerns. In the face of potentially unstable and possibly counterfeit identities, states impose durable identities in order to achieve their administrative, economic, and political aims. Passports and other documents authorizing movement and establishing identity discourage people from choosing identities inconsistent with those validated by the state.

Documents such as passports and ID cards constitute the "proof" of our identities for administrative purposes, and permit states to establish an enduring embrace of those admitted into their communities and to distinguish them from others. Our everyday acceptance of "the passport nuisance"[17] and of the frequent demands from state officials that we produce "ID" is a sign of the success with which states have monopolized the capacity to regulate movement and thus to constrain the freedom of ordinary people to come and go, as well as to identify and constrain possible interlopers. The state monopolization of the means of legitimate movement has thus rendered individual travelers dependent on state (as opposed to private) regulation of their movements in a manner previously unparalleled in human history. In this regard, people have to some extent become prisoners of their identities, which may sharply limit their opportunities to come and go across jurisdictional spaces.

Passports and identification documents, the products of elaborate bureaucracies devoted to identifying persons and regulating their mobility, have made possible this extraordinary transformation of social life – a transformation akin to those identified by Marx when he analyzed the monopolization of the means of production by capitalists, and by Weber when he discussed the modern state's expropriation of the legitimate use of violence. To these two, we must add a third type of "expropriation" in order to make sense of the modern world – the monopolization of the legitimate means of movement by modern states and the state system more broadly. While hardly seamless, the monopolization of the legitimate means of movement by states and the international state system as a whole in the modern world has been extremely successful in regulating population movements and sorting out who belongs where. It has thus been critical to states' efforts to construct putatively homogeneous "nations," although this is an aim that in the very nature of the case is impossible to achieve.

INTRODUCTION

1 See "Law to Track Foreigners Entering US Postponed," *New York Times* (West Coast edition), 4 October 1998: A4; "Agreement Resolved Many Differences Over Policy as Well as Money," *New York Times* (West Coast edition), 16 October 1998: A17.
2 See Brubaker 1992, Chapter 1; Crowley 1998.
3 See especially Wiener 1998.
4 See Soysal 1994.
5 I have myself been involved in organizing an effort toward this end, although the temporal frame and geographic reach ultimately remained more restricted than we would have wished; see Caplan & Torpey 2000.
6 My thinking on this issue has been much influenced by Bull 1995.

1 COMING AND GOING

1 Meyer 1987: 53.
2 See Foucault 1979; 1980b; 1991.
3 See, e.g., Zolberg 1978; 1983. It seems to me that Zolberg's pleas have only recently begun to be heeded; see, e.g., Skran 1995.
4 See Anderson 1991. Michael Mann (1993: 218) has noted that "Anderson's 'print capitalism' could as easily generate a transnational West as a community of nations" in the absence of the institutionalization of the latter.
5 On the "identification revolution," see Noiriel 1991; he develops the notion of "The Card and the Code" (1996, Chapter 2). In her work on laws relating to naming, Jane Caplan (2000) speaks of the emergence of a "culture of identification" during the nineteenth century.
6 For a comparative analysis of slavery and serfdom as systems of control over movement, see Kolchin 1987, especially Chapter 1, "Labor Management."
7 For an in-depth study of such persons in one country, see Beier 1985.
8 Polanyi 1944: 104 (my emphasis); see also Chambliss 1964.

9 For an analysis of the origins of modern poor relief systems, see Gorski 1996, 1997. On the "nationalization" of poor relief in Germany, see Steinmetz 1993. One may well wonder whether recent changes in US welfare law that shift responsibility from the federal down to the state level have begun to reverse this trend.

10 On such organizations, see Spruyt 1994.

11 On passport controls in the Soviet Union and China, see Torpey 1997.

12 On this issue, see Gilboy 1997.

13 See, for instance, Mann 1993; Skocpol 1978; Tilly 1990. Randall Collins used the term "penetration" as a sort of taken-for-granted shorthand for understanding the essential activities of modern states in his comments on a presentation by Michael Mann at the Center for Social Theory and Comparative History, UCLA, 27 January 1997.

14 See Habermas 1987.

15 Mann 1993: 60.

16 Ibid. 61.

17 See Scott 1998. If I may borrow the metaphor with which Scott describes how he and Stephen Marglin arrived at roughly similar views about the functioning of states, he and I seem to have taken different trains to much the same destination; his train, however, was a "local," whereas mine was an "express." That is, Scott explores a variety of ways in which modern states have sought to make societies "legible," while I have tried to focus on one particular aspect of that effort – namely, identification documents deployed for the regulation of movement.

18 Douglas 1966: 121.

19 Brubaker 1996: 24; see also Powell & Dimaggio 1991.

20 Noiriel 1996: 45.

21 See Brubaker 1992.

22 Weber 1978: 922.

23 Brubaker 1996: 16, 19.

24 Tilly 1990: 25.

25 Giddens 1987: 47. Leonard Dudley (1991) has noted that writing originated (in ancient Sumeria) not as a means of recording speech, but in order to facilitate taxation.

26 See Goffman 1963.

27 See ibid. 1961.

28 See Foucault 1979; 1980a. For a critique of the negative assessment of the visual faculty in recent French social thought and its attendant attack on Enlightenment styles of thought with their emphasis on transparency, luminosity, and, well, *enlightenment*, see Jay 1993.

29 1996 California Driver Handbook, Department of Motor Vehicles, State of California [n.p., n.d.]. My italics.

30 For a discussion of recent developments in the understanding of surveillance in modern societies, see Lyon 1994. Lyon's exposition makes clear that it is not only states that have an interest in intensified surveillance, but private economic entities as well; this book concerns only the way that

states make use of and depend upon surveillance techniques in order to control movement.

31 Foucault 1979: 189.
32 Nordman 1996: 1123–4.
33 Anderson 1974: 37–8.
34 Bertelsmann 1914: 17–18.
35 Raeff 1983: 74, 89–90.
36 5 R. II, stat. 1, c. 2 (1381) section 7, cited in Plender 1988: 85 n. 12.
37 See Warneke 1996.
38 14 Charles II c. 12. This law appears to be what Karl Polanyi refers to as the "Act of Settlement (and Removal)."
39 Bendix 1978: 501ff.
40 Matthews 1993: 1–2.
41 See Kolchin 1987.
42 On this process, see Burke 1997; Elias 1978; 1982; Tilly 1990.
43 See Brubaker 1992: 37. It is suggestive that, at least according to one historian, the term "passport" was first attested to in France during this period. See Nordman 1987: 148.
44 Polanyi 1944: 63–7. I am grateful to Peggy Somers for reminding me of the usefulness of Polanyi's classic for the analysis I am trying to develop here.

2 "ARGUS OF THE *PATRIE*"

1 See Woloch 1994: 130, 393; see also Woloch 1986.
2 See Burguière & Revel 1989: 66; Grossi 1905: 145; Nordman 1996: 1123.
3 Cobb 1970: 243.
4 Hufton 1974: 229.
5 *Cahiers des États Généraux* (Paris: Librairie Administrative de Paul Dupont, 1868) [hereinafter *Cahiers*], vol. 4: 759. See also the *cahiers* of the bourg d'Ecouen, Paris hors les murs, *Cahiers*, vol. 4: 509.
6 *Cahiers*, vol. 4: 21.
7 Lefebvre 1962: 107.
8 On the Tennis Court Oath, see Lefebvre 1947: 84–5.
9 *Le Moniteur*, vol. 2: 22–3.
10 Greer 1951: 26.
11 Lefebvre 1962: 180–1.
12 *Collection complète des lois, décrets, ordonnances, réglements, etc.*, ed. J. B. Duvergier [hereinafter *Collection complète*], vol. 1 (Paris: A. Guyot, 1834): 195–6.
13 *Le Moniteur*, vol. 5, (Jeudi, 29 juillet 1790): 242–3. It seems likely that this was the same Peuchet who edited and wrote the introduction for the section on *police* – the theory and practice of public administration – in the *Encyclopédie méthodique* in 1789. Keith Baker describes Peuchet as a man "passionate in his defense of the values of modern society." See Baker 1990: 240 and *passim*. I am grateful to Jan Goldstein for pointing out this connection.

14 *Le Moniteur*, vol. 5: 351–2.

15 Greer 1951: 24.

16 Lefebvre 1962: 170.

17 See the "Décret qui ordonne d'arrêter toutes personnes quelconques sortant du royaume, et d'empêcher toute sortie d'effets, armes, munitions, ou espèces d'or et d'argent, etc." of 21 June 1791 in *Collection complète*, vol. 3: 53. Indications of the National Assembly's stunned reaction to the announcement of the King's flight can be found in *Archives parlamentaires de 1787 a 1860* [hereafter *AP*], 1. Serie, vol. 27 (Paris: Societé d'imprimerie et librairie administratives Paul Dupont, 1887): 358.

18 This paragraph and the next are based on the account in *Le Moniteur*, vol. 8: 741–3.

19 Lefebvre 1962: 207–8.

20 *Le Moniteur*, vol. 8: 737.

21 Ibid. 738.

22 Ibid.

23 "Décret qui indiqué les formalités a observer pour sortir du royaume" of 28 June 1791, in *Collection complète*, vol. 3: 68–9.

24 See *AP*, 1. Serie, vol. 27: 563–4.

25 Greer 1951: 26; see "Décret du 1er–6 août 1791, relatif aux émigrants," *AP*, 1. Serie, vol. 29: 8–89; and "Décret portant abolition de toutes procedures instruites sur les faits relatifs a la révolution, amnestie generale en faveur des hommes de guerre, et revocation du décret du 1er août dernier, relatif aux émigrans, 14–15 septembre 1791," *Collection complète*, vol. 3: 267–8.

26 See, for example, Lefebvre 1962: 187–8, 191–2.

27 Quoted in ibid. 105.

28 Quoted in Brubaker 1992: 47.

29 For a discussion of this process, see Guiraudon 1991; Wahnich 1997; n.d.

30 Noiriel 1996: 46.

31 On the "departmentalization" of France, see Woloch 1994: 26–31. The quotation is on p. 27.

32 For a brief discussion of the consequences of the measures taken in this regard until mid-1791, see *AP*, 1. Serie, vol. 28: 722; this discussion was the prelude to the "Décret pour l'exécution du tarif des droits d'entrée et de sortie dans les relations du royaume avec l'étranger, 6 août (28 juillet et) – 22 août 1791," *Collection complète*, vol. 3: 182–202.

33 Lefebvre 1964: 295.

34 Constitution française, *Collection complète*, vol. 3: 241.

35 One hundred and seventy-five years later, in striking down as unconstitutional the denial of passports to suspected Communists wishing to travel abroad, the American Supreme Court would find that "freedom of travel is a constitutional liberty closely related to rights of free speech and association." The principal rulings were handed down in *Kent v. Dulles* (1958) and in *Aptheker v. Secretary of State* (1964). See Plender 1988: 103; Turack 1972: 11.

36 *AP*, 1. Serie, vol. 30: 621.

37 Ibid. 632.

38 Greer 1951: 26–7.
39 "Décret relatif aux émigrans," *Collection complète*, vol. 4: 14–15.
40 See Lefebvre 1962: 213–15.
41 "Arrêté pris par le directoire du département du Nord, le 17 décembre · 1791," quoted in Wahnich 1997: 96.
42 See *AP*, 1. Serie, vol. 37: 608–9.
43 Wahnich 1997: 96–7.
44 *AP*, 1. Serie, vol. 36: 618; quoted in Wahnich 1997: 107–8.
45 Quoted in Lefebvre 1962: 217.
46 "Arrêté relatif aux certificats de residence (Extrait du registre des deliberations du corps municipal, du lundi, 9 janvier 1792)," *Le Moniteur*, vol. 11: 114.
47 *Le Moniteur*, vol. 10: 622.
48 *AP*, 1. Serie, vol. 37: 149.
49 Ibid. vol. 38: 14–27.
50 See Polanyi 1944: 106, 140. Georges Lefebvre has written (1962: 185) that "Bentham drew up a plan for judicial reform, which Mirabeau presented to the Constituent Assembly." Bernard Gainot of the Institut de l'Histoire de la Révolution française doubts this, however (personal communication, 20 September 1997). The Panopticon is of course the institution for surveillance and correction about which Foucault would later make so much in *Discipline and Punish.*
51 See the short biography in Caratini 1988: 379.
52 Lefebvre 1962: 213.
53 The previous two paragraphs are based on *AP*, 1. Serie, vol. 37: 608–9.
54 The discussion of the proposed passport law on which the following account is based can be found in *AP*, 1. Serie, vol. 37: 691–4.
55 See "Décret relatif a l'organisation d'une police municipale et correctionelle, 19–22 juillet 1791," *Collection complète*, vol. 3: 114ff.
56 *AP*, 1. Serie, vol. 37: 691–4.
57 *AP*, 1. Serie, vol. 38: 38–45.
58 *AP*, 1. Serie, vol. 37: 691–4. My italics.
59 See Soboul 1989: 1089.
60 The following account is based on *AP*, 1. Serie, vol. 38: 14–27.
61 Noiriel 1996: xvii–xviii.
62 In an article of 22 July 1854 in *La Lumière* (p. 156), one Richebourg claims to have introduced the idea of the passport photograph. I am grateful to Jane Caplan for this reference.
63 The protagonists mistakenly refer to this statute as the law of 19 *janvier* 1791.
64 See Caratini 1988: 522.
65 Lefebvre 1962: 215.
66 Fussell 1980: 28.
67 "Décret relatif aux passeports," 1 février – 28 mars 1792, *Collection complète*, vol. 4: 55–6.
68 This account is drawn from *AP*, 1. Serie, vol. 38: 14–27.

69 "Décret relatif aux passeports," 1 février – 28 mars 1792, in *Collection complète*, vol. 4: 55–6.

70 "Décret relatif aux passeports," 28–29 juillet 1792, in *Collection complète*, vol. 4: 272.

71 On this point, see Brubaker 1992: 67.

72 "Décret relatif au retablissement de la libre circulation des personnes et des choses dans l'intérieur," 8 septembre 1792, *AP*, 1. Serie, vol. 49: 472–3.

73 See *AP*, 1. Serie, vol. 50: 149; "Décret relatif à la libre circulation des personnes et des choses dans l'intérieur," 19 septembre 1792, in *Collection complète*, vol. 4: 470.

74 See Nordman 1987: 149–50.

75 Noiriel 1996: xviii; see "Loi que détermine le mode de constater l'état civil des citoyens, du 20 septembre 1792," *Le Moniteur*, vol. 14, pp. 173–6. Noiriel goes on to note that, in the Napoleonic period, the government went even further toward fixing identities for administrative purposes, imposing upon all individuals "the obligation to use a single given surname [and] establishing rules for its use and transmission."

76 Quoted in Brubaker 1992: 8.

77 "Décret qui bannit a perpetuité les émigrés français, 23–25 octobre 1792," *Collection complète*, vol. 5: 27.

78 "Décret qui oblige les émigrés rentrés en France a sortir du territoire français, 10 novembre 1792," *Collection complète*, vol. 5: 42.

79 "29 novembre – 1er decembre 1792, Décret qui leve la suspension des certificats de residence en ce qui concerne les négocians, les marchands et leurs facteurs, connus pour être dans l'usage de voyager pour leurs affaires de commerce," *Collection complète*, vol. 5: 63.

80 "7 decembre 1792, Décret relatif aux passeports à accorder à ceux qui seraient dans le cas de sortir du territoire français pour leurs affaires," *Collection complète*, vol. 5: 69. Interestingly, this decree was followed the same day by a "Décret qui abolit toutes les servitudes réeles ou conditions portées par les actes d'inféodation ou d'acensement, et qui tiennent à la nature du regime féodal."

81 *AP*, 1. Serie, vol. 54: 404.

82 "22–27 janvier 1793, Décret relatif a la nouvelle forme des congés des bâtimens de commerce français et des passeports a délivrer aux bâtimens étrangers," *Collection complète*, vol. 5: 118.

83 See *Le Moniteur*, vol. 15: 498, 531–2; vol. 16: 52; Guiraudon 1991: 595; Soboul 1989: 198.

84 *AP*, 1. Serie, vol. 59: 270.

85 *Collection complète*, vol. 5: 173–4.

86 Ibid. 175.

87 "10 avril 1793, Décrets relatifs aux passeports," *Collection complète*, vol. 5: 245.

88 Lefebvre 1964: 45–8. See the "Décret concernant les peines portées contre les émigrés, 28 mars – 5 avril 1793," *Collection complète*, vol. 5: 218–28.

89 See "Décret relatif aux passeports des agens du conseil exécutif et du comité du salut public," *Collection complète*, vol. 5: 279.

90 "22–26 juin 1793, Décret relatif aux citoyens servant dans les armées dirigées contre les rebelles," *Collection complète*, vol. 5: 350.

91 See *AP*, 1. Serie, vol. 81: 626.

92 Lefebvre 1964: 68; see the "Décret relatif aux gens suspects, 17 septembre – 12 août 1793," *Collection complète*, vol. 6: 172.

93 *Le Moniteur*, vol. 18: 333.

94 Wahnich 1997: 117.

95 Guiraudon 1991: 595. Wahnich (1997: 12, 21) claims that the armband was merely proposed (as article 7 of the *Loi sur les étrangers* of 3 August 1793), but never actually carried out.

96 Lefebvre 1964: 47; Wahnich 1997: 119–20.

97 Lefebvre 1964: 40.

98 Cobb 1970: 95.

99 Lefebvre 1964: 294.

100 See *Le Moniteur*, vol. 19: 134–5.

101 See *Le Moniteur*, vol. 21: 571.

102 The measure to suppress the municipal administration of Paris came on 14 Fructidor Year II. See Soboul 1989: 811.

103 *Le Moniteur*, vol. 22: 106. For more on the contention between the municipality of Paris and the central government over the authority to regulate movement, see *Le Moniteur*, vol. 23: 250–1.

104 "Décret interpretatif de celui du 6 fructidor, concernant les passeports," *Collection complète*, vol. 7: 287.

105 See the draconian law of 5 Ventose Year III (24 February 1795), which relieved of their responsibilities and confined to surveillance in their original municipality all functionaries of whatever level who had been relieved of their posts after 10 Thermidor (28 July 1794); *Le Moniteur*, vol. 23: 548–9. On the 1795 relaxation of these restrictions for cultivators, artists, and merchants, see *Le Moniteur*, vol. 23: 693.

106 Greer 1951: 97.

107 *Le Moniteur*, vol. 24: 365.

108 See Lefebvre 1964: 144–5.

109 "Arrêté du comité de sûreté général, du 17 messidor, l'an III de la république française une et indivisible [5 juillet 1795]," *Le Moniteur*, vol. 25: 180.

110 *Le Moniteur*, vol. 25: 421.

111 "23 messidor an III (11 juillet 1795), Décret qui ordonne aux étrangers nés dans les pays avec lesquels la République est en guerre de sortir de France, s'ils n'y sont pas domiciliés, avant le premier janvier 1792," *Collection complète*, vol. 8: 185.

112 *Collection complète*, vol. 8: 301–2.

113 "24 vendémiaire an II (15 octobre 1793), Décret contenant des mesures pour l'extinction de la mendicité," *Collection complète*, vol. 6: 229–33.

114 See "2 germinal an 4 (22 mars 1796) – Arrêté du Directoire exécutif, contenant des mesures relatives a l'exécution des lois," *Collection complète*, vol. 9: 66–7.

115 Cobb 1970: 95–6.

116 *Le Moniteur*, vol. 27: 535.

117 The speaker referred to was Jean-Gérard Lacuée; see *Biographie nouvelle des contemporains*, vol. 10: 261–2.

118 This account is based on *Le Moniteur*, vol. 27: 627–30; for the law itself, see "14 ventôse an 4 (4 mars 1796), Loi qui détermine le mode de délivrance des passeports à l'étranger," *Collection complète*, vol. 9: 53. Having adopted this measure, the government almost immediately adopted another designed to reduce the issuance of passports to those using assumed names, and to punish those involved. See "17 ventôse an IV (7 mars 1796), Loi contenant des mesures pour empêcher les délivrances des passeports sous des noms supposés," *Collection complète*, vol. 9: 53–4.

119 See Souhait's remarks in the Council of 500 of 24 Ventose Year IV (14 March 1796), in *Le Moniteur*, vol. 27: 710.

120 "4 nivôse an 5 (24 December 1796), Arrêté du Directoire exécutif, qui prescrit des mesures relatives aux passeports des étrangers arrivant en France," *Collection complète*, vol. 9: 250. The Bureau (Ministry) of General Police had been created by the Committee of Public Safety at the end of Floreal Year II (second half of May 1794). See Lefebvre 1964: 122.

121 "21 germinal an 5 (10 avril 1797), Arrêté du Directoire exécutif, concernant les passeports délivrés par les ministres et envoyés des États-Unis d'Amerique," *Collection complète*, vol. 9: 339.

122 Probably the best known response was Burke's mordant *Reflections on the Revolution in France* (1790), which reflected much elite opinion.

123 See Greer 1951: 102–3; Lefebvre 1964: 197–201.

124 Plender 1988: 65; for the run-up to the law, see *Le Moniteur*, vol. 29: 22, 29, 33, 39, and 43.

125 *Collection complète*, vol. 10: 79–80.

126 Tocqueville 1955: x.

3 SWEEPING OUT AUGEAS'S STABLE

1 On this point, see the discussion in Sheehan 1989: 232–3.

2 Lüdtke 1989: 46.

3 See H. H. 1866: 222, where the author writes that "passports (*Pässe*) themselves are first mentioned under the name of 'passports' (*Passporten*) in article LXXXIX of the *Reiterbestallung* of Speyer in 1570." I am much indebted to Mathieu Deflem for passing along this valuable article.

4 H. H. 1866: 224–5.

5 Grossi 1905: 136.

6 H. H. 1866: 225.

7 Grossi 1905: 122.

8 Hansen 1961: 50.

9 See Sheehan 1989: 296–302; the quotation is from p. 301.

10 Koch 1985: 18.

11 "Allgemeines Paßreglement für gesammte Königlich-Preussische Staaten, vom 20. März 1813," *Gesetzsammlung für die königlichen preussischen Staaten* [hereinafter *Gesetzsammlung*] *1813*: 47–57.

12 Bertelsmann 1914: 18.

13 Koch 1985: 23.

14 "Allgemeines Paßreglement für gesammte Königlich-Preussische Staaten, vom 20. März 1813," *Gesetzsammlung 1813*: 47–57.

15 Sheehan 1989: 317–18; the quotation is from p. 318.

16 "Deklaration des Pass-Reglements vom 20. März 1813 in Ansehung der Frachtfuhrleute, Handwerksgesellen und Viehhaendler. Vom 20. Februar 1814," *Gesetzsammlung 1814*: 10–12. The edict was issued from the King's field headquarters at Troyes, over both his name and that of Hardenberg.

17 See Sheehan 1989: 401–6.

18 "Allgemeines Paßedikt für die Preussische Monarchie," 22 June 1817, in *Gesetzsammlung 1817*: 152ff.

19 H. H. 1866: 229–30.

20 Lüdtke 1989: 82.

21 Brubaker 1992: 69–70. The push for greater freedom of movement even extended beyond the boundaries of the Confederation itself; for an example, see the "Erklärung wegen Ausdehnung der seit 1812 zwischen der königlichen Preussischen Regierung und der Schweizerischen Eidgenossenschaft bestehenden Freizügigkeits-Übereinkunft, auf sämmtliche jetzige Königliche Preussische und zur Schweizerischen Eidgenossenschaft gehörige Lande," 25 October 1817, in *Gesetzsammlung 1817*: 1.

22 Brubaker 1992: 69–70.

23 Walker 1964: 75.

24 Ibid. 13–20, 29–30; the quotation is from p. 30.

25 Hansen 1961: 110.

26 Walker 1964: 20, 24, 30; the quotation is from p. 20.

27 See Walker 1971.

28 Hansen 1961: 170.

29 Ibid. 155–6.

30 See Polanyi 1944: 77–8, 88–9; see also Hansen 1961: 128–9.

31 For a succinct discussion of the historiographical controversy over the significance of the Speenhamland system of allowances, see Marshall 1985; the quotation here is from p. 43. I am grateful to Phil Gorski for this reference.

32 MacDonagh 1961: 26. The reality of a bicontinental, "North Atlantic" Irish society at this time – as well as many other examples that could be cited, perhaps especially including the overseas colonies of Chinese – should be taken into account by those who have only recently discovered the phenomenon of "transnationalism," or who think it new.

33 Saggar 1992: 31.

34 First British Passenger Act (43 Geo. III, cap. 56); see MacDonagh 1961: 61–4.

35 See Hobsbawm 1962: 211; MacDonagh 1961: 64–5.
36 Quoted in Hansen 1961: 104.
37 Hansen 1961: 97; MacDonagh 1961: 64–5.
38 Hansen 1961: 129–30, 242.
39 "Magna Carta, 1215," in Rothwell 1975: 320–1.
40 Hansen 1961: 131–5.
41 6 & 7 Will. IV, c. 11, in *Statutes Revised*, vol. VII, 2 & 3 William IV to 6 & 7 William IV, A. D. 1831–1836: 975–8.
42 Saggar 1992: 27.
43 Bergmann & Korth 1985: 13–14.
44 Note that *jus sanguinis* as migratory mercantilism tends to presuppose that the original population from whom citizenship may be acquired by descent constitutes "our" people; in a later context of large-scale immigration of suspect "others," it becomes a way of excluding them and their descendants from full citizenship. Of course, other political considerations – especially the national mythology concerning the matter of openness to immigrants – plays a role in these issues as well. I am grateful to Patrick Weil for pointing out that the *jus soli* principle for granting citizenship held sway under the *ancien régime*, and was thus not "republican" in inspiration as Brubaker has claimed.
45 Brubaker 1992: 69–70.
46 David Blackbourn has noted that resistance to changes in communal citizenship codes in southwestern Germany was fierce and was only overcome in the 1860s. See Blackbourn, "The Discreet Charm of the Bourgeoisie: Reappraising German History in the Nineteenth Century," in Blackbourn & Eley 1984: 191–2.
47 Walker 1971: 267.
48 Bergmann & Korth 1985: 14.
49 Brubaker 1992: 71.
50 Ibid. 65.
51 See Walker 1964: 95.
52 Steinmetz 1993: 113–14.
53 Ibid. 114.
54 Grossi 1905: 135–6; Tammeo 1906: 141; Walker 1964: 138, 142–3, 150–1.
55 See Hansen 1961: 288–90, 304.
56 This paragraph and the one following are based on the account in H. H. 1866: 230–2. Note the wide compass of the term "German states," which at this point also routinely included Austria. For more on the meaning of "national unification" in Germany, see below.
57 *Staatsangehörige*, as opposed to *Staatsbürger*, with its implication of a specific package of rights à la T. H. Marshall (1964).
58 Grossi 1905: 139–40.
59 H. H. 1866: 232–3, 238ff. See the remarks of Dr Friedenthal in *Stenographische Berichte über die Verhandlungen des Reichstages des Norddeutschen Bundes*, I. Legislatur-Periode, Session 1867 [hereinafter *Verhandlungen*], 1. Band, Berlin, 1867: 177.

60 H. H. 1866: 240–1. For a study of the rise of rail travel during the nineteenth century, see Schivelbusch 1980.
61 Hamerow 1969: 98–9.
62 Ibid. 160–1.
63 Ibid. 98.
64 Hansen 1961: 280.
65 See Hobsbawm 1975: 193–5.
66 Lüdtke 1989: 77–8; see also pp. 78–9, 82, 87, and 110.
67 The text of the treaty is reproduced in H. H. 1866: 251–3.
68 On this point, see Lüdtke 1989: 79.
69 Craig 1978: 11, 12, 18–19.
70 Steinmetz 1993: 9–10.
71 *Verhandlungen*, 2. Band, Anlagen, Berlin, 1867: 23.
72 Paragraph 3 of the 1865 passport law had included such a provision as well. In their recent treatise on passport and citizenship law, however, Bergmann and Korth (1990: 5) trace this liberal innovation to the 1867 law, presumably because of the latter's subsequent adoption as the passport law of the Empire.
73 See Tocqueville 1969, especially Volume 2.
74 On these points, see *Verhandlungen*, 2. Band: 24.
75 For these proposed amendments, see Aktenstücke 26, 31, 33, 35, and 39 in *Verhandlungen*, 2. Band: 72–3, 85.
76 The record of the debate can be found in *Verhandlungen*, 1. Band: 177–89.
77 See Hobsbawm 1975: 196.
78 Aktenstück 39, *Verhandlungen*, 2. Band: 85.
79 Craig 1978: 68–9.
80 "Gesetz über das Paßwesen," 12 October 1867, in *Bundesgesetzblatt des Norddeutschen Bundes, 1867* (Berlin, 1868): 33–5. For two brief legal commentaries, see Brunialti 1915: 679; Grossi 1905: 141.
81 *Verhandlungen*, 1. Band: 183.
82 "Gesetz über die Freizügigkeit," 1 November 1867, *Bundesgesetzblatt des Norddeutschen Bundes, 1867* (Berlin, 1868): 55–8.
83 Steinmetz 1993: 4.
84 Hobsbawm 1975: 36.
85 See Tocqueville's "Speech in the Chamber of Deputies, 27 January 1848," included as Appendix III in Tocqueville 1969, pp. 749–58. Tocqueville (1971) quotes from the relevant portions in his *Recollections*: 16–19.
86 On the weakness of the socialist movement during this period, see Hobsbawm 1975: 108–15. Still, a wave of labor unrest swept across the continent in 1868, touching Germany as well; see ibid. 112.
87 "Verordnung, betreffend die vorübergehende Einführung der Paß-Pflichtigkeit für Berlin, 26 June 1878," *Reichsgesetzblatt 1878*: 131. Although the measure was explicitly stated to be temporary, I have not found any order rescinding it.
88 I share George Steinmetz's assessment of the transformation of nineteenth-century German historiography launched by David Blackbourn and Geoff

Eley (1984) in their path-breaking book, *The Pecularities of German History*: "Eley and Blackbourn have introduced a higher level of conceptual clarity and rigor into the study of the Prussian-German state. They waste no time complaining about the weakness of an idealized middle-class liberalism, turning instead to the problem of understanding what German liberalism actually did during the Empire. They reject the certitudes of economic 'bases' determining political and ideological 'superstructures' and attend carefully to the failures as well as the successes of German governments in cementing a broad ruling-class alliance. They have mustered considerable evidence for the claim that the Prussian-German state was founded on a bourgeois basis, that Bismarckism promoted capitalism even without direct representation of the bourgeoisie, and that after 1890 the bourgeoisie was increasingly the state's privileged political partner." Steinmetz 1993: 85.

89 For an extended discussion of this point, see Geoff Eley, "The British Model and the German Road: Rethinking the Course of German History Before 1914," in Blackbourn & Eley 1984; the quotations are from pp. 144–5.

90 On the points made in this and the preceding paragraph, see Hobsbawm 1975: 88; Steinmetz 1993: 5–6.

91 See Hobsbawm 1975: 35–9. The quotations are from pp. 35–6. See also Brunialti 1915: 679.

92 Quoted in Plender 1988a: 67.

93 See Zeldin 1973: 198–9.

94 The quotation is from *La grande encyclopédie* (multiple volumes published around 1900), vol. 26: 57; see also Brunialti 1915: 676; Burguière & Revel 1989: 67; Plender 1988: 90 n. 132; Vattel 1863: 514 n. 1.

95 Bolis 1871, quoted by Senator Pierantoni in the debate over the 1901 Italian passport law, *Atti Parlamentari della Camera dei Senatori: Discussioni*, Legislatura XXIa, 1a Sessione 1900–1901 (Rome: Forzani e C. Tipografi del Senato, 1901): 922.

4 TOWARD THE "CRUSTACEAN TYPE OF NATION"

1 Zolberg 1997: 315.

2 See Higham 1988: 8; Zolberg 1978: 250–1.

3 Hansen 1961: 102; Zolberg 1978: 256.

4 Salyer 1995: 4. On the bonding system, see Hansen 1961: 257; MacDonagh 1961: 51.

5 Hansen 1961: 260; Salyer 1995: 4.

6 "An act regulating the diplomatic and consular systems of the United States," 18 August 1856, Sec. 23, *US Statutes at Large*, vol. 11: 60–1. See also United States, Department of State, Passport Office 1976: 9, 26, 31; Hunt 1898: 37–41; the quotation is on p. 41.

7 Bensel 1990: ix. On some of the difficulties of establishing national authority in the United States prior to the Civil War, see also Lipset 1979: 34–5.

8 See Foner 1970: 134–8. In one of those ironies of history, the assertion of "states' rights" came to be associated with Republican anti-slavery agitation against the federal Fugitive Slave Act of 1850. Foner notes laconically (137–8) that the radical Republicans' enthusiasm for the traditionally pro-slavery notion of states' rights was "quite remarkable in view of the conduct of the radicals during Reconstruction."

9 See Moore 1966, Chapter 3. For Lincoln's views on the war, see McPherson 1991.

10 The decision was handed down in the case of *Crandall* v. *Nevada*. See Hall 1992: 877.

11 For an intriguing discussion from a global standpoint, see McNeill 1983.

12 See Higham 1988: 15–17.

13 See Coolidge 1969: 77, 148; Zolberg 1997: 299–301.

14 The quotation is from Coolidge 1969: 160; see also Chan 1990: 62; Zolberg 1997: 300–1.

15 On the objections of the French Foreign Ministry to anti-immigration policies in late nineteenth-century France, see Noiriel 1991: 94–5.

16 Fitzgerald 1996: 114.

17 Salyer 1995: 7. For the story of working-class opposition to the Chinese in California and its role in the coming of the Chinese Exclusion Act, see Saxton 1971.

18 The law covered those of Chinese "race" rather than simply the subjects of the Emperor, despite the fact that this violated treaties with other countries, such as Canada, who objected to having to "keep" Chinese who failed to gain admission into the United States.

19 Salyer 1991: 86, n. 14.

20 See Coolidge 1969: 169.

21 See Salyer 1991: 60–1; 1995: 17–19.

22 Coolidge 1969: 183–5; the quotation is from p. 185. See also Salyer 1995: 19–20.

23 See Chan 1990: 62; Coolidge 1969: 190–208.

24 Salyer 1995: 22–3.

25 Coolidge 1969: 233. This and the two preceding paragraphs are based on Coolidge: 209–33.

26 Quoted in Salyer 1995: 26. For an excellent general discussion of immigration to the United States and of efforts to restrict it during this period, see Chan 1990.

27 Salyer 1991: 61–2; 1995: 32.

28 See United States Department of Justice, Immigration and Naturalization Service 1991: 6; Chan 1990: 62–4; Salyer 1995: 32; "An Act to amend sections four thousand and seventy-six, four thousand and seventy-eight, and four thousand and seventy-five of the Revised Statutes," 14 June 1902, *US Statutes at Large*, vol. 32, Part I: 386. Salyer contends that Chinese immigration fell under the general administration of immigration only with the creation of the Bureau of Immigration in 1903, whereas Fitzgerald argues that this took place with the Sundry Civil Act of June 6, 1900; see Fitzgerald

1996: 126. According to Plender (1988: 139–40), the practice of issuing American passports to Filipinos only came to an end when the odd coalition of anti-Filipino exclusionists and the islands' independence activists obtained the Philippines' departure from American overlordship in 1936.

29 See Fitzgerald 1996: 116, 120–3. See also United States Department of Justice, Immigration & Naturalization Service 1991: 5–6. On the overseas medical examination of would-be emigrants that was prompted by American immigration rules, see the report of the Dillingham Commission in US Congress, Senate, Committee on Immigration 1911b: 71ff.

30 Cf. Brubaker 1992: 69–70.

31 On this point, see Clark 1984: 33.

32 See the law no. 23 on emigration and the Royal Decree no. 36 on passports, both of 31 January 1901, in *Raccolta Ufficiale delle Leggi e dei Decreti del Regno d'Italia, 1901*, vol. 1 (Roma: Stamperia Reale, 1901) [hereinafter *Raccolta Ufficiale*]: 50–78 and 218–39. For a discussion of the emigration law's various provisions, see Foerster 1919: 477–86.

33 Remarks of Eugenio Valli in *Atti del Parlamento Italiano*, Camera dei Deputati, Sessione 1900, 1. della XXI Legislatura, vol. 1 (Roma: Tipografia della Camera dei Deputati, 1900): 604. For an extremely critical contemporary Italian view of American immigration restrictions and of the support for them from the American labor movement, see Tammeo 1906: 106.

34 See Pantano's remarks during the debate of 30 November 1900, in *Atti del Parlamento Italiano*, Camera dei Deputati, Sessione 1900, 1. della XXI Legislatura, vol. 1: 770.

35 On efforts to restrict the immigration of foreign radicals during this period, see Preston 1963.

36 For the attitudes of Italian elites toward emigration during this period, see Foerster 1919: 475–6; on the decline in left-wing voting in areas of high emigration, see Dowty 1987: 50–1, citing MacDonald 1963–64.

37 The quotation, which is of the Italian nationalist Enrico Corradini, is in Foerster 1919: 495. On the Libyan war, see Clark 1984: 153–6.

38 On the failures of Italian imperialist designs, their consequences for the emigration, and the 1912 citizenship law, see Foerster 1919: 486–501.

39 On the distinction between "national" and "nationalist," see Mann 1993: 32–3 and *passim*.

40 See Brubaker 1992: 85–6 and *passim*; Noiriel 1996: 55.

41 Noiriel 1991: 89.

42 See Noiriel 1996: 57.

43 Noiriel 1991: 166–9.

44 See Dallier 1914: 32–3; Noiriel 1996: 66–8.

45 Dallier 1914: 43; Noiriel 1996: 60.

46 Dallier 1914: 56–61; the quotation is from p. 58; see also Noiriel 1996: 60–1. For more on the *carnet des nomades*, see Kaluszynski 2000.

47 And not, as Bergmann and Korth suggest (1990: 5), in the First World War.

48 "Verordnung, betreffend die Paßpflichtigkeit der aus Rußland kommenden Reisenden," 2 February 1879, in *Reichsgesetzblatt 1879*: 9.

49 "Verordnung, betreffend die Paßpflichtigkeit der aus Rußland kommenden Reisenden," 14 June 1879, *Reichsgesetzblatt 1879*: 155.

50 "Verordnung, betreffend die Paßpflichtigkeit der aus Rußland kommenden Reisenden," 29 December 1880, *Reichsgesetzblatt 1881*: 1.

51 "Verordnung, betreffend die Paßpflichtigkeit der aus Rußland kommenden Reisenden," 30 June 1894, *Reichsgesetzblatt 1894*: 501.

52 On the debate over the "Polonization" of the German east as a result of labor importation, see Herbert 1990: 9–37. The quotation is from pp. 12–13.

53 See Brubaker 1992: 133.

54 Weber 1988b: 456.

55 See Weber 1988a: 504.

56 Knoke 1911: 78; quoted in Herbert 1990: 32.

57 See Herbert 1990: 34–44; the quotation is from p. 43.

58 On the anomalous stringency of passport requirements for entry into Russia during this period, see Bertelsmann 1914, "Einleitung"; Brunialti 1915: 679.

59 Preussische Verordnung of 1 December 1892, quoted in Bertelsmann 1914: 20–1.

60 Bertelsmann 1914: 18–19.

61 See Lucassen 1997: 2.

62 Plender 1988: 90 n. 132; see also Burguière & Revel 1989: 67.

63 Noiriel 1996: 61, 273–4.

64 Zolberg (1997: 312–13) notes that in England before 1905, " 'immigrant' rapidly became synonymous with Jew, a group so undesirable that they were compared unfavorably with the despised Irish and . . . categorized [in the popular mind] as close to the Chinese."

65 4 & 5 Geo. 5, c. 12, 5 August 1914, *The Public and General Acts, 1914*: 26–8. In a pattern that would recur in British history after the Second World War, the nearly simultaneous British Nationality and Status of Aliens Act 1914 (7 August 1914, 4 & 5 Geo. 5 c. 17), further described as an "Act to consolidate and amend the Enactments relating to British Nationality and the Status of Aliens," was motivated by the need to determine who exactly was an alien for purposes of alien restriction.

66 "Verordnung, betreffend die vorübergehende Einführung der Paßpflicht," 31 July 1914, *Reichsgesetzblatt 1914*: 264–5.

67 "Verordnung, betreffend anderweite Regelung der Paßpflicht," 16 December 1914, *Reichsgesetzblatt 1914*: 521–2.

68 "Verordnung, betreffend anderweite Regelung der Paßpflicht," 21 June 1916, *Reichsgesetzblatt 1916*: 599–601.

69 "Bekanntmachung, betreffend Ausführungsvorschriften zu der Paßverordnung," 24 June 1916, *Reichsgesetzblatt 1916*: 601–9.

70 "R. decreto del 6 agosto 1914, n. 803, che sospende la facoltá di emigrare ai militari del R. esercito e della R. Marina," *Raccolta Ufficiale, 1914*, vol. 3 (Rome: Stamperia Reale): 2804–5.

71 "R. decreto 2 maggio 1915, n. 635, concernente l'espatrio per ragioni di lavoro," *Raccolta Ufficiale, 1915*, vol. 2 (Rome: Stamperia Reale): 1723–7.

According to the "Decreto Luogotenenziale 23 dicembre 1915, n. 1825, che proroga sino alla fine della guerra il termine di validità stabilito nell'art. 12 del R. decreto 2 maggio 1915, n. 635, circa l'espatrio per ragioni di lavoro," (*Raccolta Ufficiale, 1915*, vol. 5 [Rome: Stamperia Reale]: 4623–4), the requirement that those going abroad to work present a labor contract before doing so was to be abolished with the end of the war.

72 "Decreto-legge del 2 maggio 1915 [n. 634], concernente il soggiorno degli stranieri in Italia," *Raccolta Ufficiale, 1915*, vol. 2 (Rome: Stamperia Reale): 1708–22.

73 "Decreto Luogotenenziale 16 marzo 1916, n. 339, che sospende temporaneamente il rilascio dei passaporti per l'estero," *Raccolta Ufficiale, 1916*, vol. 1 (Rome: Stamperia Reale): 643–4.

74 "Decreto Luogotenenziale 23 luglio 1916, n. 895, che approva le norme relative all'entrata e all'uscita di persone dal Regno," *Raccolta Ufficiale, 1916*, vol. 2 (Rome: Stamperia Reale): 1896–1918.

75 "Decreto Luogotenenziale 27 agosto 1916, riguardante la concessione dei passaporti per l'interno," *Raccolta Ufficiale, 1916*, vol. 3 (Rome: Stamperia Reale): 2369–71.

76 On the characteristics of the army fielded by Italy in the First World War, see Clark 1984: 186–8.

77 "Verordnung, über die Abänderung der Verordnung vom 21. Juni 1916, betreffend anderweite Regelung der Paßpflicht," 10 June 1919, *Reichsgesetzblatt 1919*: 516–17. Three weeks earlier, the German government had announced stiffened penalties for transgression of the passport laws and for various violations of proper procedure with respect to border controls. See "Verordnung, betreffend Strafbestimmungen für Zuwiderhandlungen gegen die Paßvorschriften," 21 May 1919, *Reichsgesetzblatt 1919*: 470–1.

78 *Aliens Order* 1920, 25 March 1920, *The Statutory Rules and Orders and Statutory Instruments Revised to 31 December 1948*, vol. II (London: His Majesty's Stationery Office, 1950): 1–48.

79 "Decreto-legge Luogotenenziale 18 maggio 1919, n. 1093, che stabilisce l'obbligo del passaporto per i cittadini che sono considerati o si presumono emigranti, fissando altresí norme per il suo rilascio e le penalitá da infliggersi ai contravventori," *Raccolta Ufficiale, 1919* vol. 3 (Rome: Tipografia delle Mantellate, 1919): 2381–4.

80 International Labour Office 1928: 85.

81 Dowty 1987: 83.

82 Executive Order No. 2285, 15 December 1915.

83 See Chan 1990: 63; Higham 1988: 203–4; the text of the law can be found at 39 Stat. 874 (1917). For some of the legal complications of American racial classifications during this period, see Haney-Lopez (1996).

84 *US Statutes at Large*, vol. 40, Part I: 559; Executive Order No. 2932, 8 August 1918.

85 Public Law #79, "An Act To regulate further the entry of aliens into the United States," 10 November 1919, *US Statutes at Large*, vol. 41, Part I: 353.

86 The quotation is from Commissioner General of Immigration Anthony Caminetti in United States, Department of Labor, Bureau of Immigration 1919: 67–8. As a member of the US House of Representatives from the state of California in the late nineteenth century, Caminetti had been active in efforts to deport Chinese criminals. See Coolidge 1969: 230.

87 See Paxton 1975: 95.

88 Letter of F. W. Berkshire, Supervising Inspector, Mexican Border District, El Paso, Texas, to Commissioner-General of Immigration, 5 February 1918, US Department of Labor, Immigration Service File No. 54261/276.

89 See United States, Department of Labor, Bureau of Immigration, 1918: 321.

90 For more about the role of the INS and the Border Patrol in ensuring labor supply to agricultural businesses in the Southwest, see Calavita 1992. I am also grateful to Professor Calavita for a personal communication (12 August 1998) clarifying my understanding of the origins of the Border Patrol.

91 The relevant history is detailed in Higham 1988, Chapter 11. Canadians and Latin Americans were exempted from the quota limitations.

92 United States, Department of Labor, Immigration and Naturalization Service 1934: 2.

93 Zolberg 1997: 308–9; see also Fitzgerald 1996: 132; Higham 1988: 324. For details on the workings of the system, see United States, Department of Labor, Immigration and Naturalization Service 1934: 2ff.

94 See Noiriel 1996, Chapter 2.

95 On the notion of the twentieth-century "protectionist state," see Strikwerda 1997.

96 On the concept of "infrastructural power" and its importance for understanding the novelty of European states since the nineteenth century, see Mann 1993: 59–61.

97 For a discussion of the role of the welfare state and its beneficiaries in the labor movement in promoting immigration restriction during this period, see Lucassen 1998.

98 This is a central theme of Mann 1993; for the case of France, see Noiriel & Offerlé 1997. My argument here parallels that of Zolberg (1997: 293, 304), who argues that the "internalist" analyses of immigration restriction adduced by American liberals such as John Higham are unable to explain the global character of the restrictionist impulse in the late nineteenth and early twentieth century, and that explanations invoking the antipathies of labor movements to immigrant competitors ignore the fact that labor movements generally lacked the power to compel legislative action in their interest.

5 FROM NATIONAL TO POSTNATIONAL?

1 See Reale 1930: 1–2.

2 Arendt 1973: 277.

3 See Skran 1995.

4 Zolberg 1978: 267.

5 See Kulischer 1948: 56. Estimates of total population movements across borders during this period range up toward 10 000 000.

6 Skran 1995: 36, 102.

7 "R. Decreto 18 marzo 1923, n. 590, relativo al rilascio dei passaporti per l'estero agli inscritti di leva ed ai militari in congedo," *Raccolta Ufficiale, 1919,* vol. 3 (Rome: Tipografia delle Mantellate, 1923): 1915–1917. On the creation of the Fascist Militia, see Clark 1984: 222.

8 Remarks in the Camera dei Deputati, 31 March 1927, quoted in Oblath 1931: 808.

9 See Levi 1947. In addition, of course, Antonio Gramsci's *Prison Notebooks* emerged from the Fascist context, but Gramsci was imprisoned rather than merely sent into internal exile in the South, a penalty the Fascist regime apparently considered punishment enough for a cultivated Turinese doctor – but not for a southern Italian revolutionary.

10 See Skran 1995: 55–6; Zolberg 1978: 272.

11 On the millet system, see Kymlicka 1995: 156–8.

12 See Skran 1995: 41–5.

13 Arendt 1973: 274–5. Macartney's comments on the results of the Versailles are trenchant: "The result of the Peace settlement was that every State in the belt of mixed population . . . now looked upon itself as a national state. But the facts were against them . . . Not one of these states was in fact uni-national, just as there was not, on the other hand, one nation all of whose members lived in a single state." Quoted in ibid. 274, n. 14.

14 See Marrus 1985: 92–4.

15 See Skran 1995: 104–5.

16 Arendt 1973: 282, n. 33.

17 Marrus 1985: 94; Skran 1995: 105.

18 See Marrus 1985: 94; Skran 1995: 106–8. Notably absent from among the signatories were the United States, Great Britain, and Italy; the latter, of course, had fallen under fascist control since the signing of the first Arrangement.

19 See Skran 1995: 108–9, 113.

20 Marrus 1985: 95.

21 Skran 1995: 105.

22 Hobsbawm 1990: 132.

23 Polanyi 1944: 202.

24 Matthews 1993: 5.

25 Fitzpatrick 1994: 92.

26 Shelley 1996: xv.

27 See Hall 1992: 877–8; Kulischer 1948: 18.

28 See Turack 1972: 9.

29 I borrow the terms, and the idea of their juxtaposition by the Nazis, from Herf 1984.

30 See Aly & Roth 1984: 55, 58–9. Despite its shortcomings, this book is by far the best monographic treatment of the complex administrative difficulties

the Germans confronted in the project of "solving" the Jewish "problem," and of how they went about tackling those obstacles. I rely on it heavily in the present discussion.

31 "Gesetz über den Widerruf von Einbürgerungen und die Aberkennung der deutschen Staatsangehörigkeit," 14 July 1933, *Reichsgesetzblatt 1933*, Part I: 430ff.; the implementing order of 26 July 1933, is to be found at *Reichsgesetzblatt 1933*, Part I: 538ff. Brief versions of the essentials of the law and the implementing order may be found in Walk 1981: 36, 42; see also Bergmann & Korth 1985: 27. For a brief discussion of the law and its significance, see Schleunes 1970: 110–11.

32 See Schmid et al. 1983, vol. 1: 97–100.

33 Aly & Roth 1984: 44–5. I have been unable to establish whether the similarities between the Nazis' "work-book" and the Soviet internal passport was coincidental or the result of conscious imitation. On the "passportization" of the USSR in the early 1930s, see Garcelon 2000; Torpey 1997.

34 See Ayass 1988: 219–21; Treuberg 1990: 89–90.

35 "Gesetz über das Paß-, das Ausländerpolizei-, und das Meldewesen sowie über das Ausweiswesen," 11 May 1937, *Reichsgesetzblatt 1937*, Part I: 589. An analogous order was adopted for Austria soon after the *Anschluss*; see "Verordnung über die Einführung des Gesetzes über das Paß-, Ausländerpolizei- und das Meldewesen sowie über das Ausweiswesen vom 11. Mai 1937 im Lande Oesterreich vom 10. Mai 1938," *Reichsgesetzblatt 1938*, Part I: 511. That the Interior Minister assumed these powers over the issuance of passports had nothing to do with the uniquely horrifying features of the Nazi regime. Rather, in a departure from practice elsewhere in Europe and in the United States, where passport matters are the province of the foreign minister, in Germany these responsibilities have always been in the domain of the Ministry of the Interior, and remain so to this day.

36 See Schulze 1942 for the main components of the original regulations and their subsequent revisions. See also Aly & Roth 1984: 39–40.

37 Schulze 1942: 3; see Aly & Roth 1984: 141–2.

38 F. Bürgdorfer, "Die Juden in Deutschland und in der Welt: Ein statistischer Beitrag zur biologischen, beruflichen und sozialen Struktur des Judentums in Deutschland," *Forschungen zur Judenfrage* Bd. 3, Hamburg 1938: 162–3, quoted in Aly & Roth 1984: 62–3.

39 Quoted in Aly & Roth 1984: 41–2.

40 "Kennkartenzwang (3. Bekanntmachung vom 23. 7. 1938)," quoted in ibid. 75–6, 78.

41 Aly & Roth 1984: 53–4.

42 "Ausländerpolizeiverordnung," 22 August 1938, *Reichsgesetzblatt 1938*, Part I: 1053–6.

43 See Schleunes 1970: 229–30.

44 This account is based on Skran 1995: 211–14; see also Yahil 1990: 94–5.

45 "Verordnung über Reisepässe von Juden," 5 October 1938, *Reichsgesetzblatt 1938*: 1342; Burleigh & Wippermann 1991: 87; Yahil 1990: 108–9.

46 See Wyman 1968, 1984.

47 Rubinstein 1997: 17. My italics.

48 This paragraph and the next are based on Skran 1995: 75–6, 113–14, 196–98.

49 Rubinstein 1997: 36–7. Needless to say, Rubinstein does not share Daniel Jonah Goldhagen's view that the Jews in Germany were surrounded by bloodthirsty "eliminationist" anti-Semites, from whom presumably Jews would not have waited so long to flee. Nor do I.

50 Aly & Roth 1984: 75.

51 See ibid. 44–6.

52 Ibid. 25–6, 78–9.

53 Quoted in ibid. 51.

54 "Vorschriften über das Meldewesen," 6 September 1939, *Reichsgesetzblatt 1939*, Part I: 1688, also in Schulze 1942: 71–8; the quotation is from the preamble in ibid. 71.

55 The letter is quoted in Aly & Roth 1984: 42–3.

56 See Browning 1986. The quotations are from pp. 501 and 512.

57 Friedman 1955: 50.

58 See ibid. and the discussion in Schwan 1997: 116–18.

59 On the "modernity" of the Holocaust, see Bauman 1991.

60 Quoted in Aly & Roth 1984: 52–3.

61 See ibid. 66–7.

62 Kipphardt 1983: 114.

63 This paragraph is based on Zolberg et al. 1989: 21–2.

64 See Marrus 1985: 310, 317–24.

65 See Zolberg et al. 1989: 22–6.

66 See articles 27 and 28 of the 1951 Convention Relating to the Status of Refugees. I clarified my understanding of the UNHCR's role in supplying travel documents to refugees in a telephone interview with Legal Counselor Jane Kochman of UNHCR, Washington, DC, 11 February 1999, and on the basis of an advisory on "Travel Documents" issued by that office, dated 29 April 1998.

67 See Plender 1988: 206, 274, 288.

68 Turack 1972: 53.

69 Ibid. 68–9.

70 See the "Begründung" of the Gesetzentwurf der Bundesregierung, Entwurf eines Paßgesetzes, Deutscher Bundestag, 10. Wahlperiode, Drucksache 10/3303, 7. Mai 1985.

71 The Legal Committee's report of September 23, 1953, can be found in Council of Europe, Consultative Assembly, Fifth Session, Third Part, 15–26 September 1953, *Documents*, Doc. 201, quoted in Turack 1972: 70.

72 See "Erste Beratung des Entwurfs eines Gesetzes über das Paßwesen," *Verhandlungen des deutschen Bundestages* [hereafter *Verhandlungen*], 164. Sitzung, Mittwoch, den 26. September 1951: 6650–1, and the "Zweite und dritte Beratung des Entwurfs eines Gesetzes über das Paßwesen," *Verhandlungen*, 176. Sitzung, Donnerstag, den 22. November 1951: 7223–35. The quotation is from p. 6650.

73 See the government's "Begründung" of the "Entwurf eines Bundesgesetzes über das Paßwesen," *Anlagen zu den Verhandlungen des deutschen Bundestages* [hereafter *Anlagen*] (1951), Drucksache 2509: 6.

74 See the "Änderungsvorschläge des Bundesrates zum Entwurf eines Bundesgesetzes über das Paßwesen," *Anlagen* (1951), Drucksache 2509: 8; remarks of Deputy Hoppe, *rapporteur* of the Ausschuß für Angelegenheiten der inneren Verwaltung, "Zweite und dritte Beratung des Entwurfs eines Gesetzes über das Paßwesen," *Verhandlungen*, 176. Sitzung, Donnerstag, den 22. November 1951: 7224; and the final version of the law, "Gesetz über das Paßwesen," 4 March 1952, *Bundesgesetzblatt 1952*, Part I: 290–2. A report of the *Industrie- und Handelstag* from this period notes that the organization was successful in achieving its aim of avoiding any exit visa requirement for trips abroad by Germans. See Deutscher Industrie- und Handelstag (DIHT), *Tätigkeitsbericht für das Geschäftsjahr 1951/52* (n.p., n.d.): 39. I was unable to learn the reasons determining the DIHT's stance in these matters because, according to Dr Jürgen Möllering, the director of the Legal Department of the organization, no materials from that year survive in the DIHT's archives. Personal communication from Dr Möllering, 19 January 1996.

75 See the remarks of KPD deputy Paul and SPD deputy Maier in "Zweite und dritte Beratung des Entwurfs eines Gesetzes über das Paßwesen," *Verhandlungen*, 176. Sitzung, Donnerstag, den 22. November 1951: 7225–6, 7232, and *passim*.

76 *US Statutes at Large*, vol. 64, part I: 993.

77 See Maier's remarks, as well as the similar criticisms of FPD deputy Neumayer, in "Zweite und dritte Beratung des Entwurfs eines Gesetzes über das Paßwesen," *Verhandlungen*, 176. Sitzung, Donnerstag, den 22. November 1951: 7230 and 7233.

78 *Verhandlungen*, 164. Sitzung, Mittwoch, den 26. September 1951: 6650. The Social Democratic representative Dr Mommer seconded the Interior Minister's views on this matter. See "Zweite und dritte Beratung," p. 7227.

79 See Chapter 4 above.

80 Plender 1988: 22, 24; the quotation is from Turack 1972: 118.

81 Turack 1972: 61, 118–19.

82 Ibid. 119; Plender 1988: 25, 83; Saggar 1992: 48.

83 "Verordnung zum Reichsbürgergesetz," November 25, 1941, *Reichsgesetzblatt 1941*, Part I: 722ff., cited in Bergmann & Korth 1990: 27.

84 The preceding paragraphs are based on Plender 1988: 135–6; Turack 1972: 120–1.

85 On the Immigration Act of 1971, see Miles & Phizacklea 1984: 69–73.

86 For the report on the proposed law by the joint committee of the Committees on Presidential Affairs, Internal Affairs, and Foreign Affairs, see Senato della Repubblica, IV Legislatura, "Relazione e testo degli articoli approvati dalle Commissioni Riunite: 1a (Affari della Presidenza del Consiglio e dell'Interno) e 3a (Affari Esteri) (Relatore Battino Vittorelli)," N. 1775-A, sul Disegno di Legge presentato dal Ministro degli Affari Esteri

di concerto col Ministro dell'Interno, di Grazia e Giustizia, ecc., nella Seduta del 13 Luglio 1966, communicata alla Presidenza il 24 luglio 1967.

87 Article 8 of the Convention for European Economic Co-operation, the constitutional instrument of the OEEC, quoted in Turack 1972: 53.

88 See "Erste Beratung des von der Bundesregierung eingebrachten Entwurfs eines Passgesetzes," Deutscher Bundestag, 10. Wahlperiode, 149. Sitzung, den 27. Juni 1985, and "Zweite und dritte Beratung des Passgesetzes," Deutscher Bundestag, 10. Wahlperiode, 202. Sitzung, den 28. Februar 1986, as well as the Greens' various proposed revisions to the law.

89 Bergmann & Korth 1990: 6–7.

90 Plender 1988: 214.

91 Turack 1972: 115.

92 See Sassen 1996.

93 On these points, see Cornelius et al. 1994.

94 Richmond 1994: 216.

95 See "Centri speciali prima dell'espulsione," *Corriere della Sera*, 20 February 1998: 3.

96 I am grateful to Susan Sterett for pointing this out to me.

97 "The Convention on International Civil Aviation, Annexes 1 to 18" (n.p.: International Civil Aviation Organization, 1991); see also "Memorandum on ICAO: The Story of the International Civil Aviation Organization" (Montreal: ICAO, 1994); "Machine Readable Travel Documents, Part I: Machine Readable Passports," 3rd edn. (Montreal: International Civil Aviation Organization, 1992).

98 Brubaker 1994: 230.

99 For an analysis of the effectiveness of controls on migration, see Zolberg forthcoming.

100 This is the main thrust of Soysal 1994.

101 See Jacobson 1997.

102 Soysal 1994: 159.

103 Arendt 1973: 230.

104 On these issues, see Marshall 1964.

105 Walzer 1983: 39.

106 See Caldeira 1996.

107 Blakely & Snyder 1997: 7.

CONCLUSION

1 Meyer 1987: 52.

2 Bertelsmann 1914: 13–17.

3 See Hannum 1987.

4 See Turack 1972: 8–9. The case in question was *Satwant Singh Sawhney* v. *Assistant Passport Officer, Government of India*, 10 April 1967. Ironically, the result of this decision was the Passport Act 1967, which enumerated the specific grounds on which the Indian government could refuse a passport

to an applicant. The 1967 Act was the first statutory regulation of a matter that theretofore had been left arbitrary.

5 Bergmann & Korth, 1990: 4.

6 Plender 1988: 150.

7 Dowty 1987: 171.

8 Ibid. 128.

9 See Bhagwati 1976.

10 Zolberg 1978: 271.

11 For a thoughtful discussion of the reasons why a liberal polity might want to restrict entry into its territory, see Whelan 1988.

12 Already in 1959 – that is, before the arrival in Europe of large numbers of "guestworkers" who have been seen as the vanguard of a reconfiguration of the relationship between citizenship and access to rights (see Soysal 1994) – a leading analyst of the role of nationality in international law put it this way: "Admission, especially of persons who wish to take up residence in the admitting State, resembles in many respects naturalization (which sometimes results): the foreign national is thus admitted to the local legal community; through his residence or actual sojourn[,] rights and obligations come into being which resemble those resulting from nationality." (Van Panhuys 1959: 55).

13 Goodwin-Gill 1978: 26.

14 Article 15 of the Universal Declaration of Human Rights (1948) states flatly, "Everyone has the right to a nationality" (UN Department of Public Information 1985). The Convention Relating to the Status of Stateless Persons was adopted in 1954, and the Convention on the Reduction of Statelessness in 1961. The quotation is from Dowty 1987: 109.

15 I am grateful to David Laitin for insisting on this point in a personal communication.

16 See Garcelon 2000; Fitzpatrick 1994; Matthews 1993; Torpey 1997; Zaslavsky & Luryi 1979.

17 Fussell 1980: 24.

REFERENCES

Aly, Goetz, & Karl-Heinz Roth. 1984. *Die restlose Erfassung: Volkszählen, Identifizieren, Aussondern im Nationalsozialismus.* Berlin: Rotbuch Verlag.

Anderson, Benedict. 1991 [1983]. *Imagined Communities: Reflections on the Origin and Spread of Nationalism.* Revised edn. New York: Verso.

Anderson, Perry. 1974. *Lineages of the Absolutist State.* New York: Verso.

Arendt, Hannah. 1973 [1948]. *The Origins of Totalitarianism.* New edn. New York: Harcourt, Brace & Company.

Ayass, Wolfgang. 1988. "Vagrants and Beggars in Hitler's Reich." In Richard J. Evans, ed., *The German Underworld: Deviants and Outcasts in German History.* New York: Routledge: 210–37.

Baker, Keith. 1990. *Inventing the French Revolution: Essays on French Political Culture in the Eighteenth Century.* New York: Cambridge University Press.

Bauman, Zygmunt. 1991 [1989]. *Modernity and the Holocaust.* Ithaca: Cornell University Press.

Beier, A. L. 1985. *Masterless Men: The Vagrancy Problem in England, 1560–1700.* London: Methuen.

Bendix, Reinhard. 1978. *Kings or People?: Power and the Mandate to Rule.* Berkeley: University of California Press.

Bensel, Richard Franklin. 1990. *Yankee Leviathan: The Origins of Central State Authority in America, 1859–1877.* New York: Cambridge University Press.

Bergmann, Wilfried, & Jürgen Korth. 1985. *Deutsches Staatsangehörigkeits- und Paßrecht: Praxishandbuch mit synoptischen Gesetzestexten.* Cologne: Carl Heymanns Verlag.

—— 1990. *Deutsches Staatsangehörigkeits- und Paßrecht: Praxishandbuch mit vollständigen Gesetzestexten.* Revised and expanded edn. 2. Halbband: Paßrecht. Cologne: Carl Heymanns Verlag.

Bertelsmann, Werner. 1914. *Das Passwesen: eine völkerrechtliche Studie.* Strassburg: J. H. Ed. Heitz.

Bhagwati, Jagdish N. 1976. *The Brain Drain and Taxation: Theory and Empirical Analysis.* vol. 2. New York: American Elsevier Publishers.

Blackbourn, David, & Geoff Eley. 1984. *The Peculiarities of German History: Bourgeois Society and Politics in Nineteenth-Century Germany.* New York: Oxford University Press.

Blakely, Edward J., & Mary Gail Snyder. 1997. *Fortress America: Gated Communities in the United States.* Washington, DC: Brookings Institution Press/Lincoln Institute of Land Policy.

Block, Fred, & Margaret R. Somers. 1984. "Beyond the Economistic Fallacy: The Holistic Social Science of Karl Polanyi." In Theda Skocpol, ed., *Vision and Method in Historical Sociology.* New York: Cambridge University Press: 47–84.

Bolis, Giovanni. 1871. *La polizia e le classe pericolose della società.* Bologna/Modena.

Browning, Christopher. 1986. "Nazi Resettlement Policy and the Search for a Solution to the Jewish Question, 1939–1941." *German Studies Review* 9: 497–519.

Brubaker, Rogers. 1992. *Citizenship and Nationhood in France and Germany.* Cambridge, MA: Harvard University Press.

—— 1994. "Are Immigration Control Efforts Really Failing?" In Cornelius, Hollifield, & Martin, eds, *Controlling Immigration: A Global Perspective.* Stanford, CA: Stanford University Press: 227–31.

—— 1996. *Nationalism Reframed: Nationhood and the National Question in the New Europe.* New York: Cambridge University Press.

Brunialti, Attilio. 1915 [?]. "Passaporti." In Pasquale Stanislao Mancini, ed., *Enciclopedia Giuridica Italiana* vol. 13, Part I. Milan: Società Editrice Libraria: 674–85.

Bull, Hedley. 1995 [1977]. *The Anarchical Society: A Study of Order in World Politics.* 2nd edn. New York: Columbia University Press.

Burguière, André, & Jacques Revel, eds. 1989. *L'Espace français* (vol. 1 of *Histoire de la France*). Paris: Editions Seuil.

Burke, Victor Lee. 1997. *The Clash of Civilizations: War-Making and State Formation in Europe.* Cambridge, MA: Polity Press.

Burleigh, Michael, & Wolfgang Wippermann. 1991. *The Racial State: Germany 1933–1945.* New York: Cambridge University Press.

Calavita, Kitty. 1992. *Inside the State: The Bracero Program, Immigration, and the I.N.S.* New York: Routledge.

Caldeira, Theresa P. R. 1996. "Fortified Enclaves: The New Urban Segregation." *Public Culture* 8(2): 303–28.

Caplan, Jane. 2000. "'This or That Particular Person': Protocols of Identification in Nineteenth-Century Europe." In Caplan & Torpey, eds, *Documenting Individual Identity: The Development of State Practices in the Modern World.* Princeton: Princeton University Press.

—— & John Torpey, eds. 2000. *Documenting Individual Identity: The Development of State Practices in the Modern World*. Princeton: Princeton University Press.

Caratini, Roger. 1988. *Dictionnaire des personnages de la Révolution*. Paris: Le Pré aux Clercs.

Chambliss, William. 1964. "A Sociological Analysis of the Law of Vagrancy." *Social Problems* 11(1): 67–77.

Chan, Sucheng. 1990. "European and Asian Immigration into the United States in Comparative Perspective, 1820s to 1920s." In Virginia Yans-Mclaughlin, ed., *Immigration Reconsidered: History, Sociology, Politics*. New York: Oxford University Press: 37–75.

Clark, Martin. 1984. *Modern Italy, 1871–1982*. New York: Longman.

Cobb, Richard C. 1970. *The Police and the People: French Popular Protest 1789–1820*. Oxford: Oxford University Press.

Coolidge, Mary Roberts. 1969 [1909]. *Chinese Immigration*. New York: Arno Press and *The New York Times*.

Cornelius, Wayne, James F. Hollifield, & Philip L. Martin, eds. 1994. *Controlling Immigration: A Global Perspective*. Stanford, CA: Stanford University Press.

Craig, Gordon. 1978. *Germany, 1866–1945*. New York: Oxford University Press.

Crowley, John. 1998. "Where Does the State Actually Start? Border, Boundary & Frontier Control in Contemporary Governance." Paper presented at the annual meeting of the International Studies Association, Minneapolis, MN, 18–20 March.

Dallier, G. 1914. *La police des étrangers a Paris et dans le département de la Seine*. Thèse de droit. Paris: A. Rousseau.

Douglas, Mary. 1966. *Purity and Danger: An Analysis of Concepts of Pollution and Taboo*. London: Routledge & Kegan Paul.

Dowty, Alan. 1987. *Closed Borders: The Contemporary Assault on Freedom of Movement*. New Haven: Yale University Press.

Dudley, Leonard M. 1991. *The Word and the Sword: How Techniques of Information and Violence Have Shaped Our World*. Cambridge, MA: Basil Blackwell.

Elias, Norbert. 1978 [1939]. *The Civilizing Process*, vol. 1: *The History of Manners*. Translated by Edmund Jephcott. New York: Pantheon.

—— 1982 [1939]. *The Civilizing Process*, vol. 2: *Power & Civility*. Translated by Edmund Jephcott. New York: Pantheon.

Fitzgerald, Keith. 1996. *The Face of the Nation: Immigration, The State, and the National Identity*. Stanford, CA: Stanford University Press.

Fitzpatrick, Sheila. 1994. *Stalin's Peasants: Resistance and Survival in the Russian Village After Collectivization*. New York: Oxford University Press.

Foerster, Robert. 1919. *The Italian Emigration of Our Times.* Cambridge, MA: Harvard University Press.

Foner, Eric. 1970. *Free Soil, Free Labor, Free Men: The Ideology of the Republican Party Before the Civil War.* New York: Oxford University Press.

Foucault, Michel. 1979. *Discipline and Punish: The Birth of the Prison.* Translated by Alan Sheridan. New York: Vintage.

—— 1980a. "The Eye of Power." In Foucault, *Power/Knowledge: Selected Interviews and Other Writings, 1972–1977,* edited by Colin Gordon. New York: Pantheon: 146–65.

—— 1980b. "Questions on Geography." In Foucault, *Power/Knowledge: Selected Interviews and Other Writings, 1972–1977,* edited by Colin Gordon. New York: Pantheon: 63–77.

—— 1991. "Governmentality." In *The Foucault Effect: Studies in Governmentality,* edited by Graham Burchell, Colin Gordon, and Peter Miller. London: Harvester Wheatsheaf: 87–104.

Friedman, Philip. 1955. "The Jewish Badge and the Yellow Star in the Nazi Era." *Historia Judaica* 17: 41–70.

Furet, François, & Mona Ozouf. 1989. *A Critical Dictionary of the French Revolution.* Translated by Arthur Goldhammer. Cambridge, MA: Belknap/Harvard.

Fussell, Paul. 1980. *Abroad: British Literary Traveling Between the Wars.* New York: Oxford University Press.

Garcelon, Marc. 2000. "Colonizing the Subject: The Genealogy and Legacy of the Soviet Internal Passport." In Caplan & Torpey, eds, *Documenting Individual Identity: The Development of State Practices in the Modern World.* Princeton: Princeton University Press.

Giddens, Anthony. 1987. *The Nation-State and Violence.* Berkeley: University of California Press.

Gilboy, Janet. 1997. "Regulatory Relaxation: International Airlines, the Immigration Service, and Illegal Travelers." Paper presented to the Annual Meeting of the Law and Society Assocation, St. Louis, MO (May).

Goffman, Erving. 1961. "On the Characteristics of Total Institutions." In Goffman, *Asylums: Essays on the Social Situation of Mental Patients and Other Inmates.* Garden City, NY: Anchor Doubleday: 1–124.

—— 1963. *Stigma: Notes on the Management of Spoiled Identity.* New York: Simon & Schuster.

Goodwin-Gill, Guy S. 1978. *International Law and the Movement of Persons Between States.* Oxford: Clarendon Press.

Gorski, Philip Steven. 1996. *The Disciplinary Revolution: Calvinism and State Formation in Early Modern Europe, 1550–1750.* Ph.D. dissertation, Department of Sociology, University of California, Berkeley.

—— 1997. "Sixteenth-Century Social Reform: Why Protestantism Mattered." Typescript, Department of Sociology, University of Wisconsin, Madison.

Greer, Donald. 1951. *The Incidence of Emigration During the French Revolution.* Cambridge, MA: Harvard University Press.

Grossi, Vincenzo. 1905. "Emigrazione." In V. E. Orlando, ed., *Diritto Amministrativo Italiano.* Milan: Società Editrice Libraria: 119–209.

Guiraudon, Virginie. 1991. "Cosmopolitism and National Priority: Attitudes Towards Foreigners in France Between 1789 and 1794." *History of European Ideas* 13 (5): 591–604.

H. H. 1866. "Die Entwicklung und Reform des deutschen Passwesens." *Deutsche Vierteljahrs-Schrift* 29 (1): 219–53.

Habermas, Jürgen. 1987. *The Theory of Communicative Action,* vol. 2: *Lifeworld and System: A Critique of Functionalist Reason.* Translated by Thomas McCarthy. Boston: Beacon Press.

Hall, Kermit L., ed. 1992. *The Oxford Companion to the Supreme Court of the United States.* New York: Oxford University Press.

Hamerow, Theodore. 1969. *The Social Foundations of German Unification, 1858–1871,* vol. 1, *Ideas and Institutions.* Princeton: Princeton University Press.

Haney-Lopez, Ian. 1996. *White By Law: The Legal Construction of Race.* New York: New York University Press.

Hannum, Hurst. 1987. *The Right to Leave and Return in International Law and Practice.* Dordrecht/Boston/Lancaster: Martinus Nijhoff Publishers.

Hansen, Marcus Lee. 1961 [1940]. *The Atlantic Migration, 1607–1860.* New York: Harper Torchbooks.

Herbert, Ulrich. 1990. *A History of Foreign Labor in Germany, 1880–1980: Seasonal Workers/Forced Laborers/Guest Workers.* Translated by William Templer. Ann Arbor: University of Michigan Press.

Herf, Jeffrey. 1984. *Reactionary Modernism: Technology, Culture, and Politics in Weimar and the Third Reich.* New York: Cambridge University Press.

Higham, John. 1988 [1955]. *Strangers in the Land: Patterns of American Nativism, 1860–1925.* New Brunswick, NJ: Rutgers University Press.

Hobsbawm E. J. 1962. *The Age of Revolution: Europe 1789–1848.* London: Weidenfeld and Nicolson.

—— 1975. *The Age of Capital, 1848–1875.* London: Weidenfeld and Nicolson.

—— 1990. *Nations and Nationalism Since 1780.* New York: Cambridge University Press.

Hufton, Olwen. 1974. *The Poor of Eighteenth-Century France, 1750–1789.* Oxford: Clarendon Press.

Hunt, Gaillard. 1898. *The American Passport: Its History and a Digest of Laws, Rulings, and Regulations Governing its Issuance by the Department of State.* Washington: Government Printing Office.

International Labour Office. 1928. *Migration Laws and Treaties,* vol. 1: *Emigration Laws and Regulations.* Geneva: International Labour Office.

Jacobson, David. 1997. *Rights Across Borders: Immigration and the Decline of Citizenship.* Baltimore: Johns Hopkins University Press.

Jay, Martin. 1993. *Downcast Eyes: The Denigration of Vision in Twentieth Century French Thought.* Berkeley: University of California Press.

Kaluszynski, Martine. 2000. "The Republic's Identity." In Caplan and Torpey, eds, *Documenting Individual Identity: The Development of State Practices in the Modern World.* Princeton: Princeton University Press.

Kipphardt, Heinar. 1983. *Bruder Eichmann.* Reinbek bei Hamburg: Rowohlt.

Knoke, Anton. 1911. *Ausländische Wanderarbeiter in Deutschland.* Leipzig: A. Deichert.

Koch, Rainer. 1985. *Deutsche Geschichte 1815–1848: Restauration oder Vormärz?.* Stuttgart: W. Kohlhammer.

Kolchin, Peter. 1987. *Unfree Labor: American Slavery and Russian Serfdom.* Cambridge, MA: Harvard University Press.

Kulischer, Eugene M. 1948. *Europe on the Move: War and Population Changes, 1917–1947.* New York: Columbia University Press.

Kymlicka, Will. 1995. *Multicultural Citizenship: A Liberal Theory of Minority Rights.* New York: Oxford University Press.

Lefebvre, Georges. 1947. *The Coming of the French Revolution.* Translated by R. R. Palmer. Princeton: Princeton University Press.

—— 1962 [1957]. *The French Revolution,* vol. 1: *From Its Origins to 1793.* Translated by Elizabeth Moss Evanson. New York: Columbia University Press.

—— 1964 [1957]. *The French Revolution,* vol. 2: *From 1793 to 1799.* Translated by John Hall Stewart and James Friguglietti. New York: Columbia University Press.

Levi, Carlo. 1947. *Christ Stopped at Eboli: The Story of a Year.* Translated by Frances Frenaye. New York: Farrar, Strauss and Co.

Lipset, Seymour Martin. 1979 [1963]. *The First New Nation: The United States in Historical and Comparative Perspective.* New York: W. W. Norton.

Lucassen, Leo. 1997. "The Invention of the Alien: Immigration Controls in an Emerging Welfare State and the Implementation at the Local Level in the Netherlands (1918–1940)." Paper presented at the Annual Meeting of the Social Science History Assocation, Washington, DC, 16–18 October.

—— 1998. "The Great War and the Origins of Migration Control in Western Europe and the United States (1880–1920)." In Anita Böcker, et al., eds, *Regulation of Migration: International Experiences.* Amsterdam: Het Spinhuis: 45–72.

Lüdtke, Alf. 1989. *Police and State in Prussia, 1815–1850.* Translated by Pete Burgess. New York: Cambridge University Press.

Lyon, David. 1994. *The Electronic Eye: The Rise of Surveillance Society.* Minneapolis: University of Minnesota Press.

MacDonagh, Oliver. 1961. *A Pattern of Government Growth, 1800–1860: The Passenger Acts and Their Enforcement.* London: Macgibbon and Kee.

MacDonald, John S. 1963–64. "Agricultural Organization, Migration, and Labour Militancy in Rural Italy." *Economic History Review* 2d ser. 16: 61–75.

Mann, Michael. 1993. *The Sources of Social Power*, vol. 2: *The Rise of Classes and Nation-States, 1760–1914.* New York: Cambridge University Press.

Marrus, Michael. 1985. *The Unwanted: European Refugees in the Twentieth Century.* New York: Oxford University Press.

Marshall, J. D. 1985. *The Old Poor Law, 1795–1834.* 2nd edn. London: Macmillan.

Marshall, T. H. 1964. "Citizenship and Social Class." In Marshall, *Class, Citizenship, and Social Development.* Garden City, NY: Doubleday: 65–122.

Matthews, Mervyn. 1993. *The Passport Society: Controlling Movement in Russia and the USSR.* Boulder, CO: Westview Press.

McNeill, William. 1983. *The Great Frontier: Freedom and Hierarchy in Modern Times.* Princeton: Princeton University Press.

McPherson, James M. 1991. *Abraham Lincoln and the Second American Revolution.* New York: Oxford University Press.

Meyer, John. 1987 [1980]. "The World Polity and the Authority of the Nation-State." In George M. Thomas, et al., eds, *Institutional Structure: Constituting State, Society, and the Individual.* Newbury Park, CA: Sage.

Miles, Robert, and Annie Phizacklea. 1984. *White Man's Country – Racism in British Politics.* London: Pluto Press.

Moore, Barrington, Jr. 1966. *Social Origins of Dictatorship and Democracy: Lord and Peasant in the Making of the Modern World.* Boston: Beacon Press.

Noiriel, Gérard. 1991. *La tyrannie du national: Le droit d'asile en Europe, 1793–1993.* Paris: Calmann-Levy.

—— 1996 [1988]. *The French Melting Pot: Immigration, Citizenship, and National Identity.* Translated by Geoffroy de Laforcade. Minneapolis: University of Minnesota Press.

—— & Michel Offerlé. 1997. "Citizenship and Nationality in Nineteenth-Century France." In Jytte Klausen & Louise A. Tilly, eds, *European Integration in Social and Historical Perspective: 1850 to the Present.* New York: Rowman & Littlefield: 71–84.

Nordman, Daniel. 1987. "Sauf-Conduits et passeports, en France, à la Renaissance." In Jean Céard & Jean-Claude Margolin, eds, *Voyager à la Renaissance: Actes du colloque de Tours 30 juin – 13 juillet 1983.* Paris: Maisonneuve et Larose: 145–58.

—— 1996. "Sauf-Conduits et passeports." In Lucien Bely, ed., *Dictionnaire de l'Ancien Régime.* Paris: Presses Universitaires de France: 1122–4.

Oblath, Attilio. 1931. "Italian Emigration and Colonisation Policy." *International Labour Review* 23 (June): 805–34.

Paxton, Robert. 1975. *Europe in the Twentieth Century.* New York: Harcourt Brace Jovanovich.

Plender, Richard. 1988 [1972]. *International Migration Law.* 2nd revised edn. Dordrecht: Martinus Nijhoff.

Polanyi, Karl. 1944. *The Great Transformation: The Political and Economic Origins of Our Time.* Boston: Beacon Press.

Powell, Walter W. and Paul Dimaggio, eds. 1991. *The New Institutionalism in Organizational Analysis.* Chicago: University of Chicago Press.

Preston, William. 1963. *Aliens and Dissenters: Federal Suppression of Radicals, 1903–1933.* Cambridge, MA: Harvard University Press.

Raeff, Marc. 1983. *The Well-Ordered Police State: Social and Institutional Change Through Law in the Germanies and Russia, 1600–1800.* New Haven, CT: Yale University Press.

Reale, Egidio. 1930. *Le régime des passeports et la société des nations.* Paris: Librairie A. Rousseau.

Richmond, Anthony. 1994. *Global Apartheid: Refugees, Racism, and the New World Order.* New York: Oxford University Press.

Rothwell, Harry. 1975. *English Historical Documents, 1189–1327.* Vol. 3. London: Eyre & Spottiswoode.

Rubinstein, William D. 1997. *The Myth of Rescue: Why the Democracies Could Not Have Saved More Jews from the Nazis.* New York: Routledge.

Saggar, Shamit. 1992. *Race and Politics in Britain.* Hemel Hempstead: Harvester Wheatsheaf.

Salyer, Lucy. 1991. "'Laws as Harsh as Tigers': Enforcement of the Chinese Exclusion Law, 1891–1924." In Sucheng Chan, ed., *Entry Denied: Exclusion and the Chinese Community in America, 1882–1943.* Philadelphia: Temple University Press: 57–93.

—— 1995. *Laws Harsh as Tigers: Chinese Immigrants and the Shaping of Modern Immigration Law.* Chapel Hill, NC: University of North Carolina Press.

Sassen, Saskia. 1996. *Losing Control?: Sovereignty in an Age of Globalization.* New York: Columbia University Press.

Saxton, Alexander Plaisted. 1971. *The Indispensable Enemy: Labor and the Anti-Chinese Movement in California.* Berkeley: University of California Press.

Schivelbusch, Wolfgang. 1880. *The Railway Journey: Trains and Travel in the Nineteenth Century.* Oxford: Basil Blackwell.

Schleunes, Karl A. 1970. *The Twisted Road to Auschwitz: Nazi Policy Towards German Jews, 1933–1939.* Urbana, IL: University of Illinois Press.

Schmid, Hans-Dieter, et al. 1983. *Juden unterm Hakenkreuz: Dokumente und Berichte zur Verfolgung und Vernichtung der Juden durch die Nationalsozialisten 1933–1945.* 2 vols. Düsseldorf: Schwann.

Schulze, Georg. 1942. *Die Reichsmeldeordnung und die sonstigen Vorschriften über das Meldewesen und über die Volkskartei.* 2. (vermehrte) Auflage. Dresden: Kommunal-Verlag Sachsen Kurt Gruber K.-G.

Schwan, Gesine. 1997. *Politik und Schuld: Die zerstörerische Macht des Schweigens.* Frankfurt am Main: Fischer.

Scott, James C. 1998. *Seeing Like a State: How Certain Schemes to Improve the Human Condition Have Failed.* New Haven: Yale University Press.

Sheehan, James J. 1989. *German History, 1770–1866.* New York: Oxford University Press.

Shelley, Louise I. 1996. *Policing Soviet Society: The Evolution of State Control.* New York: Routledge.

Skocpol, Theda. 1978. *States and Social Revolutions: A Comparative Analysis of France, Russia, and China.* New York: Cambridge University Press.

Skran, Claudena. 1995. *Refugees in Inter-War Europe: The Emergence of a Regime.* Oxford: Clarendon Press.

Soboul, Albert, ed. 1989. *Dictionnaire Historique de la Révolution Française.* Paris: Presses Universitaires de France.

Soysal, Yasemin. 1994. *Limits of Citizenship: Migrants and Postnational Membership in Europe.* Chicago: University of Chicago Press.

Spruyt, Hendrik. 1994. *The Sovereign State and its Competitors.* Princeton: Princeton University Press.

Steinmetz, George. 1993. *Regulating the Social: The Welfare State and Local Politics in Imperial Germany.* Princeton: Princeton University Press.

Strikwerda, Carl. 1997. "Reinterpreting the History of European Integration: Business, Labor, and Social Citizenship in Twentieth-Century Europe." In Jytte Klausen & Louise A. Tilly, eds, *European Integration in Social and Historical Perspective: 1850 to the Present.* New York: Rowman & Littlefield: 51–73.

Tammeo, Giuseppe. 1906. "Emigrazione." In Pasquale Stanislao Mancini, ed., *Enciclopedia Giuridica Italiana: Esposizione Ordinata e*

Completa dello Stato degli ultimi Progressi della Scienza, della Legislazione e della Giurisprudenza vol. 5, Part 2. Milan: Società Editrice Libraria: 1–160.

Tilly, Charles. 1990. *Coercion, Capital, and European States, A. D. 990–1992*. Oxford: Basil Blackwell.

Tocqueville, Alexis de. 1955 [1856]. *The Old Regime and the French Revolution*. Translated by Stuart Gilbert. Garden City, NY: Anchor Doubleday.

—— 1969 [1835/1840]. *Democracy in America*. Translated by George Lawrence. Edited by J. P. Mayer. Garden City, New York: Anchor Doubleday.

—— 1971 [1893]. *Recollections*. Translated by George Lawrence. Edited by J. P. Mayer and A. P. Kerr. Garden City, NY: Anchor Doubleday.

Torpey, John. 1997. "Revolutions and Freedom of Movement: An Analysis of Passport Controls in the French, Russian, and Chinese Revolutions." *Theory and Society* 26: 837–68.

Treuberg, Eberhard von. 1990. *Mythos Nichtseßhaftigkeit: Zur Geschichte des wissenschaftlichen, staatlichen, und privatwohltätigen Umgangs mit einem diskriminierten Phänomen*. Bielefeld: Verlag Soziale Hilfe.

Turack, Daniel C. 1972. *The Passport in International Law*. Lexington, MA: Lexington Books.

United Nations. n.d. *Human Rights Fact Sheet No. 20: Human Rights and Refugees*. New York: United Nations.

United Nations. Department of Public Information. 1985. *The International Bill of Human Rights*. New York: United Nations.

United States. Congress. Senate. Committee on Immigration. 1911a. *Abstracts of Reports of the Immigration Commission* [aka the Dillingham Commission]. Committee on Immigration, United States Senate, 61st Congress, 3rd session. 5 December 1910. Washington, DC: Government Printing Office.

United States. Congress. Senate. Committee on Immigration. 1911b. *Reports of the Immigration Commission*, vol. 4: *Emigration Conditions in Europe*. Washington, DC: Government Printing Office.

United States. Department of Justice. Immigration and Naturalization Service. 1991. *An Immigrant Nation: United States Regulation of Immigration, 1798–1991*. Washington, DC: US Government Printing Office.

United States. Department of Labor. Bureau of Immigration. Multiple years, 1917–1921. *Annual Report of the Commissioner General of Immigration to the Secretary of Labor*. Washington, DC: US Government Printing Office.

United States. Department of Labor. Immigration and Naturalization Service. 1934. "American Consular Procedure and Technical

INDEX

Lightning Source UK Ltd.
Milton Keynes UK
UKOW041345061212

203268UK00003B/125/A